Vidal Sassoon was born in London in 1928.
He began his hairdressing career as an apprentice
during the Second World War. Today, his name is still
associated with the salons and the hairdressing schools
he founded in the 1960s. He lives in London and
Beverly Hills, and in 2009 he was made a
CBE in the Queen's Birthday Honours.

Vidal Sassoon

VIDAL

The Autobiography

PAN BOOKS

First published 2010 by Macmillan

First published in paperback 2011 by Pan Books
an imprint of Pan Macmillan, a division of Macmillan Publishers Limited
Pan Macmillan, 20 New Wharf Road, London N1 9RR
Basingstoke and Oxford
Associated companies throughout the world
www.panmacmillan.com

ISBN 978-0-330-52129-1

1 3 5 7 9 8 6 4 2

A CIP catalogue record for this book is available from
the British Library.

Printed in the UK by CPI Mackays, Chatham, ME5 8TD

Visit **www.panmacmillan.com** to read more about all our books
and to buy them. You will also find features, author interviews and
news of any author events, and you can sign up for e-newsletters
so that you're always first to hear about our new releases.

To my girl Ronnie,
my wife, my fortress and safe harbour,
who I cherish with all my heart.

Contents

List of Illustrations

Unless indicated otherwise pictures are courtesy of the author.

1. My mother with me in her arms.
2. Mother with Ivor, aged two and a half and myself aged five.
3. Me, aged six.
4. With Ivor at the orphanage, when I was eight and he was five and a half.
5. Nathan G and Mother.
6. With Ivor, on a trip back to the orphanage when we were adults.
7. Adolph Cohen's salon.
8. With Ivor and friends at Larkswood Pool.
9. In Israel in 1948.
10. With Colin Fisher and Jack Aptaker, my Israeli army friends and comrades.
11. Mr 'Teasy-Weasy': Raymond at the height of his fame. (Getty Images)
12. One of my first competitions.
13. With the first-prize cup after a competition.
14. The Vidal Sassoon Salon at 171 New Bond Street.
15. With Elaine. (By courtesy of Elaine Sassoon)
16. Grace Coddington modelling the 'Five Point Cut'. (David Montgomery /Vidal Sasson Inc.)
17. With Adolph Cohen, watching him giving a model one of my geometric cuts.

List of Illustrations

List of Illustrations

Acknowledgements

My literary agents, Georgina Capel and Anita Land, of Capel and Land, had been after me for a couple of years to tell the stories of my life. I always said I was too young. Then I reached eighty. I agreed but had conditions. Georgina promised to find me the best writer available. I said I was doing it myself. When she asked if I could write, I sent her some material. She called me and said, 'Yes, you can write, but you're going to need a fabulous editor.' Well, they did better than that. They introduced me to Sally Abbey, an extraordinary freelance editor who immediately found my voice – which I was always scared would be lost with a ghostwriter.

Eighteen months ago, Mary Langford turned up through an agency in America where I wrote this book. She is very experienced in working with authors and a first-class stenographer. I thought I was hiring someone who would transcribe my random thoughts, but she has been so much more than that. Between Sally and Mary I learned how to think book-wise rather than speech-wise. The English language has always fascinated me, and to have the luck of not one, but two, teachers to give my ramblings structure and meaning has indeed been a joy and a lesson in life that I will not forget. At eighty-two, I've been learning a whole new craft and feel like I've been apprenticing under two dedicated pros. I owe them both my deepest thanks and respect.

A special thanks goes to my editor at Macmillan, Georgina Morley, who had the vision to commission the memoirs of this old

Acknowledgements

hairdresser and whose excellent understanding of great storytelling has added much to the pacing and flow of this book. Her enthusiasm and encouragement along the way has helped keep everybody on track. I must also thank editorial manager, Tania Adams, who has patiently put up with numerous late additions to the text and ensured that everything is where it should be.

I am especially grateful to Marilyn Esquivel, my finance manager and personal assistant, whose reliability and loyalty have never wavered. She visited the dusty archives countless times and painstakingly weeded through thousands of photos to find and assemble the best ones for this book.

Our dear friend, Martyn Lawrence-Bullard, apart from being a designer of great note, is one of the most generous men I know. He introduced me to Georgina Capel and I've often thought that had it not been for Martyn, this book might not have happened at all.

I would also like to acknowledge the following people for adding greatly to my life:

The world of fashion would have been far less colourful without Mary Quant (obviously), Barbara Hulanicki of Biba, Zandra Rhodes, Marion Foale and Sally Tuffin (known fondly as 'Huffin' and Puffin'), Kiki Byrne, Caroline Charles, Jean Muir and Vivienne Westwood.

Stanley Alwyn, my first barber in Shaftesbury Avenue who spiced up his haircuts with raucous jokes.

Janet Salisbury, housekeeper extraordinaire from the north of England, who came with my first flat in Curzon Street. Wives came and went but Janet always stayed.

Lord David Puttnam, filmmaker *par excellence*, a friend from the old days who I first met when he was agent to David Bailey and who has never forgotten his old mates. I don't know who I like and admire more – him or his lovely wife Patsy. A rare couple indeed.

Acknowledgements

Norman Lear, a gentle soul with the power of a giant who taught me so much when I served on his board for People for the American Way. He is an American of distinction and truly a great man.

My deepest admiration for my dear friends Dame Gail Ronson for her graciousness, charm and ability to affect change, and Gerald Ronson for his lifetime commitment to moral courage that gives inspiration to so many.

Sergeant Jim McGarry, policeman and body guard – who has a wonderful nature and managed to keep me alive during a dangerous episode of my life.

Chaim Topol, *the* fiddler on the roof, who took me with him on a day trip to Lebanon during the war in 1981.

Jeremy Irons and Sinéad Cusack, for a great and unforgettable weekend at their castle in Ireland.

Tony Rizzo, a true hero who, through the Alternative Hair Show, has raised over seven million pounds to combat leukemia after the death of his own son, Valentino, at the age of three. I feel proud to say he started with me, and I thank him for giving me a truly wonderful evening to celebrate my fifty years in hair at the Royal Albert Hall.

My congratulations and admiration to Peter Green – one of the original group of young hairdressers who moved with me from London to New York in 1965 to open our first US salon – having published two books, he is now working on a third. Who said hairdressers can't write?

Billie Currie, who has my enormous admiration for saving Ronnie's ribs, and possibly her life, in a crush against the barriers outside the entrance to an Alexander McQueen fashion show.

On a purely sartorial level, my thanks must go to Hedi Slimane for making the best lapels since Giorgio Armani.

Acknowledgements

Shortly before finishing this book I caught pneumonia and was knocked off my feet for a few weeks. You sure find out who your friends are when the chips are down. I want to thank and acknowledge the following people for their love and support during those difficult days:

My dear friend for over fifty years, the brilliant John Heyman and his exquisite wife Nizza, whose love and friendship I cherish.

Dr Steven Zax, an excellent surgeon and close friend for more than thirty years, who many moons ago allowed me to introduce him to my beloved land of Israel and eventually became a first-class ambassador for the country.

Cheryl Calhoun, my trusted advisor and confidante of more than three decades.

My gentle friend, David Philp, who came to hospital nearly every day to read me a page or two of Proust's *The Remembrance of Things Past*, while his wife, Hunter, brought in takeout Chinese.

Denis O'Neill, the screenwriter, and a very special buddy, who brought fresh croissants most hospital mornings and all the soccer news of the day. He's a man whose wealth of knowledge I admire and whose generosity of spirit lifts mine. Six years ago he tried to produce a screenplay based on my life but nobody was interested. Thank you Denis. Maybe they'll listen now.

Nancy Heller – our darling friend – a true Jewish mother who is always good for chicken soup, chocolate chip cookies, hugs and kisses, and her husband, Fred Specktor, for his faithful friendship and gutsy disposition towards life.

Etienne Taenaka, our wonderful friend who visited to give me Japanese baths, shaves and a great haircut, and his partner, Ron Wheeler, a Yaley, who keeps me on my toes intellectually.

Debbie and Curt Tweddell, who dropped their busy lives in

Acknowledgements

Cincinnati to come to Los Angeles and lend their love and support when we needed them.

Karen Sheehy, our devoted friend who takes loving care of us and our precious dogs, and is always there when we need her.

Jorge Melgar, a gentle man from Guatemala, who has worked with us in our home for almost twenty years. He has the best disposition and his kindness and caring for my wife and me has been extraordinary.

Rick Gold – my doctor, humorist and magic man – who has saved my life on numerous occasions.

Liza Bruce and her husband Nicholas Alvis-Vega who called each and every day and sent lovely cards. They have become our dearest friends in London.

My homeopath, Dr Soram Singh Khalsa, who for decades has looked into my eyes to tell me whether I am well or not, and has kept me going longer than I wish to say.

I also want to thank Loree Rodkin, Annie Philbin, Kim and Michael McCarty, Michael Green, Ian La Frenais, Kim Klosterman, Michael Lowe, Jim and Fran Allen, Zaha Hadid, Candy and Freddy DeMann, and all those friends whose love and caring sustained me and kept me going while I recovered.

And an extra special thanks to my daughter Eden, who seemed to be always by my side when I needed her; my son Elan, who flew in from Boston and stayed at just the right time, my niece Esther, who sent her love from afar, and my nephew Simon, who cared for me in a way that touched my heart and one which I will never forget.

I cannot possibly say enough about my Ronnie. She was at the hospital day and night, bringing me home-cooked meals, and looking after my every need. I have never felt so loved. Without her tremendous support throughout my illness, and throughout the writing of this book, I'm not sure it would have ever gone to print.

Last, but far from least, the thousands of hairdressers that have trained and worked with us since the fifties and carried the work forward, who I would love to mention personally but space simply will not allow. I am fortunate enough to know that many of the finest hairdressers in the world have passed through my door and made their mark. Some of you dedicated yourselves to this vision of ours then took your creativity elsewhere, with brilliant results. I have a long list of people who have worked with our organization for twenty-five years or more and are still working with us now. Then there are the many young stylists in the salon today who are creating beautiful work and more than keeping up the standards of the past. This is your story, as well as mine, and I'm so grateful that you helped make it happen.

In the midst of winter, I found there was,
within me, an invincible summer.

– Albert Camus

Prologue

There were times in the sixties and seventies when the press were literally camped outside my Bond Street salon, snapping the new haircuts as they walked out of the door, even photographing the staff themselves wearing the latest looks. In our heyday we were chased down the street, followed by a pack of screaming girls. Once we started on the geometric bobs, I had magazine editors continually on the end of the phone line for an exclusive. I had top models and actresses fighting to get an appointment. We were working fourteen-hour days. At the end of the day when the team and I went out for a drink, guess what we talked about? We lived and breathed hair. It wasn't work to me, it was a passion.

But one night a week was sacrosanct. Friday-night dinner at my mother's house in Kilburn was something I never missed. In some ways it was an antidote to all the fashion and razzamatazz, high jinks and crazy parties, and in other ways it complemented it rather nicely. It provided perspective when things looked in danger of getting out of hand.

My mother, Betty, was old school. Traditional. She was very

religious. But though she had turned to God, she didn't try to convert people. For the Friday dinner she would always say to me, 'Darling, bring whoever you like.' And I did, from photographers like Brian Duffy to actresses like Nancy Kwan or the singer Beverly Todd. She liked to meet people of all nationalities and persuasions. There were often a dozen or more people there. 'If everyone got together there wouldn't be room for hate,' she used to say as she served the delicious chicken soup that she had spent all day preparing. Brian Duffy loved to get into philosophical debates with my mother. He would pretend he was a fascist or a communist, depending on his mood, just to create an argument. Mother would always pay him back in kind. After the horrors of the Holocaust, she became an ardent Zionist. We used to have secret political meetings at our house in Bow, with me or my brother stationed on a nearby corner to check the police didn't decide to come in and break it up. We were very used to Mother and her pamphlets. She was always fighting for some cause or other.

My mother passionately believed that people should know about other people and their culture – then there would be less intolerance in the world. She was very political but she didn't force it down your throat. They were lovely, lively evenings. My friends enjoyed them too. It was something special to be at my mother's. She made the best lokshen and the best matzo ball soup. She had an answer for everything. If you asked her what the historic rationale was for matzo ball soup she would answer, 'It will keep you out of hospital and get you into the synagogue.' She liked a mixture of people so there would be different points of view; she liked a discussion. Her family was originally from Spain and you only needed to say the word 'Spanish' and out would come the castanets.

She was very proud of us children, but if she thought I was in danger of getting big-headed she would say, 'If you think Vidal's OK you should meet his brother – he's the clever one.' My brother, Ivor, was always at those Friday-night dinners too, and he would just laugh. We were in business together and both starting to share the roller-coaster ride of success. But Ivor could do no wrong in her eyes – all her special put-downs were reserved for me, her first-born. After the 'Five Point' haircut I was all over the press, but she just said, 'It's a very nice article, dear. Now let's eat.'

It was at one of those dinners that I told her how glad I was that she had hauled me, aged fourteen, into Professor Cohen's on the Whitechapel Road to be an apprentice. How grateful I was that she had insisted I stuck it out when I came home complaining about scrubbing floors and polishing mirrors. How on earth did she know that I would find my vocation in hairdressing? She just nodded wisely when I asked her that. 'There are some things only a mother knows.'

My mum might have been traditional but she was not at all straight-laced – she loved coming into the West End to see us. She adored coming to the parties we had at the salon. Dressed up to the nines, she would sweep in and introduce herself to aristocrats, artists and pop stars. 'I haven't put all this time and effort into you to not get a bit back now,' she would mutter as she wafted past me with a glass of champagne. She wanted to see for herself what Swinging London was getting up to.

And in the end that is why I'm glad that Professor Cohen made a good crimper out of me. My scissors have lifted me out of Petticoat Lane in the East End of London and have taken me all over the world. My mother, too. They have been the passport to a life we could never have dreamt of. I've met prime ministers

and Hollywood directors, screen legends and football super-
stars. I've cut the hair and listened to the secrets of some of the
most beautiful women in the world, and all because of one great
lady and her belief in me.

1

An East End Childhood

My mother died on 19 August 1997. She had lived ninety-seven years, three months and twenty-one days. I'd known her almost seventy years and had always looked up to her; she was the one stable force in my life when I was a child.

She came from a large family. Her brothers were born in Kiev, the capital city of the Ukraine, but in the late 1890s the family fled the violent anti-Semitism there and emigrated to England. Most Jewish immigrants during that time found their way to the East End of London, to Aldgate and Whitechapel, which, being close to the docks, were the hub of the community. And that's where my mother, Betty Bellin, was born in 1900. Surrounded by grinding poverty, she resolved early on to make the best of her life.

My father, Jack Sassoon, was born in Salonika, in the northern part of Greece. Blessed with both good looks and charm, it is easy to see why my mother was smitten with him when they met in 1925. Two years later, in 1927, they married and moved to Shepherds Bush, where there was a large community of Greek Jews.

Dad cajoled others into trusting him. A con artist who had the gift of the gab, he made people believe what he wanted them to believe. His brothers had also come to England and dealt in fine-quality Turkish and Eastern carpets, but his playboy manner did not sit well with them. Eventually, they asked him to find work elsewhere. Working or not, this carefree, debonair man was adored by the Greek community in Shepherds Bush. His love for life – and women – was a source of great attraction for those who did not have to rely on his ability to earn a living.

My mother always glossed over the bad bits of her life, but some years ago she was going through a box of faded pictures and started talking about the old days, when we used to live on a pittance. Her reminiscences piqued my curiosity. 'Mum,' I asked, 'what was the worst moment of your life?'

She paused for a moment, and then said, 'When you were three years old, Vidalico, and your brother six months, we were evicted and had nowhere to live.' (Mum always called me 'Vidalico'. The name 'Vidal' had been in my family for years. It was passed down to the first-born from grandfather to grandson, always skipping a generation.) As she spoke, her voice cracked and it was obvious that it still hurt her.

My brother, Ivor, and I were both born in Shepherds Bush, but when my father abandoned us for another woman, leaving my mother bereft, it was clear we could not stay there. I was later told my father spoke seven languages and had sex in all of them. And his casual attitude to earning a living left her unable to pay the rent on the house where we lived. Her problems seemed to be mounting day by day and she dreaded the thought of eviction. So, in the dead of night, she packed a few belongings and photographs that she treasured, and moved Ivor and me to my aunt

Katie's, her elder sister's. One of my father's brothers drove us to Katie's two-room tenement on Wentworth Street in Petticoat Lane, the very heart of the East End. Her husband had died, so she was raising her three children by herself. But despite her own troubles, she invited my mother, Ivor and me into the fold and her tiny flat. We kids slept on mattresses in one room, but Ivor was lucky; he had his own crib.

Life was very tough but, as she cuddled Ivor and me, telling us that we were her special little people, my mother would talk about the great times the future would bring. She always saw the good side of everything and everyone, especially the two of us. She never crumbled, and even as children, Ivor and I knew that she could make things right.

Mum was a large-boned, tall woman, with a curvaceous figure, an exotic look and a face that would cause passers-by to stare at her captivating olive-brown eyes. When the three of us were together, with her arms around us, we felt like a proper family. But I knew there was something missing in her life.

Our aunt Katie was living precariously close to the poverty line. But she was a robust woman with enormous vitality and a bellowing laugh. She had to laugh. There were seven of us living in her two rooms. The tenement itself was a vast, gloomy rabbit warren of ugly little flats. There were no bathrooms, no internal toilets – just cold running water in tiny kitchens. The roof was falling apart and leaked – sometimes water simply poured through it. There was one toilet shared by four families on the landing outside. To get to the toilet meant leaving through the front door and walking or running to the end of the landing. Once, in the early hours of a freezing winter morning, I had to queue for the toilet as two people were already ahead of me. In the winter, at night, frost collected on the toilet walls, and the seat was only kept warm by the person who occupied it before you. The frigid, damp air would invade the body and the soul. It was a quick dash both ways.

All we could see from our windows was the greyness of the tenements across the street. There was ugliness all around, and yet my aunt Katie and her family had a spirit and a humour that rose above the dingy circumstances of life in our crowded home. Aunt Katie's children, Kitty, Amelia and Sonny, were older than us and always kept an eye out to make sure that I wasn't getting myself into any scrapes or bother. As Ivor was just a baby, he needed extra loving care and was always the centre of attention.

There weren't many visitors to our flat, but I do remember Uncle Morrie, my mother's brother. Very patriotic, Morrie had volunteered for the army at the age of seventeen, during the First World War. After basic training, he was sent to the Dardanelles with his regiment, but he was wounded in the head and was never quite the same again. He was a simple man who seemed lost and bewildered by all that had happened to him. It was sometimes a little scary for us kids as he'd wander off into sentences that we could not understand, but he was kind and gentle, and was often found in our kitchen talking quietly to himself.

In the corner of our tenement was Mrs Cohen's bakery. The whole lane was familiar with Mrs Cohen's kind heart and caustic tongue, but it was her bagels that sustained us when we were hungry. Mrs Cohen served from a small counter and there were breads of every kind on display, but it was in a kitchen at the back of the shop where she performed her magic. She baked the most delicious cakes and bagels, and if the wind was blowing in just the right direction, the delectable smells of cinnamon, nutmeg and warm bread would waft into our tiny flat, making us feel instantly ravenous, but with money so tight we had to get used to ignoring the hunger pangs. Another torment was the seductive smell of Mrs Feinstein's latkes – crisp little pancakes made of grated potatoes. She cooked them in her tiny shop in the tenement but sold them in the street. They were delicious, but we could rarely afford such treats.

There is one episode I will always remember. Ivor, who was three at the time, asked Mum if he could go down to Mrs Cohen's and get a bagel. Mum gave in to his pleading, handed me two pennies and told me to look after him.

Mrs Cohen gave us the usual grumbling spiel about always wanting something for nothing, so was delighted when I handed over the two coppers. Clutching our bagels, Ivor and I walked out of Mrs Cohen's into the market stalls and general chaos of Petticoat Lane. Suddenly I was alone. I'd lost my brother. I couldn't find him anywhere. I ran upstairs to tell Mum, and within fifteen minutes, everybody we knew in the neighbourhood was looking for Ivor.

Two hours later, he was found behind one of the stalls, lying in a banana box. Ivor had gone there to savour his bagel in private, munching it a little at a time. When we finally came across him, he was sound asleep, with a half-smile of contentment on his face.

I never lost him again.

Home-life was a little on the cramped side, but some evenings my mother would push the threadbare furniture to one side and entertain us all with her Spanish dancing. There was an exotic flourish of her skirts as she started to sing and play the castanets. She had a poised grace and style to her dancing, which my cousins Kitty and Amelia tried to emulate. The dance was not as easy as it looked and we laughed a lot at their attempts to keep up. When she did not want us children to understand, Mum would speak in either Ladino (the Jewish form of Spanish) or Yiddish, depending on which side of the family she was talking to.

In the streets outside, we played football – the chap whose ball it was usually had the privilege of being centre forward. When the first thud of the ball was heard, a bunch of street urchins and ragamuffins just like us would emerge from the nearby streets and alleyways, as if from nowhere. Life had a certain rhythm to it where football was involved. Coats or jackets were used as goal posts and kicking a ball about did no favours to the hand-me-down shoes most of us wore. As night-time fell and the market folded up, we all went our separate ways.

Dinnertime was a balancing act. Trying to feed seven people on a shoestring budget and a very small table took enormous dexterity on the part of Aunt Katie. Stew was the name of the game, especially vegetable stew. Sometimes, when we could afford meat, there were beef and lamb stews and, on very rare occasions, fish stew.

❖

When I was five, everything changed. Aunt Katie's girls were growing up and although we were too young to become inquisitive, it was felt that it was better we part. Mum approached the Jewish authorities and Ivor and I were accepted into the Spanish and Portuguese Jewish Orphanage in Lauderdale Road, Maida Vale, next door to the synagogue. But sadly for me, as Ivor was only three, it would be eighteen months before he was permitted to join me.

My mother sat me down and told me that I would be going

away to this new school within the next two weeks. She promised I would be well looked after and would get a good education. I didn't care about an education; I did not want to leave home. I knew how much I would miss Mum's wonderful touch as she hugged Ivor and me each night before we went to bed. That night, I fell asleep hugging my skinny little brother and wondered when I would see him again.

I was going to miss the neighbourhood, too. The lane was my life – the smells of the street, the shops, the kindness and humour of the barrow boys. We got up to all sorts of pranks. I did not know what my mother did to provide for our very basic living, but during the long hours she was at work, Ivor and I ran around the feet of the crowd and on occasion pinched fruit from the barrows. We were so much a part of the lane scene, I'm sure the barrow boys looked the other way, knowing we were hungry. Wentworth Street was a huge playground to us kids and I remember being happy most of the time. I had got used to muddling along with Aunt Katie and my cousins, so why couldn't things stay the same? I had lost my father when I was three, and my brother in Petticoat Lane when I was five. Now, only a few weeks later, being told that I was to be taken away from the whole family, I was certain I was being punished. I felt scared, unwanted and unloved.

On the dreaded day, as my mother and I walked through the main doors of the orphanage, I took in the smell of this dark, ugly building and felt sick to my stomach. I knew I had to stop her leaving me there. I grabbed her skirt and just wouldn't let go. Through my tears I begged and pleaded, 'Mama, no! No, Mama. No!'

The man on duty took hold of the hands that were tightly gripping my mother's skirt and gently separated me from her.

Mum was crying, too, but she made one last effort to reassure me that this would be good for me. As she reached the door and turned towards me, I saw the tears running down her cheeks. She put her hands to her lips and threw kisses in my direction as she headed slowly out through the door. I felt I was all alone – a feeling that would stay with me a long, long time.

I was given a quick tour of my new home. There were dormitories on four floors; two for girls and two for boys. I was shown my quarters and a bed was assigned to me towards the end of the room. I laid my head down and started to cry, and although there were many boys in the room at the time, they left me alone. They knew all too well how I felt.

After a while, I heard footsteps at the side of my bed. A master had come into the room. He placed his hand on my shoulder and told me everything would be fine. I turned and saw a kind face and wanted desperately to believe him. But as I looked around the room, the drabness hit me. The walls were grey, the beds were iron cots, the room was orderly and spotless. It was just for sleeping in.

But there was a playroom on the first floor that we all shared. There were books for different age groups, and colouring books and crayons for the younger kids like me. On any given day, four of my fellow inmates could be seen playing table tennis, while a couple of kids would always be wrestling in the corner. There was a radio, and the stations were constantly being changed by the kid closest to it, as nobody seemed to like the same programme. My new surroundings had nothing of the excitement of Wentworth Street, where we didn't even have a playroom, and I wished hard and often that I was back there.

I asked when I could see my mother and was told that visiting day was one Sunday each month. *One Sunday each month?*

I was bereft. But I kept my feelings to myself. I felt different from the other boys, lost in surroundings that I never quite got used to.

The man who had put his hand on my shoulder was the headmaster, Daniel Mendoza, who took a special interest in me from the moment I arrived. He told me how lucky I was to be there, and insisted I grab the opportunities to study and learn. My confidence grew as he encouraged me, and he quickly became the father figure I had never had. But it was not to last. Masters came and went, and after two years Mr Mendoza left too. But his influence remained and I will always be grateful for the optimism he instilled in us boys. During those two years, he taught us the value of using our imagination and natural talents. But, for me, the most important thing the wonderful Mr Mendoza did was give me back my zest for life.

A year and a half after I arrived at the orphanage, it was Ivor's turn to leave Petticoat Lane and we were reunited. I was so relieved to see my little brother again and took him for a tour of the building, explaining the different rooms as we went – where we were allowed to go and where we weren't. I felt very protective as I showed him round his new home. Fortunately, he settled in quite well. Ivor was very wise for his years and listening to us you would not have been able to tell that there was any age difference.

I spent nearly seven years at the orphanage. And though I've been told many times that I must have had a terrible childhood, in fact that was not always the case. The orphanage had a bath – a rare luxury in those days. I was often found in it. There was a big yard out back, and as I loved football and had a ready-made squad of my fellow orphans to play with, I was able to succumb to its temptation every day. But I remember being hungry much of the time; we all were. The portions of food at mealtimes were rather small. Although cooked well, it was not quite enough, and I often left the table with an empty feeling in my stomach. There were never second helpings, and like Oliver Twist, there was no point in asking for more. And of course I always longed to see my mother, who was only allowed to visit us once a month and never permitted to take us out.

The masters were mostly kind but they made it clear that we were among the unfortunates of this world, often reminding us of this fact, and telling us that we were being looked after by the community and we should respect this and be grateful. They seemed compelled to say, 'Remember, this is an *orphanage*.' None of us thought for one moment that it was Buckingham Palace. Aside from trying to turn us into decent, civilized members of society, one of their responsibilities was to see that we were all tucked in bed at an appropriate time each night. There was one master, Mr Shine, who was regularly on dormitory duty. A terrifying man who played on our fear, he would inspect our underpants and if there were any 'pertaining marks of negligence', we were given six of the best with the back of a brush. Fortunately, the authorities that governed us agreed that his views on small boys and hygiene weren't the norm, and he was quickly got rid of.

We all went to school at Essendine Road Elementary. It was a Christian school of about a thousand kids in a tough neighbourhood, but its pupils were mostly well disciplined. Coming from the nearby orphanage, we naturally drew attention to ourselves as we walked in pairs through Paddington Recreation Ground to get there. There were frequent taunts of 'Yid' from the other kids. Among other things, they would chant, 'All Jews have long noses,' and we'd return the compliment with our own, 'All Yocks have funny cocks.'

Each year there was a Sports Day, and when I was ten, I won the hundred-yard dash in front of the whole school. I was elated because I had beaten some damn good runners, and although it upset one or two of my fellow athletes that an outsider had become champion, others congratulated me with genuine enthusiasm and sportsmanship. The need to win has never left me.

There was one particularly memorable family at the orphanage – the Addises, originally from Manchester. Albert, the eldest, was head boy. He was powerful, a bit of a bully, and we all took great care not to cross his path. Raymond and Dennis were twins my age and we became great friends. Raymond was a great scrapper and much to our delight would take on anybody. Dennis and I would watch and cheer him on. Raymond and I fought once, over what I can't remember, but the black eye I received for my troubles should have been photographed for posterity; it was a shiner that was admired by all.

The synagogue needed choir boys and we were all forced to audition. It says something about the shortage of natural talent that somehow I was selected. We wore black robes and choir-boy hats and sang in Hebrew, which meant that none of us understood a word we were singing. The bass singer, a Mr Diaz, who had been there for years, rehearsed us and actually turned our miserable voices into something quite passable. In fact, at times we sounded rather angelic. I had a high soprano voice, which I disinherited immediately after leaving the synagogue. But I was chosen to sing solo, and that gave me a feeling of belonging, which meant a lot to me. Not only that, it also gave me a chance to see my mother, because she was allowed to come to the synagogue every Saturday to hear me sing and she'd wave to me from the balcony.

But trouble was brewing. When it came to rules and regulations, I was the odd boy out. I often decided to do things my own way. One Saturday afternoon after choir, I decided I'd had enough of the discipline at the orphanage and ran away. I wondered, Should I go to the East End and try to find my mother, or to Shepherds Bush, where my mother's great friend, Auntie Polly, lived? I decided on the latter.

Auntie Polly was a relative of my father; a thin, elegant lady to whom people often went with their troubles. I don't really know what drew me to her, but it was closer to Maida Vale and I had strong memories of her house, as prior to moving to the orphanage we were always visiting there. Also I thought I'd be able to see my father again. As I was only ten and had no money or other means to get to Auntie Polly's house, I walked all the way. She immediately called my father, who, later that evening, came to her house. He did not show me any kindness or love, but just took me straight back to the orphanage.

I had expected so much more from our reunion. I knew my mother loved me, but my father's total neglect had only made me want his love and recognition more. I'd been longing to see him for more than half my life.

It was not to be. I can still remember the incredible sadness I felt when he rejected me again. His face, as he left, had no tenderness. He was already somewhere else. Numbly, I watched him pull out of the driveway. I never saw him again.

My mother was informed and came at once to the orphanage. She was heartbroken. I had never seen her so distressed; tears were running down her face. In between sobs she kept saying, 'Don't you know that *I'm* the one who truly cares for you?' She couldn't bear that I had turned to my father's family when things got tough. I stroked her face as she cuddled me and told her that I did not know where she lived since she had found a different job and moved from Aunt Katie's.

No one had run away from the orphanage before, and I remember a meeting where we were allowed to speak our thoughts. There was only one thought and I expressed it: we all wanted more food. The portions did become larger, which gave me the respect of my fellow inmates for about nine and a half minutes.

✧

On 1 September 1939, we heard on the radio news that Nazi Germany had attacked Poland. On 3 September, France and Britain declared war on Germany. It's a date I'll never forget. All children of school age and younger were evacuated from London and sent off to the country. We orphans were given a bag to put a few precious belongings in. Mine consisted of a handful of clothes and a beaten-up pair of toe-curling shoes.

We were taken to a railway station, where we were given nametags. Suddenly my brother and I and all our fellow orphans were on trains with hundreds of thousands of other kids, moving out of London. For an eleven-year-old boy, largely unaware of the terrifying aspects of war, it was an incredible adventure. We left the station at about ten o'clock in the morning and three or four hours later the train stopped at a place called Trowbridge, in Wiltshire. From there, we were bussed to Holt, a small village of a thousand people, which had two pubs but otherwise seemed a rather unremarkable place, given the early promise of the train journey across rolling countryside. It did, though, have a splendid village green where, in the summer months, each Sunday after church, the religion of cricket was practised, as I was soon to discover.

The authorities tried to keep sisters, brothers and other relatives together as much as possible, and Ivor and I found ourselves greeted by an extremely tall family, a Mr and Mrs Lucas and their young, leggy daughter, Veronica. We were to spend a year with them in a tiny house off the lane that led to the school. There was a row of four modest houses all together and the Lucases lived in the second one along. It was small but comfortable, with what seemed to me a very country smell and atmosphere, sort of damp, and yet inviting at the same time. They had a Labrador called Spot and he lived outside in the front garden in his own house, a kennel. We got to take him through the village to the open fields each day. It was the first time I'd ever seen cows or sheep in such large numbers. They outnumbered the village people tenfold.

Mr Lucas worked in what was now a munitions factory in Melksham, about three miles away, and he'd bike both ways as the bus service was very limited. He was secretive about his war work, which I found intriguing. Mrs Lucas looked after the house and made sure that her daughter did not become too interested in a certain eleven-year-old lad from London. Veronica was a graceful young blonde with blue eyes, and many of my school chums had a crush on her. I learned to keep a respectful distance as her mother's gaze, though generally kindly, became a good deal more fierce when it came to the honour of her only daughter.

In a school not more than a hundred yards from the Lucases' house, Ivor and I and the rest of the kids from the orphanage made friends with the local children. They had a strange accent, which I learned was West Country. I'd never heard English spoken this way before, and mentioned it to Veronica, who said she felt the same way about our Cockney accents.

The British government had come to an agreement pre-war with the German government that 10,000 Jewish children from Germany would be allowed to enter Britain, and a group of these children were also evacuated to Holt. They only spoke German – which was even stranger to me than West Country – and were put in a class by themselves while learning English. At the age of eleven, I could say *'Guten tag!'* on a daily basis but very little else, though we soon discovered a common language that we could all understand. Everybody played football, and our friendships grew from the feet up.

I was a very bad student. I could not come to grips with anything that really didn't interest me and my grades were abysmal, with the exception of mental arithmetic, which I was good at. There was one teacher, Mr Jones, who intrigued us all. He was Welsh, and even as a young boy I realized that his aptitude for language was extraordinary. He captured my imagination with his lyrical voice. I wondered if I would ever speak with such clarity. He'd use word play and verbal quips, and would occasionally spout poetry to us in his most dramatic voice. He was also the master who taught mental arithmetic, and after a session in which I had done particularly well, he looked at me and said, 'Sassoon, it is a pleasure to see that you have gaps of intelligence between bouts of ignorance.' I wrote it down because I knew I would not remember it otherwise. I liked Mr Jones a lot.

A year after we had arrived in the village, my mother and a Mr Nathan Goldberg arrived in Holt. My mother had recently become Mrs Nathan Goldberg and though Ivor and I knew she was remarrying, we had not yet met the gentleman or got to grips with the idea of a stepfather. In the autumn of 1940, they rented a small house from a local farmer. They thanked the Lucases profusely for having looked after us so well, and moved us in with them. My brother and I were in shock. I had not lived with my mother since I was five and Ivor not since he was four and there was also this strange man who had suddenly come into our lives.

We took things slowly. Mum was aware that we weren't going to take to the idea of our new dad overnight, but gradually we found out many things about Nathan G, as we came to call him. Back in London, he had worked as a foreman in a tailoring factory. He was a machinist who had had a dozen people working under his direction. Tailoring was what he had done all his life. But he had given up this well-paying job to be with my mother, and was now employed by a laundry in Trowbridge. The work was hard and the pay was little. But there was something about Nathan G that soon endeared him to Ivor and me. He would come home, put on his slippers, relax into his favourite armchair, and listen to Gigli and Caruso, two of the great tenors that he loved. He was a big opera fan – something that Ivor and I hadn't even heard of then. He read philosophy and taught me to write thoughts down as they came to me, a habit that has stuck with me all my life.

Nathan G also had style. When dressed in a suit, a handkerchief always flourished from his top pocket. The trilby hat that he wore at a slight angle gave him the appearance of a toff. He was a well-built man, quite powerful, and in his younger days boxed semi-professionally. For the young and uneducated, fighting was one of the only ways to break free from the ugliness of poverty. His ambition was to win some big fights and earn enough cash to leave. Nathan G never became a champ, but he was passionate when talking of his closest friend, Ted 'Kid' Lewis, who did. He was an East End fighter who proudly wore the Star of David on his trunks and became Welterweight Champion of the World. Nathan G was never more animated than when he proudly related to Ivor and me some of the great fights that Ted 'Kid' Lewis fought and won. Lewis had handsomely beaten an American boxer, Jack Britton, in New York to claim the world title. The whole country had apparently gone crazy about the victory, and even though the fight didn't finish until after four in the morning, people ran out into the streets, dancing and singing into the late hours of the morning.

Slowly, Nathan G became our dad and Ivor and I learned to love him. Later I realized just how much I had learned from him and how lucky my mother had been to meet this man who would transform our lives. The small house that we rented cost five shillings a week. His wages at the laundry were only three pounds a week, four with overtime. This didn't seem to concern him, though, as he loved my mother dearly, and they would walk hand-in-hand through the village with a devotion that was obvious to all.

There was a modest shop in the village that satisfied most of our needs. It had a little of everything, including one or two items that always surprised me, like the latest jazz records and magazines that weren't meant to be seen by children. Nathan G, by then a regular customer, was told by the proprietor that they needed a newspaper boy to do the afternoon round. The evening papers arrived from London at around 4.30 and Nathan G thought I was the obvious choice to deliver them. He told me about the paper-round job with such enthusiasm it was hard to resist. He told me it was five days a week with the weekends off – but think of the independence it would buy me! He talked to me about values, making sure that I understood that half of the salary I was to receive, which was three shillings and sixpence a week, should go to my mother. He said that even at twelve years old, which I was then, one could not live free and that it was important to contribute to the family income.

Transport was supplied, as the newspaper round came with a bicycle. I'd bike to the railway station each day. I'd pick up two dozen papers, which were literally thrown from a slow-moving train, and go on my rounds. I soon discovered that the village had far too many BEWARE OF THE DOG signs. But I was never bitten, and being able to give my mum a shilling at the end of the week was very rewarding.

The job was curiously fascinating, as I learned so much more about the village. There was a huge estate owned by Lady Cecilie Goff, whose magnificent gardens were internationally renowned. It was also rumoured that she was a great friend of the Queen. I never saw her or her gardens, for as soon as I rang the bell, a housemaid would arrive at the side gate to pick up the newspaper.

Then there was the young couple who lived in a gorgeous house with a swimming pool. They looked as though they had stepped straight out of a Hollywood movie, as they were rather beautiful. I saw them embrace on a few occasions, and visions of them making violent love accompanied me on the rest of the newspaper round – I was still only twelve, but the teenage hormones were already there in full force.

Generally, though, I was delivering to ordinary people who wanted to see the news in print. There were nods of recognition and sometimes even a hello as I threw the papers into the doorways. There was one man, a Mr Harris, who screamed blue murder at the proprietor, saying that he hadn't received his newspaper for a week. I had inadvertently thrown his paper into the wrong doorway and it was gratefully accepted by the person who lived there, thinking it was a present from the shop owner. Luckily, it was all sorted out and I wasn't fired, despite Mr Harris's angry mutterings: 'You can't trust those bloody evacuees from London.' There were no other incidents of note and I kept the job for a year and a bit.

Saturday was a day when many of our dreams came to pass. At two o'clock, Dad (for I had come to think of Nathan G as that now) would take Ivor and me on the bus from the village green to Trowbridge. Trowbridge had two cinemas and Dad would choose something he thought was suitable. The show was always three hours long, opening with a cartoon, then the British Movietone News, which covered the war, a B-movie (which was very B) and then the main event. Errol Flynn had always been my favourite action man, but I remember watching Tyrone Power as Jesse James. I was riveted. After that, Errol Flynn definitely took second place in my fantasies of being a he-man.

After we left the cinema, Dad would take us into a bookshop and we would walk around while he talked about the magic of finding so many beautiful books, some by very famous writers, in one place. He would say, 'Open a book, feel it, smell it, and one day you will be old enough to read it and understand its message.' We couldn't afford to buy anything, though, but that extraordinary ritual has stayed with me. To this day I keep a well-stocked library in my house and another in a little guest house. Being around books has always enticed me to learn. Back then Ivor and I would stand open-mouthed in awe at Nathan G's knowledge. There was no doubt in our minds that he was a very wise man.

At the age of fourteen, practically to the day – which for me was 17 January – you were literally pitched out of school to make way for some other semi-literate who would have to suffer the insults I had. The school-leaving age was fourteen, not fourteen and a few days, so after my birthday, that was it. Unless you were extraordinarily bright and had won a scholarship, or had money for further education, you went to work. Giving up my news-paper job for something full-time held little concern for me except that I was rather sad that the bicycle had to go.

There was a large factory in Holt by the name of Bevins that made gauntlets for the RAF and gloves for its other customers. It employed half the village. I was taken on at twelve shillings a week, which seemed a fortune to me – until I remembered Mum would get six.

Glove cutting was a craft that had to be learned. It took experience to know exactly how to stretch the leather and use the shears, and I was open-mouthed watching the truly profes-sional glove cutters doing what they did. My job was to cut the straps that would eventually be sewn to the gauntlets. I learned to be very precise, as apart from one end of the strap being sewn to the gauntlet, at the other end I would have to cut a slight circle for the snap. I'm not sure I believe in divine intuition, but it seems worthy of note that in my very first full-time job, I had a pair of shears in my hand.

The general patter of the cutters had a country flavour to it. I did not hear too much chatter about the war, but was well informed about how many pints of beer they had drunk the night before. They were good-natured and generous and kidded me a lot. Knowing I was Jewish, they looked for horns growing out of my head and pretended to be disappointed when they couldn't find any. Of course I knew they were joking and felt no animos-ity at all from anyone.

I left after only three months and on my last day, with an

uncanny sense of the ridiculous, I turned up wearing plastic horns. The whole floor saw the funny side of this and the foreman gave me a big hug. I left the horns with him for posterity.

Our eighteen months in the country with Mum and Nathan G had united us as a family but the work at the laundry was affecting his health, and he was subsidizing our stay in the country with his savings, which were rapidly dwindling. So, after two and a half years in Wiltshire, we said goodbye to the Lucases and all our other friends and moved back to London.

Because of the continuous bombing there were few properties available to rent, but my mother found an old house in Lawrence Road, Bow. It needed a lot of work, but the landlord saw no point in refurbishing it as a bomb could have taken it down the following day. This unstable residence had a sitting room, a dining room, a kitchen, which also served as a bathroom, two bedrooms on the upstairs floor and, as usual, a well-used toilet out back. We were back to the old East End way of life.

✧

I needed to find a job and I had heard they were looking for lads in the City of London who would take messages down to the docks, so I made my way over to a small office in the City and applied.

The officer behind the desk was patient as I enthusiastically rattled on about my qualifications. He listened to me with obvious amusement, and when I stopped talking, he said, 'Son, we don't need a genius for this job. All we need is a kid with a bike. Do you have one?'

'No,' I said, feeling my hopes drain away.

'Well, son, unless you're a long-distance runner, go pinch one.'

Pinch a bike? He wasn't serious, was he?

As ever, Dad came to the rescue and a second-hand bike was quickly purchased. I got the job, which turned out to be arduous but interesting, as the German Air Force was each night rearranging the streets of London, and my route from the City to the docks seemed to change daily. I got used to seeing bodies and blood, and hearing cries of agony as people who had been injured were rushed to hospital.

We were sleeping in the shelters, down on the platforms of the Underground station. There were always sing-songs, which lifted everybody's spirits. Vera Lynn was of course very popular then and we all knew the words to her biggest wartime hit, 'The White Cliffs of Dover'. As I joined in the singing, I could only imagine the strength of those white cliffs and the bluebirds winging their way over them across the Channel to France – a freedom that was not open to me.

At night, a bunch of us fourteen-year-old lads would wander around the shelter watching the young girls get ready for bed. We were naughty, but they were very pretty. Between six and seven each morning, my family would make our way back to the house, which was close by. Dad's track record as a first class craftsman meant that he was welcomed back to his original position with open arms. He used the kitchen/bathroom first, as he had to be at work by eight o'clock. Ivor and I always argued over who should be second. He was very persuasive.

That same year, Ivor, who was top of his class in school, won a scholarship to the Regent Street Polytechnic. The whole school had evacuated to Minehead in Somerset, on the west coast of England, and Ivor joined them there. He was always brilliant, and his headmaster, Dr Bernard Worsnop, asked to see my mother. At their meeting, he defined Ivor as Oxford or

Cambridge material and suggested that he should have extra tuition. Sadly, we never had the money.

I was now earning a small amount of cash, and although I had left the orphanage some three years earlier, I still had fantasies about the hot baths there. But there was a way to relive those rare moments of luxury, as I had discovered!

Once a week, I could go to the local public baths in Stepney Green and bask in the piping-hot water. It was an enormous space that housed about thirty baths, and typically two or three attendants were on duty. Each person had their own private cubicle, but there was no ceiling to each bathroom, only a giant roof very high up, so sound travelled well throughout. When a customer left the bath, one of the attendants with a big broom and bucket of soap would scrub it clean and start filling it with hot water for the next person in line. Each of the bathrooms was numbered and if the water cooled as you were luxuriating, you would shout, almost sing, your number to the attendant: 'Hot water number twenty-three ... Hot water number twenty-three ... Hot water number twenty-three ...' This would continue until the attendant came to number twenty-three and poured hot water into the bath. Then the next cubicle would take up the song: 'Hot water number twenty-four ...' As the attendant stopped pouring water into the baths, a chorus of happy bathers would croak in unison, 'Ooh ... ahh ... lovely.'

I usually felt clean for about two days. Back at the house in Bow, we would lock ourselves in the kitchen one at a time, boil some water on the gas stove, and with a flannel, soap and vigour, wash the necessary parts daily.

Oh, to be an orphan again ...

2

Professor Cohen

I enjoyed my job as a bike messenger, learning the alleyways and shortcuts through the city, whizzing along, indulging in fantasies of espionage, of capturing an enemy agent and becoming a hero overnight. My mother got to hear about all the fun I was having, and after three months of this decided that she and I had to talk.

She sat me down and told me of her ambitions for me. I listened, but didn't really take it in. She talked of hairdressing as a profession, but I wanted to become a footballer. I could not imagine myself backcombing hair and winding up rollers for a living. My mother was an expert at holding her own; she could take any side of an argument and win. She told me about a dream she had had – a vision of my future – adding, 'Sorry, son. A premonition is a premonition.' I vigorously protested but she was having none of my nonsense.

On the appointed day, she dressed me in my finest – which was the smarter of my two pairs of trousers – and, totally against my will, frog-marched me into the salon of Adolph Cohen at 101 Whitechapel Road. Mr Cohen was *the* hairdresser of the

East End. He had enormous respect in the neighbourhood, especially among the ladies, and was fondly nicknamed 'the Professor'. He was not only an excellent craftsman, he was also highly regarded as a wigmaker. There was a well-earned admiration for him in hairdressing circles, Mum had told me on the bus on the way over.

Mr Cohen greeted us with a warm smile. He was all of five foot two but had the presence and personality of a much larger man and an attitude that made us feel immediately welcome. After about fifteen minutes of conversation with mainly my mother talking, he stopped her in mid-flow with, 'You do know that we charge a fee of one hundred guineas to teach an apprentice? Even if he's a natural and picks the craft up easily, it will take at least two years of study, and many more before he becomes truly good.'

My mother looked so terribly dejected, I thought she might faint. I held her arm gently. Finally, she collected herself. 'But, Mr Cohen, we don't have one hundred buttons.'

There was nothing more to be said. We shook hands and walked to the door. I opened the door for my mother and doffed my cap to Mr Cohen, leading my mother into the street. I couldn't have been happier. I could now go about the business of trying to become an ace striker. We hadn't walked two yards before the door of the salon opened behind us. We heard Mr Cohen call out, 'Excuse me,' and turned towards him. 'You seem to have very good manners, young man. Start Monday and forget the fee.'

He looked at my mother with the look of a man who had just done his good deed for the century. Tears rolled down my mum's face out of pure joy.

As for me, I was in total shock. I couldn't believe that after fifteen minutes of listening to my mother's greatest-ever sales pitch, my life had gone downhill so drastically. I was about to become an *apprentice ladies' hairdresser*. What could I possibly tell my mates? I sat in silence on the bus that took us back to Bow. My mum understood how I felt. How could I – a young, virile athlete – succumb to my mother's wishes?

For two or three days, my spirits were lower than low. I wanted to be alone. But at 8.30 the following Monday morning, I was in Adolph Cohen's salon, scrubbing floors and cleaning mirrors, along with several other young apprentices. The only amusement I had was in wondering whether the parents of the other apprentices, who had paid one hundred guineas for their children to learn the craft, knew that they were also scrubbing floors and cleaning mirrors. But all the women who usually did this job were in factories doing war work.

I was told what my salary would be over the two-year period of my apprenticeship. I would start on five shillings a week, with a five-shilling rise every six months. At the end of my apprenticeship, I would be making the princely sum of one pound. I was advised by one of the more advanced juniors at the salon that I would do well to become an excellent shampoo boy, as tips would become a vital part of my earnings.

Professor Cohen made it clear that a good appearance was essential. His first rule was that all male apprentices must have a crease in their trousers every morning. When I tried to point out that there was a war on and we were sleeping in the Underground, I was told in no uncertain terms that I should find a way. I soon discovered that putting my trousers inside a folded blanket that was then slept on didn't do a bad job at all. My nails also had to be clean. This was done partly by shampooing so many heads. Walking through the London rubble after a night's bombing made shining shoes a difficult feat, yet Mr Cohen would not allow unpolished shoes in his salon. In the small pack that we carried our equipment in I learned to carry a tin of shoe polish and a rag. Professor Cohen was an extreme disciplinarian and never wavered from the standards he set.

The salon was on two floors with a cellar. As clients entered on the ground floor, they were greeted by a receptionist, who, it would appear, was only taught how to smile and nothing else. But it was a tough job. So many of the clients had problems as a result of the war, the shortages and rationing, and the receptionists had to have a warm way about them to help the clients feel at ease and to relax some jangled nerves. During my two-year apprenticeship, there were at least twelve receptionists. Many left to join the army on the basis that it was easier and certainly more fun than dealing with clients on a short fuse.

The reception area had a showcase of wigs, combs and brushes that were for sale, but being wartime the choices were few. It was also appointed with well-worn furniture that had clearly seen better days. Many of the clients would sit and gossip to one another while waiting for their stylists. I would often catch parts of their conversations and was frequently left wondering who was doing what to whom.

I had a bet with Renee, a fellow apprentice, that I could walk to Aldgate, about half a mile away, wearing one of Mr Cohen's wigs and not be noticed. I went into a cubicle with a red wig parted on the left side and set in waves, ends flipped up. I put it on, then fixed my cap at a jaunty angle and, feeling like one of the Three Musketeers, I took to the streets. All that was missing was a cape and a sword.

Odd as I looked, I won the bet. But when Mr Cohen saw me walking back into his emporium, he was beside himself with fury, convinced that I was making a mockery of his wig. In fact, I would have to say the Professor was most unprofessorial on this occasion. I hadn't realized he was so attached to the wig, especially as it suited me rather well. I was high-spirited and a little devilish perhaps, but when Mr Cohen realized I meant no harm, he calmly accepted my apology.

The real drama, however, took place in the salon itself, where each client had their own private cubicle. Taped to the wall in each cubicle was a typewritten notice that read: MADAM, DURING AN AIR RAID, YOU ARE PERMED AT YOUR OWN RISK.

This was no idle warning as the perms in those days were quite primitive. The perming machine was plugged into the mains and had rods attached which the client's hair was wrapped round. Each rod was then covered with an electrical heating device. She couldn't have moved even if she had wanted to. When the air-raid warning sounded, I was obliged to say, 'Excuse me, madam. I'm going down to the shelter. I promise I'll be back.' Then we went down to the shelter, which was actually the cellar of the salon. The machine itself was run by electricity, and the one duty of an apprentice was to turn the electricity off before leaving for the shelter along with the rest of the staff and those clients who were not being permed.

Eventually, the 'all clear' would sound and we'd diligently return to our clients, some of whom still sat grasping the sides of their chairs, cursing whoever it was who invented perms. They had heard the bombs exploding, but were trapped in their seats. It took courage to have a perm during wartime.

On one occasion, I realized to my horror that through my

laxity, I had forgotten to turn off the machine. At that time there were two very popular looks. One was the 'Maria Cut', as worn by Ingrid Bergman in *For Whom the Bell Tolls*, a film about the Spanish Civil War, and was very, *very* short. The other was named for Rita Hayworth, a major Hollywood star then, whose long, curly mane was much copied by young would-be glamour girls.

My unfortunate client had not got the look she came in for. 'Rita Hayworth' had inadvertently become a 'Maria' – all her hair had been burnt off. I was horrified. Fortunately for me, the lady in question had a stoic attitude to adversity coupled with a strong sense of the ridiculous, and when the boss had rectified my mistake by giving her the perfect cropped cut, she looked at me and said, 'Son, not bad for wartime.'

Although each client sat in a private cubicle to have their hair cut and set, they still had to walk to a communal area to have it washed. It was a very busy salon, visited by the local A-list, secretaries, nurses from the nearby London Hospital and many young women in their army, navy or air force uniforms. Hairdressing gowns were the last thing the garment factories were manufacturing in 1942, so ours were old but always clean. I got used to the demands of the clientele, and didn't mind at all answering the call of a beautiful girl who wanted a magazine or a relaxing head massage.

As an apprentice, I spent the first few months learning how to shampoo and massage scalps correctly. Whenever the clients had departed, the Professor or one of his top stylists would teach us how to make waves and curls on old wigs. Even then I thought it was tedious. It was to be six months before I cut my first head of hair. Obviously we could not be trusted with the clients, so we had to pick someone from a few rungs further down the social ladder. A little way down Whitechapel Road was Rowton House – the local dosshouse. Every drunk and social misfit checked into this establishment at one time or another and was allowed to sleep and, if they so desired, shower.

Professor Cohen said to me, 'Vidal, go to Rowton House and find yourself a model. No one is expecting you to do a creative haircut, as you hardly know how to hold a pair of scissors. But I promise you, the model you choose will not know the difference.'

It must have been destiny. There sitting in a chair in the hallway was a hulking great creature, six foot six of wild man who must have weighed at least eighteen stone. When the call had gone out at Rowton House for anyone who needed a haircut, Dr Patrick Joseph Aloysius O'Shaughnessy's fate was suddenly in my hands.

As we were walking up Whitechapel Road towards the salon, he looked down at me and said, 'So *you're* the young limey lad that's going to give this fine upstanding Irishman a haircut.'

On the way to the salon, he was singing out of tune. When I asked him what songs they were, he grinned. 'Irish Republican ditties, but don't tell a soul.'

He swept into the salon like Lord Wellington home from the wars, and Patrick O'Shaughnessy's booming voice greeted one and all. I took him into the very last cubicle, where he discarded his jacket and my nostrils caught his smell. I looked at him and said, 'Please excuse me for a moment.'

When I came back, I handed him a bar of soap and a towel. As I led him to the basin, he got my meaning, and scrubbed his face and neck. I then vigorously shampooed his hair, and brought him back into the cubicle. He chattered away non-stop, gathering momentum as he told me that the problems between

England and Ireland were because the Irish spoke and wrote English far better than the English did. His gift of the blarney actually helped – I could cut his hair freely while he attacked the whole system we lived by.

Naturally I was copying what I had seen done by the experts in the salon, and although the cut was pretty awful, the scissors felt very comfortable in my hand. When I finished the job, he examined it carefully in the big mirror in front of him. Then I held up another mirror so that he could see the back, which he studied with equal care.

Nodding in gentle approval, he said, 'Most elegant. Some day you will be a fine barber.'

As he left, he promised to tip me most generously on his next visit, and actually wanted to make an appointment for the following month. I told him we didn't take appointments for models, but I would come to Rowton House and find him – which I did.

Over the next year, I learned about Synge, Joyce and Beckett, along with several other Irish literary greats. When I first met Patrick O'Shaughnessy, I hadn't a clue who any of these people were. But even an inebriated soul with no particular ambition in sight can be a teacher. I will never forget him.

Eventually, after many models and about eighteen months, I was given my first client. She was middle-aged and plump, had sandy-coloured hair, and even then I was looking for her facial bone structure – which was nonexistent. My effort did not particularly grace her looks, and the Professor had to come and add the finishing touches. Nonetheless, I was gaining confidence, and even when I wasn't cutting, I found myself holding a pair of scissors. I was beginning to enjoy the challenge, but even with the benefit of hindsight I cannot say I was brighter or better than any of the other apprentices. In fact, I still wasn't at all sure that my mother's premonition had been right.

❖

In 1945, Robert Zackham, who had just spent five years in the army, was discharged and came to work at Adolph Cohen's. He had been a hairdresser before his army service. He would bring sandwiches to work and the two of us would often go to the park to enjoy lunch; his adorable wife, Phyllis, who he introduced me to, would always pack an extra sandwich for me. Phyl, as she was known by all, was a small blonde with a big heart and a delightful Cockney accent. Mum also made sandwiches. Robert and I both had very healthy appetites and we would share those, too. He would tell stories of his younger days of learning hairdressing, and of being a very good amateur boxer, winning all his fights except one, which he lost to Arthur Danahar. Danahar eventually turned professional and became the Welterweight Champion of Great Britain. After being beaten by him, Robert gave up boxing for hairdressing full-time – which we both considered a very smart move.

There was a restaurant across the street called Joe's, and the kids whose parents had paid the one hundred guineas for their apprenticeship always had lunch there. It must have been nice to have rich parents. Some of the apprentices would occasionally come in with new shoes, and I used to feel so envious. Mine had to last. Every penny counted. Half my five shillings a week had to go to my mother. Once Professor Cohen said, 'There's a stain on your trousers.' I used to wear one pair while the other was at the cleaners. When I explained, he said, 'With your tips, go and get some second-hand ones.' I knew him well enough by this stage to refrain from pointing out that I had much more exciting plans for that money than boring old trousers – especially ones that had been worn by someone else.

During the days before the invasion of Europe, convoys of American and British troops, tanks and supply lorries passed the salon every day, on their way to the Channel ports. As the troops drove past, they would see the sign bearing the name ADOLPH COHEN. You can imagine the shouts that came our way. The least complimentary was, 'We're coming to get you, Adolph!' and I remember one sergeant screaming, 'And we'll be back for you, too, Cohen!' Another comment was, 'Cohen, how did you get a name like Adolph?' Everyone's morale was high and we would all laugh except Professor Cohen, who was never quite sure how serious they were.

Even in those precarious days, vanity was not far from the minds of our clients. The use of highlights had not been invented, but being blonde was very much the order of the day. In fact, whether a client was a blonde, a redhead or a brunette, the one thing they wanted was change. Mr Cohen would enter the cubicle where the client was sitting, and after a brief conversation about her needs, he would pronounce: 'Vidal, make a bleach for this client.'

In those days a 'bleach' consisted of a white bleach powder, H_2O_2 and 880 – basically peroxide and ammonia. The powder would not work alone without the peroxide and ammonia. In order to activate the bleaching process, I would carefully mix the peroxide with the powder in a small glass bowl, using a spatula to perform the work, then very gently take the lid partially off the ammonia bottle and pour two or three drops into the substance. I had to be very careful because dropping the ammonia bottle would have cleared the sinuses of the whole street, creating more chaos than a German air raid. I would give the bowl to Mr Cohen, who would put it on a tray-on-wheels and proceed to part the client's hair, colouring the roots. When the bleach had done its work, I was told to shampoo the head of the client, often left quite tender from the primitive bleaching process. I had to be very gentle, as burns from the bleach, which left sores on the head, were not as rare as one might hope.

Professor Cohen explained every step of the colouring process in exacting detail. I have much to thank him for, apart from the enormous fee that he didn't charge me. He spent a great deal of time with me, teaching me the basics with much patience, and he instilled in me the belief that hairdressing, at its best, is an art form that requires discipline. He would often stay late with me, after everyone had gone home, to explain something technical. He made it clear it was no bother to him. He lived right there above the shop so didn't have far to travel. When I remember him now, the word 'dignity' comes to mind – the cuffs of his crisply pressed trousers resting perfectly on his well-shined shoes, his greying hair combed to perfection, and his masterly manner with the clients. Each of them felt that he was there only for her. Adolph Cohen had such great pride in the craft of hairdressing it was contagious. He was not called 'Professor' for nothing. He actually knew everything there was to know about hair and would share his knowledge graciously. Slowly, over the period I was with him, something in me stopped fighting my early resistance to hairdressing.

Most evenings my family would gather round the radio and promptly at nine o'clock would hear: 'Here is the news, and this is Alvar Lidell reading it.' If not Alvar Lidell, it was Stuart Hibberd. For me, their crisp, precise pronunciation epitomized how English should be spoken. The English language held a great fascination for me and even at a young age, I understood that there was a vast world of possibilities out there for those who could master it. But apart from those two marvellous newsreaders, I didn't know many people who spoke it well. Our half-day was a Wednesday, which – fortunately for me – was also the theatre matinee day. If I had enough tips from shampooing, I would take a number 25 bus from the East End to the West End. I would buy a ticket from one of the many theatres on Shaftesbury Avenue or the Haymarket and stand at the back, elbow to elbow with others who couldn't afford a seat, and watch England's finest actors practising their craft.

I watched with awe the works of great playwrights – Chekhov, Ibsen, Shaw, Feydeau – but I never wanted to be an actor. The thought of learning a play word for word terrified me. But I did want to emulate their fine voices. With my East End accent, it was difficult, but it didn't stop me trying. After many visits to the theatre, the sounds became familiar and gradually voice and ear became as one. I found myself drifting apart from some of my East End mates, who would laugh at me for trying to talk posh, but I did not let it deter me. There were many other East Enders like me, with ambition, who wanted to make their mark. And so they did.

War or no war, people still had lives to live. At the end of the week, on my one full day off, I used to visit Petticoat Lane. It still meant so much to me and on Sundays the atmosphere there was something really special. One beautiful spring day, I got to thinking of Mrs Cohen, who had been so kind to Ivor and me when we were just nippers, and I bought her a little bouquet of flowers. I walked into her bakery and the gift took her totally by surprise. She tutted for a moment and, shaking her head, she said, 'One day you might, if a miracle happens, be somebody.' Then she added, 'Now buy some bagels.' I did – and couldn't resist buying some of Mrs Feinstein's delicious latkes too.

One of my old friends, Jackie Joseph, was a market lad, otherwise known as a barrow boy. Barrow boys had stalls and a certain space from which to sell their wares. Jackie lifted weights and had the perfect physique; he also had the patter that would draw a crowd. He sold dresses, skirts and lingerie, and would entice the ladies by stripping to the waist. He was rugged-looking and the girls adored him. He could talk for two hours without repeating a noun. A stand-up comic selling his wares, one of his great lines was known by all. Mesmerizing the crowd, he'd hold up a dress and say, 'You've all heard of Christian Dior?'

'Yes!' the crowd would chant. 'Yes!'

'Then who am I?' he would shout.

And the crowd would chant, 'Yiddisher Dior!'

Displaying the dress more fully, he'd say to a pretty girl in the crowd, 'Five shillings, darling, but for *you* half price, and we'll throw in a pair of knickers.'

As you turned from Wentworth Street into what is now Middlesex Street, the street name might have changed but the lane didn't. Nathan G's brother, known as 'Kosher Jack', worked in a butcher's shop there. He was a big, powerful man who, during the war, became the chief air-raid-warden of the neighbourhood. He was a daredevil, saving many lives; a real Cockney hero who was later honoured by the City of London.

As you walked to the end of the street, there, right on the corner was young Tubby Isaacs, selling beautiful edible eels, and cockles, and mussels, alive, alive oh. All these delicacies were swishing around in individual buckets, and there was always a long queue of seafood addicts who found Tubby Isaacs's nosh irresistible.

There was a record stall where the latest jazz and blues albums were sold. It was frequented by the gangs and well watched by the police. I got to know many of the villains, but I don't think I ever saw a disturbance there. They came to enjoy the sounds, as I did. It was the heyday of the Big Bands – Ellington and Basie – and the soothing tones of Sinatra, Billie Holiday, Tony Bennett and Billy Eckstine. I can still remember the record I bought of Eckstine singing 'Everything I Have Is Yours' with 'Hold Me Close to You' on the other side. Tips must have been really good that week.

✧

After two and a half years under Mr Cohen's wing, I told him that I was restless and had set my sights outside the East End. He tried to persuade me to stay, but seeing I was unconvinced, he suggested that if I was going to move on, to always seek the best. He recommended I try my luck with Raymond, who was fast becoming the most famous hairdresser in the country.

It was time to move up west, and with an ego unmatched by my limited talents, I decided to take Mr Cohen's advice. As I found myself in front of the House of Raymond on Albermarle Street, Mayfair, excitement overcame me. Approaching the receptionist, my Cockney accent seemed to come through. She gave me an inquisitive look as I said, 'Could I see Mr Raymond?' Her look became even more disdainful as I added, 'I know he's the number one hair man in the business. I think he could teach me a few things.'

I suddenly realized I had made an enormous mistake as she

looked at me condescendingly and said, 'No, you can't see Mr Raymond, and if you are looking for a job, I suggest you study the language before you come back. And by the way, the language is English.'

I had blown it. But I refused to give up and soon found a job through my cousin Amelia. She had also become a hairdresser and a very good one, and worked for a man named Teddy Gilties, who had two salons: one in Shaftesbury Avenue and the other in Piccadilly, near the famous Windmill Theatre.

He employed me in the Shaftesbury Avenue salon, which had a name that seemed far more suited to a greasy-spoon cafe than to a West End hair salon – Mac & George. The manager, a Mr Phil Levi, who had just come out of the army and had a very carefree attitude, would answer the phone, 'Mac & George, we can't help it,' or, 'Mac & George, we only sell fish and chips after five o'clock.' This came to the ear of Mr Gilties, who instead of changing the name of the salon changed the manager.

The glamour of the clientele that came through Mac & George in 1945 was dazzling. I was finally sure then that I had chosen the right profession. Even though I was only seventeen and slightly naïve, I knew a beautiful body when I saw one, but a whole succession of these delightful ladies created a longing within me that at the time was unfulfilled. There was one girl, Peggy, who let me in on the secret. She said, 'Darling, didn't you know we're all on the game?' When she saw my look of surprise at her candour, she immediately reassured me that not only did it provide her with a good living, it was great fun as well. She was particularly brazen and would tell me of her adventures the night before. Her clients were mainly flyboys in the British, American, French and Polish air force squadrons. They were Peggy's guests for the night. Many of them were flying the next day, and not knowing whether it would be their last, they intended to have a marvellous night before. It cost them a hundred pounds for the treat, which in those days was a lot of money. Peggy's Polish could not be used in normal conversation, but she knew all the words that mattered. When I left Mac & George after three months, I had learned far more about sex than hair.

If I wasn't learning, I lost interest, so I could not keep a job. I was constantly being fired. I worked for three months at Henri of Knightsbridge. Mr Henri was a tall, eccentric gentleman with a slight stoop and an Eastern European accent. Always elegantly dressed, his manner demanded respect. But he didn't always get it or give it. If a client or stylist displeased him in any way, he would in anger say, 'Get out of *mein* shop and go to Harrods!' Harrods was next door, a vast emporium where you could buy anything and everything of quality, rather as it is today. He obviously felt that the standard of hairdressing at the Harrods salon was vastly inferior to his own.

One afternoon I was working on a client and there was nothing about her, her look or her manner, that inspired me. When I finished and put the scissors and comb down, she said to me, 'I don't like my hair.'

I looked her in the eye and said, 'I don't like it either but it's the best I could do with what you have.'

She shrieked, 'Call Mr Henri!' Hearing the scream, he came quickly. She turned to him and said, 'I told this young man that I did not like my hair. He had the audacity to tell me he did not like it either.'

'Do not worry, madam,' Mr Henri assured her. 'I will get a more experienced stylist to look after you.' Turning to me, he said furiously, 'As for you, you're fired. Get out of *mein* shop and go to Harrods!'

I went with joy. Nothing at Mr Henri's had given me the feeling that I was making progress. The clientele was dull and boring and wore clothes and hair that did them no favours. They were a bunch of old biddies and the tedium was exasperating. Being fired came as a blessing; I wasn't learning anything. And if I wasn't learning, I wasn't improving, and I was determined to be the best I could be.

✧

In 1946, a year after the end of the war, I became passionately involved in something very different from hairdressing. It became clear from radio reports that the problems in Palestine were escalating. Mother was a Zionist to the core of her being and our house was full of Zionist literature. She would hold meetings in our living room in Bow and became known for the strength of her views. She would invite speakers to come and though what they had to tell us was sometimes grim, there was also an extraordinary sense that we were on the brink of great change; that there might at last be a Jewish homeland. There was fighting between the different factions in Palestine, with the British trying to keep the peace, and there was bloodshed on both sides. Being British and Jewish gave me an uncomfortable sense of divided loyalties. Before the meetings, Nathan G sent me to the corner of Lawrence Road to ensure that only two or three people came to the house at a time, so as not to arouse suspicion. I sent them in small groups with short intervals in between. We obviously did not want the neighbours to know that a crowd of thirty to forty Zionists was gathering. It didn't take long before my mother's views rubbed off on me.

There was one speaker in particular who convinced me that there was an urgent need for a Jewish state. He argued powerfully that had the Germans crossed the Channel, the indigenous anti-Semitism within European Christian culture, mixed with Nazi propaganda, would have created a situation in England that would have led to the death of a good percentage of Britain's 350,000 Jews. The atrocities of the Holocaust could never be repeated as long as there was a strong Israel.

Oswald Mosley, the pre-war leader of the British Union of Fascists, had been released from house arrest after the war ended, and under his leadership the fascists were on the march again, screaming profanities, always leading with 'We've got to get rid of the Yids!'

We were the strangers in their nest. We Jews were, so they thought, an easy target. I do not know the exact day when we decided to return the hate in kind, but the horror of the images coming from Auschwitz, Dachau, Buchenwald, Belsen and seemingly so many other places triggered our sense of survival. We'd all heard of the heroics of Mordechai Anielewicz and his few hundred followers in the Warsaw Ghetto Uprising, which encouraged us even more. It had taken a Nazi division almost a month to wipe out the ghetto fighters. 'Never again' became a command, not just a slogan.

The idea of forming a group to fight fascism street by street was the brainchild of Morris Beckman, who had served in the British Merchant Navy during the war. He had survived two torpedo attacks and came home to Hackney to find fascism at his front door. In March 1946 he called a meeting, and forty-three Jewish ex-servicemen and -women, many of whom were decorated war heroes, attended and decided to stop the fascists in the streets of Britain.

Leaders in different areas of London were chosen for their courage, their physical strength and their ability to bring others into the fray. In the East End, Big Jackie Myerovitch was a fighter we all looked up to, and word spread rapidly around the community. All able-bodied youngsters who had the heart wanted to belong to the 43 Group, as it was now called. Monday night at the Mile End Arena was fight night, and I'd often see Jackie there. He came to one of Mother's meetings that spring and didn't have to do much convincing to enlist another recruit. I had just turned eighteen.

There was one member of the Group who particularly inspired us – Gerry Flamberg. He was a sergeant in the paratroopers who had won the Military Medal for extraordinary courage in saving many of his comrades at Arnhem. As a street-fighter, no one would have wanted to meet Gerry in a dark alley. He was a big man with a wonderful sense of humour, laughing and joking his way through life – *except* when it came to fighting the fascists. His passion, urgency and fighting spirit were contagious. Jackie Myerovitch introduced me to him and he became a great friend. We would have followed him wherever the battle raged. It was an honour to be a young man fighting with this group of Jewish ex-servicemen who had distinguished themselves so ably during the war. Their honours included a Victoria Cross, Military Medals, Distinguished Service Orders, Distinguished Flying Crosses and Distinguished Service Medals. They had led the fight against fascism from the front and they were the toughest of the tough.

Word of the 43 Group continued to spread and suddenly there were hundreds of volunteers to challenge the fascist Black Shirts at all their meetings. One evening in Kilburn, we chased the fascists into a pub and were ourselves chased by the police. They arrested three of us. It took a long time to get to the police station, which was only a few streets away. Two policemen held one of my comrades, Mo Levy, while a sergeant pounded him, beating him everywhere but the face, at the same time calling us 'dirty Jew bastards', 'fucking Yids who Hitler missed' and 'sons of foreign whores'. I could not believe I was in the heart of London, listening to his hate. It was terrifying.

The following morning in front of the judge, we pleaded our case against the sergeant. The judge gave us a look of scorn. 'This is not Nazi Germany,' he said. 'Our police would never act like that. Now go home, be good boys, and don't let me see you again.'

And I thought we were being good boys, by cleaning the streets of fascist garbage.

On another occasion there was a brawl that left a nasty bruise on the side of my face. When I walked into work the following morning, a client said to me, 'Good Lord, Vidal, you look terrible. What happened?'

I said, 'Oh nothing, madam. I just tripped over a hairpin.'

I used that flippant remark often to stop concerned people from asking further questions. We had been advised never to talk about the 43 Group to people who did not belong. Neither my employer at this time, nor any of my employers during the time I was with the 43 Group were aware of my political activities. The bruise stayed with me for about two weeks. Obviously I was hit by somebody who was wearing a heavy ring. It could have been worse; he could have been sporting a knuckle-duster.

Because of their military training, the leaders of the 43 Group knew that youngsters like me needed to be taught the proper methods of self-defence. Gymnasiums were opened and we used them frequently. Apart from the physical training, we were taught numerous tactical manoeuvres and were always being warned never to get cut off from the main group.

Unfortunately, one night three of us were separated from the others in the Hackney area. We were running through streets when we heard footsteps some fifty yards or so behind us. As we turned a corner, we jumped a fence into a front garden when suddenly a door opened and a woman's voice whispered loudly, 'This way!' and in a flash the three of us were sheltered in her house. I could see she wasn't Jewish by the cross she wore and I asked her why she had helped us.

This brave lady, who probably saved us from an awful beating, answered in a hushed voice, 'My husband was killed in the war and I hate the fascist bastards.' She wouldn't give us her name and asked us not to look her up, and when I said, 'Why?' she replied, 'I have to live with these people.'

The British Fascist Movement did not grow; it got smaller. It was extraordinary how forty-three ex-servicemen could inspire London's youngsters to help them smash the fascists in the streets. It taught me that if I cared enough, and had the ability and determination to fight on, I could change how people thought and acted. The 43 Group made me aware that anything was possible. And everything was.

3

Private Sassoon

I honestly cannot remember in which London salon I was next employed, but I do know that when I arrived home one evening after another frustrating day behind the chair, my mother said jokingly, 'You've just received a letter from the Queen.' Actually they were my call-up papers and I soon found myself enlisted in the Royal Air Force. The war might have ended but every young man of eighteen and over still had to do National Service. A couple of months later I was sent to Yatesbury in Wiltshire for basic training. It was very different to the beautiful village we'd been evacuated to. Yatesbury was ugly – not a place you would choose to take your family for your holidays – and the camp seemed to have all the necessary equipment to make your life as uncomfortable as possible. Despite all this, I found myself enjoying the physicality of basic training.

In an attempt to show respect to other cultures and religions, the armed forces allowed us to go home for certain religious holidays. That year the Jewish servicemen were given leave to be with our families for Yom Kippur, the Jewish Day of Atonement, one of the holiest days of the year. I took my mother to the

Lauderdale Road Synagogue, where the Rabbi talked of the Holocaust, of gas chambers built to wipe out a whole race of men, women and children, and of how being born Jewish in Europe was a crime that meant certain death. People left the synagogue white-faced with shock. The appalling truth about the death camps was fairly new in people's minds and the horror of it was difficult to digest. It was the saddest Yom Kippur any of us would ever remember.

A day later, back at camp, I could not rid myself of these hideous thoughts even as I was squaring off on the parade-ground. I hadn't noticed who was next to me, but when I touched his shoulder as was required, he said, 'Who are you pushing, you fucking Jew bastard?'

At that moment, all the frustration and anger within me exploded. I don't think I'd ever hit anybody with the intent to maim them permanently until that moment, but seconds later, he was horizontal and I was on top of him, banging his head on the parade-ground concrete. It took six people to pull us apart and I was immediately hauled in front of the young duty officer. I told him what had been said to me and this was verified by others who had overheard it. When the officer had heard the full story, my antagonist was brought before him looking the worse for wear. The officer lectured him for a full five minutes in front of me, on his ugly thoughts, his stupidity, arrogance and ignorance. He talked about the war and hatred. He told the young airman that from now on, he would have to watch his step very carefully, and then dismissed him.

Then something extraordinary happened. Fighting on the parade ground was a severe offence and he could have made things very uncomfortable for me. Instead, he apologized for the abuse I had taken. 'There are always people who play foul. Just try and stay out of trouble, Sassoon.' I thought I noticed a smile at the corner of his mouth as he dismissed me. Unfortunately it didn't end there.

There was a group of fairly rough guys within our squad who were troublemakers, but happily I had made friends with the toughest kid in the outfit, Jimmy Cosgrove, from the Gorbals in Glasgow. From the stories he told, it was clear that his father was even tougher than he was. Nobody in Glasgow messed with Jimmy's father. When Jimmy came home in the wee hours of the morning, his father would be waiting. 'Jimmy, you've been galvanizin' roond the toon till awl hours of the night. I'll mascara ya!'

A music lover like me, Jimmy was particularly into jazz, and we used to revel in the talents of Coleman Hawkins, Louis Armstrong and others. He was involved with bands in Glasgow and knew quite a few Jewish musicians. After the incident on the parade ground, which seemed to have the whole camp talking, Jimmy said, 'If there are any more problems, me and my lads will be with you.'

For a while, all was quiet. Then, one day, it all started again. We were in our huts after a hard day's training. Among us was a young *yeshiva* (Jewish religious school) student who, because of his daily workouts, was just beginning to realize that he had muscles as well as a brain. Like everyone who did basic training, his body became fine-tuned. He had no intention of using his muscles for fighting, but was a disciplinarian about developing his power to think. His name was Eisenstein, and a group of moronic thugs were dancing around his bed chanting, 'Eisenstein, rise 'n' shine and piss off back to Palestine.'

Eisenstein was lean in body, but wise of head – not unfriendly, but a loner who often studied the Bible. Just like the rest of us, he was sent to Yatesbury to serve and never complained. It was hard to work out what his feelings really were as he had a Trappist monk-like attitude against the spoken word. He laid back on his bunk quite calmly while being told to piss off back to Palestine, which annoyed his antagonists even more.

After they had been hurling abuse for a while, Jimmy Cosgrove and his lads walked over in disbelief at what they were hearing. Jimmy turned to me, saying, 'Let me handle this.'

They walked to the other end of this long hut. I followed them. There was a tension in the air and it looked like it was going to get very ugly. Jimmy turned to the leader of these ignoramuses. 'OK. You've had your fun, but if I hear one more word, I promise you it will be hospital time.'

They were fit young men ready to fight for any cause, good or bad, but Jimmy had such a presence that closed fists slowly opened and common sense won the day. A clean record was important, and the thugs realized that had there been a big dust-up, their days in the RAF could be numbered.

As everything simmered down, an excellent tenor voice from Eisenstein's bunk sang, 'One day I will rise 'n' shine and piss off back to Palestine.'

The tension slowly ebbed away and there was much laughter. But even though my roommate had risen above the taunts, I'd had enough. I told Jimmy I had to get away from these mentally deficient arseholes. He said, 'Where are you going?'

'For a long walk,' I said. 'Look after Eisenstein.'

He gave me a hug and wished me luck. I grabbed my belongings and with only a general sense of where I was in the country, walked the many miles to a railway station. I waited hours for a train to London. Eventually one came and I climbed aboard, quite a lot the worse for wear. It seemed to stop at every station, but nothing was very quick in Britain at the time.

When I arrived home it was not to the loving welcome that I needed. Instead my mother – at her most commanding – stared at me in furious disbelief and said, 'You've done what? You've gone AWOL?' She made it clear that I was an absolute disgrace to the family and she was going to call the authorities immediately. There was no empathy in her voice, only anger, and when the Military Police came she presented herself and told them I was absent without leave. She then turned her back and walked into the kitchen without saying goodbye.

I felt terribly confused but allowed myself to be led out to the waiting car without saying anything. I was taken to I know not where, but it wasn't in London, and was presented in front of a group of stern-looking officers. They reviewed my record and the officer in the middle said, 'You and trouble seem to have a sound relationship. If we send you back to your unit, will you promise not to cause any more disturbances?'

I said, 'Sir, you will get no trouble from me, but I will not put up with racist abuse of any kind.'

I was asked to leave the room and waited for about ten minutes. Then the two officers who had so kindly escorted me this far put me back into the army vehicle and drove for an hour or so further. All I could tell from the road signs was that I ended up somewhere near Wolverhampton. To my horror, I found myself in the psychiatric ward of a military hospital. Some of the other inhabitants were clearly very disturbed. One young man kept screaming, 'It's all imagination. Take me home to me mother.' Others seemed to be bound to their beds.

I was sedated and woke up five or six days later, having been drugged sufficiently so that I could hardly remember a moment of my plight. I was then given a medical discharge and sent home.

In the sixty-four years since this happened, I have never told a soul about it. I wasn't proud of what I'd done, but neither was I ashamed. Now I don't even think of the reasons why I became such a rebel. Over the course of the following year, my medical discharge preyed on my mind. I had terrible mood swings and asked myself if I had been dishonourable. But then perhaps it was the RAF that had behaved dishonourably. After what had happened throughout Nazi Europe, it became more and more obvious to me that Her Majesty's government did not want to deal with anti-Semitism of any kind. And perhaps, too, having so many high-spirited men cooped up together without a common goal or higher purpose made it inevitable that some were going to become brutes and turn against their so-called comrades.

✧

I was now back at home, in our semi-bombed-out house in Bow, where much of the limited fresh water we got was rain coming through the roof. It took years before our plea for a new dwelling was answered, as there were many people far worse off than we were and their needs were greater than ours. Finally our name came up for a council flat in Kilburn and we were overjoyed to be moving into a well-built home with proper facilities. There was a much bigger kitchen with a separate larder, and Mother would swear that the chicken soup tasted better in Kilburn. There were three bedrooms, a lovely dining room and a spacious living room where Dad would sit most contentedly reading from his library or listening to his favourite operas. But my favourite room by miles was the bathroom. I would lie in a hot bath for what seemed like an hour, singing, 'Hot water, please, for number one . . . Hot water, please, for number one . . .' and then, 'Ooh . . . ahh . . . lovely.' Even though I was turning the water on and off myself, I couldn't resist revelling in the chanting of the public baths I used to frequent in Stepney. There was also a delightful courtyard where the more affluent residents could park their cars. Our living conditions had improved so much that everything about London took on a new glow.

It was the late forties and hair was everywhere except where I thought it should be. It was red, it was blonde, it was brown, it was black, it was grey, and for me it was total frustration. I'd wear dark glasses even in winter to block out the silhouettes of the rigid hairstyles that passed me on the street. The rock-hard sets held in place by heavy lacquer seemed to rob the women doomed to wear them of their sexuality and allure. To be fair, there was also some very beautiful hairdressing done, but it was 'hair dressing' – certainly not the chic styles I was beginning to imagine. Yet, without the skills to bring my imaginings to life, I was still lost in a faraway dream.

Some evenings I would visit the Italian, British or French hairdressing academies in the West End, where you were free to question the teachers. I often did. Many of them looked on me as a bloody nuisance and I'm sure they hoped that I would find other things to do on the evenings they were due to teach. Occasionally, a man called Freddy French demonstrated. He was very different from the other teachers and I made a point of being introduced to him, as I admired his individuality. He had a grand salon in Curzon Place, Mayfair, and had his own way of styling hair. What was fascinating was that whenever a client came out of the dryer, every head was brushed into a shape. No other implement was used except a brush. His work was spectacularly different and he taught many top craftsmen his methods. *At last a visionary!* He was way ahead of his time and through him I caught a glimpse of the future.

During the course of the next eighteen months, I worked for some very able people. There was Henry DeCosta in Mayfair – a tall man with flair who preferred to work quietly in a corner; Charles Plumridge in Bayswater – a showman with great style, he must have invented the word 'extrovert'; then I was employed in the Putney branch of Richard Henry (owned by Richard Conway and Henry Redman, this group had many salons around London). Henry had been wounded during the war and suffered from violent headaches; Richard Conway was a brilliant businessman who spent a lot of time with us expounding his ideas and we all appreciated him. It soon seemed I was becoming a branch hairdresser because my next job took me to Bernard Beerman and Sydney Gaby, who had a Mayfair salon. Me, they put in their branch at Maida Vale. They were all brilliantly gifted and very well known in the craft, and I was hungry to learn as much as I could from each of them.

By 1948 I was twenty years old, and without intending to I had spent the past year and a half working at four different salons. I was looking for something in hairdressing that I couldn't find, but there was another side to life that had me well and truly hooked – boxing. Fight nights in London were very exciting as I knew many of the boxers personally, partly because of my friendships with the East End fighters I had grown up with and partly because many of these gyms were open to members of the 43 Group and so I had entry into them. The sheer determination of the men training seeped into me, and I marvelled at the raw courage that it must have taken for a fighter to become a champion.

Tony Hiller worked out in an East End gym I frequented. In the ring, he was a 150-pound terror. Outside it, he saw himself as the British Irving Berlin. He had a big decision to make: did he want to be a fighter or a songwriter? He chose the latter and went on to write and produce some huge international hits, including 'United We Stand', 'Angelo' and 'Save Your Kisses for Me', which was number one in twenty-seven countries and sold over five million singles. Tony was a close buddy and we still often meet when I'm in London, and he reminds me of the old days and how many punters he put down.

Occasionally Dad would come with me; he always liked reminding me that in his day they had real champions. Big Jackie Myerovitch, the leader of the 43 Group in the East End who had saved my arse on more than one occasion, had aspirations of becoming a professional heavyweight champion. Naturally we were close and I watched him often as an amateur – he'd never lost a fight. But during one terrible evening fighting the Black Shirts, he was knifed. He spent weeks in hospital and never returned to the ring.

Mickey Duff was another fighter I knew. He was like Sugar Ray Robinson without the punch. To watch him spar was like watching Fred Astaire dance. He had every move in the book. Mickey almost became a contender and there was no question in my mind that had he been born with punching power, we would have had another great champion. As it is, he ended up managing champions, and the last time I saw him was when he brought Frank Bruno to Las Vegas.

But it was Mo Levy with whom I chased the ladies. We'd hang out together at the Stepney Girls' Club, hoping to get lucky. Mo was the one who was beaten up by the police in Kilburn. He and I took our first holiday together at Blankenberge, a Belgian seaside resort near Bruges. I met a darling girl there, obviously from a very good family because she was chaperoned. After two weeks we were still just good friends. Mo, on the other hand, was sleeping with the chaperone and having a marvellous time. It was my first trip to foreign parts but it was not to be my last. Soon I would be travelling even further away from home.

✧

On 29 November 1947, the newly created United Nations had voted in favour of an Israeli state. There was elation in the hearts of Jews worldwide, and for everyone who had been appalled by the shocking truth of the Holocaust. The British government couldn't wait to get out of Palestine, and they joyfully relinquished their Mandate on 14 May 1948. Once the British Army had left, volunteers streamed to Israel and I was one of them. Nothing and no one could have stopped me signing on.

Getting there was circuitous. We left London one at a time as we were aware we were being watched by the British authorities, who knew we were going to Israel and took a dim view of it. I remember being sent from London to Paris, to an address on the avenue de la Grande-Armée, where I was thoroughly vetted, then sent to Marseilles to await either a boat or an old Dakota, which would fly us to Israel.

In Marseilles there was an enormous displaced persons camp called Le Camp du Grand Arénas, filled with those who had somehow survived the terrors of the concentration camps and were soon to be taken to a safe haven – Israel. While waiting my turn to go, I had to spend five weeks at Grand Arénas listening to tales of horror from Holocaust survivors that seemed completely unbelievable, and yet they happened.

Many of the surviving victims could not – or would not – talk about their horrific experiences. Those who did left me mortified by what they shared. Their degradation was so complete that they could not comprehend the promise of a new land. They were broken people – emaciated, with sunken cheeks and hollow eyes that just stared into nothingness. Most were still skeletally thin and could only eat small portions of food; the Nazis had starved them and their stomachs could not yet take in a full meal. Doctors, nurses and psychiatrists who were brought into the camps by the new Israeli government had to slowly bring them back to a condition where they were recognizably human. Seeing this terrible suffering at first-hand, and living among those whose only crime was being born a Jew left an indelible mark on me.

One evening, a lost soul opened his heart and told me how his only son had been taken from him to the gas chambers. He cried in my arms and, holding him, I could not keep back the tears. Five weeks at Grand Arénas left me in a state of disbelief. How could this have been allowed to happen? Having seen so much suffering at the camp, and having lived through so much racial hatred and bigotry as a child and young man, the intolerance showed by so many made me deeply angry. One thought kept running through my mind: *Did Auschwitz have to happen before Israel became a reality?*

At last came the longed-for news; I would be leaving on the next Dakota to Israel. Our old plane could not fly there directly, so we stopped to refuel in Rome and again in Athens. Eventually we landed at a small airfield in Haifa, the largest city in the north of Israel. As I arrived in Haifa, a city of great beauty, my spirits soared. It was an historic day for me. I had finally touched the ground of a new nation called Israel. As I walked to the terminal I realized that for the first time in my life I was somewhere where history was being made.

There was no time to lose. On 15 May 1948, Egypt, Syria,

Jordan, Lebanon and Iraq had invaded Israel, launching the Arab-Israeli War. Morocco, Sudan, Yemen and Saudi Arabia also sent troops. With a population of only 600,000 Jews, no one old enough to fight could be excused. Everyone in Israel joined this giant effort to survive.

Three months before I'd left for Israel, at the beginning of April 1948, I had been invited to a rather large hall in London. When I arrived there, there seemed to be hundreds of 43 Group members in attendance. I knew something important was going to happen as there were Group members guarding the building and the streets surrounding it. As we settled in, I looked up at the stage where many leaders of the 43 Group were seated.

After the opening *shalom* to all present, an Israeli Palmach* army officer was introduced by rank only; no name was given. He spoke with a passion that had most of us spellbound. He talked of Israel as a beautiful woman who seduced all who came. He talked of the strength of the people, the extraordinary growth and beauty of its agriculture, and how the *kibbutzniks* had made the desert green. He offered us the opportunity to be part of a new nation. He talked of Britain leaving Palestine and said that although the Foreign Office was pro-Arab, there were many Britons serving there who, having seen the extraordinary ability of the Jews to re-create the land, became pro-Zionist.

He told us of the Palmach and some of the actions in which he had served. He spoke at length of Captain Orde Wingate, a British officer who had helped train many of the young Israelis. He inspired us with the wisdom of common sense that, without

---

* The Palmach was a fighting force formed in the *kibbutzim* and, like all other independent groups, became part of the Haganah, Israel's official army, in May 1948, and was renamed the Zeva Haganah Le-Yisrael (the Israel Defense Forces).

a country, the Jews would eventually be nonexistent, as the Holocaust could be a precedent to what might come next. When he stopped speaking, there was a thoughtful silence and then a two- or three-minute standing ovation.

There was no doubt in my mind. That officer's obvious love for his land and my mother's conviction made it imperative that I should be in Israel as soon as it was legally possible.

Now that magical day had finally arrived. Hundreds of volunteers were gathered at a Haifa medical centre. My name was eventually called and a doctor gave me a thorough medical examination. I was five foot ten and weighed eleven stone and six pounds and, thanks to my 43 Group training, I was passed A-1 fit and accepted. They asked me if I wanted to be in a battalion of volunteers from overseas. I said, 'Not really. I want to join the Palmach.'

The day after, together with three others 'Anglos', as they called us – Shimmy Goldberg, an American from Altoona, Pennsylvania; Colin Fisher, a Londoner who was an old comrade from the 43 Group; and Jack Aptaker, part Australian/part Londoner – I became a Palmachnik. The rest of our unit was made up of *kibbutzniks* from Lake Hula, then a fishing *kibbutz*. Apart from their excellent physical condition, they were all remarkably clever. Many of the refugees from Germany and other European countries who had joined the *kibbutzim* were university professors, and they had taught these young *kibbutzniks* to think. They were far better educated than I was and they had been training since childhood; we four Anglos had some catching up to do. We were sent immediately to Tel Mond, which was the basic training camp for the Palmach.

I've never worked so hard in my life. The training was excruciating. After a long and arduous day, we would sometimes hit the sack exhausted at 9 p.m., only to be woken at 2 a.m. for an hour and a half's running and walking with a full heavy pack. We would then crash about 3.30, only to be woken again at 6.30 for another full day's training, even though we'd had so little sleep the night before. It was the toughest two months I'd ever experienced.

One day during training, our *makh lakah* (unit) was running through a large orchard. We were sweaty and tired, and were given five minutes to rest. It was an orange grove and we succumbed to the temptation to pick the fruit and squeeze the juice into our parched mouths. Suddenly there was a shout, and the farmer who owned the orchard chased us from his field. It was a sight to see – forty-four of Israel's young finest being chased by a middle-aged farmer and sworn at in Hebrew. Close combat, which included martial arts, was an intrinsic part of our daily routine, as we were taught that if we showed confidence when we were close to the enemy, they would lose theirs. That wasn't the case with the farmer.

After training our group was bussed to the northern Negev and became part of Gedood Shleeshee, or the Third Battalion. That night we were taken by scouts through the Arab lines to Kibbutz Nir Am. Whenever we heard Arabic being spoken, we would freeze until the scouts gave us the signal to go ahead. This happened on three occasions. I felt the adrenalin rush of involvement and I knew then, for me, the excitement had just begun. It was almost as if we were making a movie in the desert – except we weren't firing blanks. This was the real thing.

There were three *kibbutzim* close together – Nir Am, Dorot and Beeri – and the Israelis were walking groups of forty to fifty soldiers through the Arab lines to them every night. During the summer and early autumn of 1948, many thousands of Israeli soldiers arrived at *kibbutzim* in this fashion, trained and well prepared for the battle ahead. We knew the situation was dire and were told constantly that we could only lose one war, and if it was this one, there would be no Israel. Our scouts went out every night to reconnoitre the enemy lines and re-examine their positions.

My first direct action was a personal disaster. We had taken a hill and the enemy was running for cover. An Egyptian armoured car then came over the hill towards us, and as we were just infantry with no armoured vehicles, we were now the ones doing the running. Suddenly, my belt snapped. My trousers fell down around my hips, but I didn't dare put down my gun. We were so short of arms, losing a weapon was out of the question. Forty-three of our company of forty-four men were back in their original positions, while I was about forty yards behind, trying my utmost to run while holding my gun in one hand and my trousers up with the other.

News of my exploit got around, and for about a month soldiers I didn't even know would look at me and start laughing. The embarrassment stayed with me, but there's no doubt it was a memorable lesson in self-preservation and only served to reinforce the camaraderie that made us a first-class outfit.

Shimmy, Colin, Jack and I shared a hut; two bunk beds on either side of the entrance and very little else to commend it. Jack was a hypochondriac. He had vitamins of all kinds and pills for any given situation. When a bomb hit the barracks, his entire supply was dispersed in all directions. I don't know how he managed it, but he survived the blow.

Shimmy had read the classics and showed off his knowledge at every opportunity, but we forgave him. He also boasted a pair of American Army boots, real beauties that came halfway up the calf. He was a size ten, as were Colin and I, and we made a pact that if Shimmy got wounded, we'd toss a coin for his boots. The rest of us wore standard-issue footwear, which had no glamour to them at all, but they took our feet in the right direction.

Colin, who came from a similar background to me, was blessed with very good brains and had won a scholarship to university. He also looked unbelievably like Paul Newman. Many of the girls of the *kibbutz* fancied him, much to the dismay of the rest of us. Colin was also the best marksman and on occasion, when needed, was called to act as a sniper. I was so proud of him that I once allowed him to use my shaving cream and razor – no small gesture on my part. I knew my life was in their hands, and I was so glad of it.

The war was about to begin in earnest. The Egyptians, with tanks and armoured cars, were advancing through the Negev with their air support. They had captured the main road leading to the heart of Israel and had to be stopped. The campaign would last for seventeen days. Our first objective was the village of Beit Hanun, on the edge of the Gaza Strip. We took it after some heavy, bloody fighting, for the Egyptians knew what we were planning to do. We had to take back the road – whoever held the road held the advantage. Our orders had been to take the hill overlooking the road and then to capture Beit Hanun at the foot of the hill. The hill was the highest of three and from it you could see the city of Gaza, less than six miles away.

Our commanding officer, Lieutenant Dov Carmeli, was a towering figure and very courageous. Leading from the front, he gave the order to attack. We seemed to surprise the Egyptians. It was 4.30 in the morning and very dark, and we were halfway up the hill before they knew what had hit them. On the twelfth day, we took that hill, although we suffered many casualties. The medics were by our side almost immediately and their prompt care of the wounded surely saved their lives.

Those of us who were unhurt were ordered to dig trenches because we weren't going anywhere. Colin and I were frantically digging and suddenly something snapped in my back. I could not lift a spade. Colin grunted and said, 'What a time to get lumbago.' There was a burst of shrapnel and Colin fell. Automatically I leapt towards him. Again my back snapped – this time back into place. I rolled Colin over. There was a hole right through his helmet. He was barely conscious and there was no medic at hand. I knew then I had to assess the damage quickly. Slowly I eased off his helmet, not knowing how much of his head would come with it. But there wasn't so much as a trickle of blood. The shrapnel had not even parted his hair, though it *had* left two mighty holes in his helmet – one on the way in; the other on the way out. Lucky boy, he only suffered a slight case of concussion.

We knew the dugout would be our home until reinforcements could fight their way through to join us and consolidate our precarious position. Two Besas, the heaviest type of machine gun, purchased from Czechoslovakia (our main source of supply in those days) were quickly brought into position on the hill, which for the army's purpose was named Hill Eighteen. Four gunners who were Besa experts joined us. The Egyptians attacked constantly. The bombing and shelling were designed to soften us up for a frontal attack. Time and again they tried to storm that hill. Time and again we beat them back with our two- and three-inch mortars, our heavy Czech machine guns, Stens and rifles. The Besas did the most damage; they made a mess of the Egyptian armoured vehicles on the road beneath us. In return, the

Egyptian Air Force threw everything they had at us. It suddenly occurred to me that we were really in one hell of a war.

We lived on that hill for six days. Our food came out of cans and our sleeping quarters were the trenches that we had dug. We were beginning to smell rather badly. Water was for drinking, not washing, and was strictly rationed. Our bodies, particularly our legs, were covered with desert sores. Yet morale remained high. It was partly due to the spirit of our commanding officer, Dov Carmeli. He was only a year older than me, but he had the experience of a veteran. He seemed to be everywhere – calm, quietly spoken and outwardly supremely confident. We drew strength from him, and we needed every ounce of it, particularly as our numbers began to dwindle. We four Anglos were honoured to be serving with a *sabra* outfit – in theory a unit composed of people who were born in Israel – but there were so few of us now that the loss of a man meant much more than a gap in the ranks. It was like the death of a brother, for battle had welded us into a fighting family.

Once, when we were blasting away at the advancing Egyptians, I glanced round and saw a *sabra* running towards me, bent double. He was carrying a can of bully beef and I grinned at the thought of food. Suddenly there was the scream of a shell. It burst nearby, showering me with sand. When I raised my head, I saw the bully beef can rolling slowly downhill. Then I saw the *sabra*. Half his head was missing.

I felt physically ill. Still propped on my elbows, my Sten gun hot in my hand, I vomited. It was not just the death of a man who a few minutes earlier had been risking his life to bring me food. It was not just the sight of the wound. It was much more personal. I had known Eliahu well. We boys from London had teased him, called him a hick from the sticks because he had grown up in a *kibbutz*. He had teased us back, calling us a bunch of city slickers, saying, 'When you were playing with toy trains, I had a rifle in my hands.' That was true. He had known war since the age of eleven, when his military training had begun. By fifteen he was a veteran.

We had teased him, too, about Sarah. She had grown up with him. They were engaged to be married and we'd been invited to the wedding. Sarah had helped us to take Beit Hanun. She was there at the height of the battle, bandaging the wounded, reloading for us, firing herself whenever there was a spare gun and a gap to be filled.

Eliahu's death was made even more tragic by the fact that twenty-four hours later we won the battle for Hill Eighteen. Our troops in the rear broke through, establishing our lines of communication, consolidating them. Reinforcements poured in, and now it was our turn to attack. Fire poured down on that vital road, which was soon clogged with shattered trucks, armoured cars and tanks.

While all this was going on, the Israeli Air Force was bombing the Egyptians, going back to base, reloading and then bombing the Egyptians again. This happened four times in the span of six hours. Shortly thereafter, Israeli headquarters intercepted a message from the Egyptian headquarters on the ground to Cairo:

> *We are being bombed by a vast Israeli Air Force*
> *and our road is blocked.*

But it was not over yet. A well-aimed bullet pierced Jack through the shoulder. If it had only been Shimmy, Colin or I could have had his boots. We lost Jack to the medics, knowing that if all went well, he would have a comfortable bed in a Tel Aviv hospital by nightfall. They removed the bullet the following day and by the time Jack was released, the action on Hill Eighteen was over.

Towards the end of the conflict, a shell came too close for comfort and shattered Colin's leg. We were worried he might lose it, but the doctors in Tel Aviv did a magnificent job in saving his leg. The fact that he only walked with a limp for the rest of his life was a miracle.

Of the forty-two of us who had taken the hill, twenty-five walked away from it. The rest left on stretchers, and seven of them were dead. The *kibbutzniks* had grown so accustomed to death, they got used to the reality that boys they had lived with and been to school with had fallen all around them. It just made them even more determined. Though the enemy we faced greatly outnumbered us, I knew after taking the hill that we would not lose this war, even if we had to fight five armies on four different fronts.

There was a moment of quiet and the boys from Lake Hula used the time to mourn their dead brothers. We Anglos had got to know all of them and shared in their grief. Although I had seen death in the Blitz on London, I had never seen death as shattering as this.

Shimmy turned out to be an absolute rock, a good soldier who never lost his boots. He and I were both sound in body but mentally exhausted. All we wanted was hot water and soap. I'd never been seventeen days without a shower. As we were relieved of duty by another unit and trucks took us back to Kibbutz Nir Am, our emotions were mixed. We had won the battle, but had lost too many healthy young men in the process.

In their desperate action to take back the hill, the Egyptians had suffered enormous losses and despite the loss of my own friends, I could not help feeling strangely sorry for them. They were conscripts who were far from their homes. They had no desire to be there and no reason to be there either, except an order from some faceless men in Cairo.

We were the lucky ones. We knew why we were there. As I sat back in that truck, however, I was in no mood to philosophize. I was heading for comparative paradise.

We were driven to Kibbutz Nir Am, where the *sabras* welcomed us with one of the greatest luxuries I have ever known – showers. We stood under them laughing, carrying on like a mob of schoolboys after a football match. The water cascaded down on us, streaking away the filth of days and washing away some of the grimmer memories, too.

After we had showered, we were given clean uniforms and I can still remember the thrill of slipping a cool, freshly ironed shirt over my head. I felt a wonderful sense of satisfaction, of having been in Israel when needed, and the *kibbutz* mounted a victory party that I shall never forget.

First they barbecued a lamb. No meat had ever tasted so tender. The fresh vegetables grown at the *kibbutz* were offered in plentiful supply. The accordions began to play and the girls pulled us to our feet. We danced with them until exhaustion overcame us. I left the dance and the laughter and sat down on my own in the dusk. I was alone but felt a sense of great pride. It was not a night for being humble. From the Holocaust to this was a magnificent stride forward.

And then I saw Sarah. She, too, was a little apart from the rest. She was not dancing because for her there could be only one partner – Eliahu, the man who had carried that tin of bully beef to me and had died on the hill.

I went over to her and we chatted for a while about everything except the war. Then she said, 'Did you hear that they've named your hill? They're calling it Hill Carmeli, after your officer. On the radio, his superior asked him if he could hold out. He said, "Yes, but send in the air force."'

I was lucky to be on that hill; even more lucky to walk off it. The name stuck. It is known as Hill Carmeli to this day.

Sarah then changed the subject. She smiled at me and said, 'What are your plans now, Vidal?'

'I'll go home, I suppose,' I said. 'Back to work.'

'Home? You mean you're leaving Israel?'

I tried to explain to her about my parents back in England, how they needed me.

She looked sad. 'This is your home, Vidal. This is your country. It's not enough just to fight for it. You must stay to help build it.'

As she walked away, I fell silent. Sarah's words had a telling grip on my heart.

I was still in Israel three months later in February 1949, when an armistice with Egypt was signed. I had been there less than a year but Israel had taken hold of me. A great new democracy was born and I had a very small part in making it happen. It was a privilege I would never forget and part of me was wondering whether I should stay in this vibrant new country.

But then I received a telegram from Mum:

STEPDAD'S HAD A HEART ATTACK STOP COME
BACK TO LONDON AND EARN A LIVING STOP

I knew my days in Israel were over. But my involvement never ceased.

4

West End Boy

I left the relative quiet of the warm desert where the air was pure and scented with oranges. Having turned parts of the desert around the *kibbutzim* into fertile land through sheer back-breaking work, the Israelis were blessed with lush fields of delicious fruits and vegetables that fed the population from miles around. In sharp contrast, the day I arrived back in London the city was fog-bound. It was grey and sombre, and black soot seemed to discharge itself from every chimney.

It took me a little time to get used to the city of my birth and my first meeting with my family as I arrived home was quite emotional. My mother, brother and stepdad greeted me excitedly at the front door and we all hugged. Mother cried and Nathan G told his favourite Kafka story about the Messiah coming the day after he was supposed to, which made me feel even more the returning hero. He seemed reluctant to discuss his health when I asked, but just said that he had been taking the doctor's medicine and would soon be right as rain. Ivor and I simply put our arms round one another and then everybody seemed to talk at once. All the family had questions about Israel's miraculous victory and Mother wanted to see my campaign medals. I had none. It was not the custom in 1948 for the Israeli Army to give decorations. I told them I was just a private; not even generals got medals. There was a mood of euphoria in the country that I had just left and I brought it back with me. It took about half an hour before Mother said, 'I've got your scissors all wrapped up and put in a drawer.' She didn't know that at that moment I had no inclination to go back into hairdressing.

The following day I went to the post office. I had just under a hundred pounds in savings, which was the total extent of my wealth. I gave my brother twenty-five of it. He had kindly cared for our parents during my absence, even though as an indentured clerk to a firm of chartered accountants he could not help them financially. For the next five weeks I lived on the money I had left. I had come home a warrior with my head full of ideals, but it didn't take long for me to be brought down to earth. I couldn't find a job; I had no skills. So I called a colleague from the 43 Group, Johnny Winbourne, who was wonderfully well connected. The only thing he could find for me was a cloakroom job in a nightclub in the West End, which didn't start till eleven at night and finished at four in the morning. Where would I sleep? Public transport stopped at midnight.

Eventually I waved the white flag. I took my scissors out of the drawer and went to find a job in the only craft that I had a limited knowledge of. A salon called Romaine's in the Edgware Road had an opening for a stylist. Albert Simmons, one of the owners, interviewed me. He thought I'd come for a job as an apprentice, as I looked so young. I was twenty-one and had fought in a war, but I still looked like a teenager. Eventually he was convinced I had some experience and I was asked to start the following Monday. As I left the salon, I saw Albert's partner,

Leonard Stein, who was styling a client and smoking a cigarette at the same time. Nothing could have been further from Professor Cohen's work ethic and dignified manner, but I was down to my last five pounds and had no ambitions to change the health habits of the Edgware Road.

Monday arrived and so did I.

Albert Simmons was an extraordinary character. He spent as much time inventing gadgets in the basement of the salon as he did running the business. Many a fighter pilot flying at night, for instance, owes his life to a gyroscopic instrument invented by Albert. It told the pilot precisely where he was in relation to the ground even after a wild bout of aerobatics. Albert made a fair amount of money from that device, and the way he invested it was typical of him. He bought an old funeral parlour in Torquay, turned it into a hairdressing salon and used the mortuary as his storeroom. He was a remarkable individual – a philosopher, an eccentric and a man whose advice to me over the years was often very sound, but sometimes quite wacky.

Apart from Albert there was Leslie Green, the manager. He had been captured during the war, and just after the war ended was let out of an Italian prisoner-of-war camp, so for him the Edgware Road was pure heaven. Leslie had fallen madly for one of his top stylists, Connie Baker. They worked closely on ideas and seemed to live in the salon, practising their craft. They made hairdressing fun and encouraged us in our work. Leslie particularly created a real excitement about hair styling. Harold Leighton (born Harold Lipski) was just sixteen when I arrived at Romaine's, but he was already an extremely talented craftsman with an artist's imagination, and he later went on to international success. Gerard London added to the creative energy at Romaine's by being the king of the chignon. Every Friday one particular client would arrive at the salon and Gerard would perform his magic as we watched. To create a perfectly balanced chignon took great skill, and to keep it in place for a whole week meant that the client had to rest her head on blocks, Japanese style, as she slept. But she obviously thought it was worth it. What really struck me about Romaine's was the buzz. There was nothing special about the Edgware Road in 1949, but there was something very special about the salon and I immediately found myself wrapped up in it all.

In those days, competition work was the ideal way of showing one's talent. Leslie took me to meet his mentor, Silvio Camillo, at his salon in a nondescript part of South London. I was astounded that this simple salon had produced a man who had won every major international competition. I also became totally fascinated with Silvio's techniques. I went to his salon on a weekly basis and he would charge me three pounds ten for an evening's lesson. My total salary was only seven pounds a week, but with a percentage of my gross take plus tips, I usually took home fifteen, so I could well afford Silvio and look after the folks at home, too.

Silvio was born in Glasgow of Italian parents and was a gentle soul. He and his wife lived very quietly in a well-designed flat above the salon. I watched in awe as he formed shapes that made hair stand in sculptural masterpieces with just his hands. He encouraged me to reach for my dreams, to treat my hands as the instruments of my art and to visualize the shapes through the mirror. He was a complete original and he taught me balance, control and an awareness of bone structure. He was a man with few pretensions. He did not look for fame; it came to him. He was truly inspirational, and under his tutelage I won two national tournaments and came third in an international competition. The truth is, I lost many more than I won, however, because I hadn't yet found what I was looking for in hair.

The restless feeling that I had experienced at Adolph Cohen's returned, and after two years at Romaine's it was time to move on. A job opened at Dumas in Albermarle Street and I was hired. It was a big break. At last, I was in Mayfair! Mayfair in those days was the Big Apple of hairdressing. It was the top echelon of hair and being in a salon there gave me a real sense of pride. One of my dreams had been fulfilled, and I settled down to work under the auspices of Frank Blaschke and Maurice Gross.

It was while I was working at Dumas that something really bizarre happened. Each morning on my way to work, I had a conundrum – train or bus? This particular morning I decided to take the train. The carriage that I entered was full. For those who couldn't find a seat, there was a hanging strap to hold on to. Hanging on next to me was an exquisite-looking girl with extraordinary eyes and a face that any hairdresser would kill to work with. I approached her and gave her a Dumas card with my name on it. She introduced herself as Vera Day and told me that her ambition was to be an actress, but that she had not yet graced the stage in a West End production. I suggested that while she was waiting to become a star, she would make a superb model. Was she interested? She was obviously used to being chatted up, but nevertheless she said she'd think about it.

I got a call from Vera two or three days later and invited her to the salon, where she caused an instant stir. Her entrance alone turned the eye of every hairdresser in the salon. Frank Blaschke, my boss and a superb competition worker, was totally bewitched by her and immediately the rotter stole her from me. After that they were inseparable, working together for the next big hair event.

Some time after Vera's first visit to the salon, I got a call there from a young body-builder by the name of Arthur Mason, nick-named 'Garth', after the muscular hero of the *Daily Mirror*'s comic strip. Like me he was from the East End. I knew Arthur, but had no idea he was dating Vera Day. Now, out of the blue, he warned me: 'If you don't stop messing with my bird, Vera, you'll be in deep trouble.'

'Arthur,' I said, 'it's all completely professional. She's modelling for the boss. All I did was introduce them.'

This cut no ice. 'You'll get yours!' he snapped and rang off.

A few days later there was an extraordinary commotion in the reception area. Two people were yelling at the top of their voices. This was Mayfair. This sort of thing wasn't supposed to happen here. I left the salon and went to reception and there was Arthur, blowing his top, pulling Vera – who was resisting madly – out of the salon and scaring the living daylights out of the two receptionists, who happened to be the wives of the owners. Like a fool, I went over and whispered, 'Arthur, you're out of line. You cannot behave this way here.'

'Really?' he said, and the next thing I knew, I felt a terrific thump above my jaw. I knew I stood no chance in a fair fight with Arthur Mason, so I hugged him as closely as possible as he was swinging at me. I felt the power of those fists as he beat me, but still clung to him as tightly as I could. I bit him in the neck – my teeth seemed to be the only weapon I had available. Clients were running back and forth in a daze while Arthur and I were now on the floor, rolling towards the reception desk. One or two of the more courageous clients were trying to whack Arthur with their

My mother with me in her arms.

Mother with Ivor, aged
two and a half and
myself aged five.

Me, aged six.

With Ivor at the orphanage,
when I was eight and he was
five and a half.

With Ivor, on a trip back to the orphange when we were adults.

Nathan G and Mother.

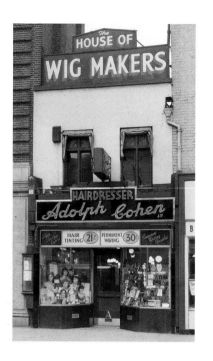

Adolph Cohen's salon.

With Ivor and friends at Larkswood Pool.

In Israel in 1948.

With Colin Fisher and Jack Aptaker,
my Israeli army friends and comrades.

Mr 'Teasy-Weasy':
Raymond at the
height of his fame.

One of my first
competitions.

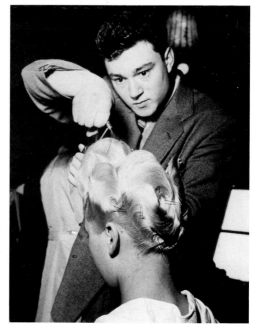

With the first-prize cup after a competition.

The Vidal Sassoon salon at
171 New Bond Street.

With Elaine.

umbrellas, but when they missed him, it was me who was on the receiving end. Inadvertently, I think I caught more of their venom than he did. Suddenly the desk, which was enormously heavy, toppled over, pinning my leg underneath it. It was like a scene from a Feydeau farce until the police arrived, when some sort of order was restored.

Arthur had become rather tranquil and Vera, who had not stopped battling, was led away to a neutral corner. There was a lot of blood but unfortunately it was not from Arthur's neck. It was mine, and the extreme pain in my leg did not bode well for any aspirations I might have had of dancing that weekend in a jitterbug competition.

The police took the facts, then asked, 'Would you like to charge Mr Mason?'

I looked up incredulously. 'Charge him? Of course not. He's a friend of mine – or was.'

One of the coppers said, almost under his breath, 'Do you have any more friends like him in your neighbourhood?'

Arthur was warned by the police not to come anywhere near the premises again, and apart from me having to take a taxi home and being forced to rest in bed for one week and up and limping for another, there was no real harm done.

Big Jackie Myerovitch, having heard of the day's events, called Arthur and told him he'd taken a diabolical liberty, but as he was a member of the 43 Group who had done a lot of good for the cause (and a lot of damage to the enemy at close quarters – which I can also vouch for) nothing but an apology was in order. Soon I received a four-page letter, which had a certain roguish flavour to it, in which Arthur apologized profusely, adding that if I ever needed a favour, to let him know. I felt, as I read, that had that clenched, angry fist held a pen for any length of time, the world might have been blessed by another gifted East End writer, and I would not have been beaten up in the first place.

Peace and tranquillity reigned once again in Mayfair, and slowly the bruises faded from my face and body. I went back to Dumas and there waiting for me was my two weeks' back salary, plus the commission I would have made – a nice little bonus for winning that particular skirmish.

Being laid up for two weeks meant I had to find another model rather quickly for the Gold Star Competition at the Park Lane Hotel. Vera was continuing to model for Frank and, boy, was I envious. None of the girls I saw and interviewed seemed to have the killer look that said to a jury, 'How could you *not* vote for me?' I was left with a girl who had an extraordinary body but a very average face structure. I lost my inspiration. The enthusiasm and confidence were not there. In fact, when I look back on it, I don't think *I* was there; I was completely uninspired. Mr Average had taken over my whole being. I was placed thirty-sixth out of thirty-eight – it was like being back at Essendine Road Elementary School. I knew then that my competition days were over.

The following day at Dumas I completely lost it. My work was bad and, in a fit of temper, I threw my scissors in the air. They stuck in the ceiling. Without mentioning my intentions to a soul, I put on my coat and scarf and left as if going to lunch. Lunch was a very late one, but it was in Paris, where I stayed for two weeks. Having called home, though, my conscience was clear. The Left Bank was excitement in itself and I welcomed the change of scenery. Paris had a daring that I loved and I found myself a cheap room in a street full of cheap rooms – very Bohemian, with lots of students. I decided to forget hair and have a wild time. I went to clubs at night, art galleries during the day, conversed in my semi-literate French, and slowly a feeling of peace came over me. When I got back to London I was quite amazed that my job with Dumas was still open for me, though that evening I was dressed down by both Mr Gross and Mr Blaschke. I remember the words 'reliability' and 'commitment to clients' featuring heavily. I worked at Dumas happily for another few months until that buzz in my brain came back to haunt me. *You need a change.*

The House of Raymond was just around the corner, and this time a charming receptionist gave me an appointment to see him. I was in awe of him immediately. He had a commanding presence and an infamous way with women. Athletically built, he was the original 'Italian stallion' and the ladies queued for him to attend to them. For reasons known only to him, Raymond spent some time with me and asked me to return later that week to do a test. It went well but I knew without question that what I'd done was neither especially creative nor particularly innovative. Nevertheless, I was hired.

As was my way, I had not told any of the clients at Dumas that I was leaving. I could not bring myself to steal from people who had been good to me and taught me so much. But with Raymond it wouldn't even have been necessary. He seemed to have an excess of clients. His publicity as 'the' hairdresser was strengthened by the fact that he was also Britain's number one extrovert. A superb equestrian, during Ascot week he rode his horse down the course in a pink morning suit, much to the delight of the crowd. There was no hat in the Ascot enclosure that could challenge Raymond at his best.

During the fifties he had a television show on every Friday evening and after my mother's chicken soup, whoever had been invited that night would watch it with us whether they wanted to or not. We watched in awe as Raymond, with great panache, would create look after look. And just as you thought he had finished, there was the final flourish – the little embellishment that made all the difference. He would take a small piece of hair, twist it with his finger and thumb and call it a teasy-weasy. Sometimes there were more than three or four teasy-weasies on one head of hair. The press had a field day and because of that show, he became known throughout the country as 'Mr Teasy-Weasy'. For a man who was built like a bulldog and whose hobby was amateur wrestling, the name seemed slightly incongruous.

I worked for him for about a year, watching his every move as he cut and pruned hair into shape with just a pair of scissors. Back then everybody else used thinning shears, a razor and a pair of scissors. But Raymond used only scissors. His technique was hard to learn – you needed agile wrists and a great feeling for hair as you matched the desired shape to the client's bone structure.

Not even Beau Brummell could have made a better entrance than Raymond as he stepped into the salon. He would hum, often holding a cigarette, looking incredibly *soigné*. His elegant, custom-made suits, always with a handkerchief dripping from the top pocket, had such an air of authority that I felt like Charlie Chaplin's little tramp standing next to him. He weaved magic through his work and made us feel we were doing so, too. There was only one Raymond.

When I wasn't observing Raymond, I was watching Louis Spinoza, who had been with him for a decade. He had special hands and his style and skill were greatly appreciated by his vast clientele and other young hairdressers like me.

One afternoon I was called to Raymond's office. He invited

me to sit down. He talked of the future, asking me if I would like to be a junior partner in the new Cardiff salon that was opening in a store named Howells. I'd never been to Wales but I agreed to go and take a look.

I was met in Cardiff by one of Raymond's partners, Tony Standish, who introduced me to some of the hairdressers who had been hired for the Howells opening. He showed me around the salon, pointing out features that he thought would beautify it, and then took me to high tea, which the department store did in great style. The event was led and orchestrated by Howell's top management and there were so many assorted goodies to eat, it seemed to me there would be no reason to eat again after a Welsh high tea. Life was good. I seemed to be needed and my natural enthusiasm was moving me in the right direction.

The next morning I met with Raymond. I asked him two questions. Would it be possible to have cards made, saying, 'Vidal – Artistic Director, Raymond's in Cardiff'? The answer was a swift 'No. That is not company policy.' Number two question was: 'If I create a look and it's photographed and used by the company, can I have my name attached to the picture at Raymond's?' Again, the answer was, 'No. It is not company policy.'

It was then that I knew I had to turn the offer down. And as many of Raymond's excellent managers and staff had found out about my trip to Cardiff, it was better that I leave immediately. I was both sad and unemployed again, but my old sandwich sharer, Robert Zackham, soon came to my rescue.

'How about teaching my staff twice a week? We could have evening sessions in two of my top salons.'

The offer was made even more enticing because Leslie Green, who had been my mentor at Romaine's in the Edgware

Road, was now Robert's partner. I soon found that on each occasion that I taught, I learned to express myself with more integrity, and I quickly realized that what I had learned both at Dumas and at Raymond's I could share with Robert Zackham's staff, all of whom were hungry for knowledge. Robert paid well and the work also taught me how to grab an audience.

I enjoyed teaching. It taught me things, too. But at the back of my mind an idea had taken root: what I really wanted was to have a salon of my own, with my name above the door. But how?

✧

Lila Burkeman, who had been a client of mine at Raymond's, had kept in touch and whenever we spoke, her first question was always the same: 'When are we going to open the salon?' I called her, and this time before she could ask I said, 'Now.' She suggested I meet with her husband and his brother and she organized a dinner later that week. Why did I need partners? Quite simply, I had no money. Whatever I had earned went to keep my family, as my stepdad's heart condition did not allow him to work and my brother, Ivor, was still studying to become a chartered accountant. So it was imperative that if I was to open a salon, I would need financial backers.

Sitting with Lila and these two charming gentlemen who listened intently, I told them how I was going to change the world of hairdressing. They kindly did not say, 'You must be kidding,' and allowed me to elaborate my thoughts and feelings about hair. I told them architecture was one of my great inspirations – architects had created form and shape and changed the look of cities. Some of the great fashion designers had cut cloth in a chic modern way, but hair – hair had remained stagnant and needed a new beginning. I felt it was my destiny. I dreamt of hair as an art form, giving the lead to other art forms.

Before the meeting, I had taken Lila to see a vacant third-floor space in Bond Street that I'd had my eye on. She had immediately seen its potential, so at the meeting she butted in to describe how utterly perfect that 700 square feet would be. She said a salon could be built for between £3,000 and £4,000 and it would be an exciting new venture for them that would fit with their business interests. Monty, Lila's husband, was in the clothing trade, and Charles was a property developer.

The meeting went well, although I had not mentioned we would be starting from scratch, as my own clientele had dispersed some months back; nor did I mention that I would not be hiring old-school hairdressers but young apprentices, whom I would train myself. Had I told them all this, they might well have wished me luck and shown me the door. But Lila, an angel at my side, had set the scene and with her confidence and my passionate monologue, we won the day.

That magical night in 1954, I walked the streets of London for what seemed an eternity. Imagine! *I* would be the innovator and I only had to answer to my inner voice. The magic had started. As I walked past 108 New Bond Street, I got the urge to break in and cut a head of hair, but I had to wait three months while the salon was built.

It was to be constructed by Richard Henry, who I had worked for in Putney. They had now expanded into building salons, so our relationship was a good one and they tolerated my idiosyncrasies. I wanted the salon to look like the hair that I envisaged. I wanted to eliminate the superfluous for clean, simple lines with no frills.

I got what I wanted and we opened on time. I was twenty-six

and I'll never forget walking up Bond Street, first thing on the Monday morning we opened. I was the first there. All you could see from downstairs were two photographs of my hair work in the window and my name in a fancy-looking script. My pulse quickened and I could feel my heart racing. I had no idea who – if anyone – to expect. I had not called any of my clientele from Raymond's. People had to find me for themselves. By the time I got into the tiny lift – I used to joke that if two people got in together, one would exit pregnant – I had a skip in my step. Boy, was I excited!

The staff that I had hired included – and I must mention her first because she stayed with me for eleven years until she married – Maria Sugarman. Maria was Jewish and was born in Poland, but she was a natural blonde with blue eyes. Taken in by a Christian family during the war, she learned the Catholic rituals and, thanks to her Aryan looks, was never questioned by the Nazi authorities. In the salon, she was wonderfully passionate and had great artistry, with a natural stamina envied by most of her friends and colleagues. Hugh Howe, a young Welsh lad fond of quoting Dylan Thomas, and John Martin, whose family I knew, were also part of the early team. Then along came Peter Laurance Taylor with a résumé I believe he wrote himself. Laurance, as he liked to be known, told me he was one of Raymond's top colourists, but I'd never seen him there. He was a total extrovert, and against my better judgement I decided to take a chance with him. He added much to the salon's atmosphere, often coming to work in outrageous outfits. One extraordinarily hot day, he arrived in pink pyjamas, with a safety pin for a zipper. I immediately offered him a second safety pin, laughingly saying, 'Now I see it, now I won't.' The staff and clients had all got used to his antics and nobody seemed to mind. Fortuitously, he was also a natural with colour and his contribution was substantial. Finally, I decided I needed a receptionist with a certain voice quality, and who should answer the advert but a lovely young lady called Elaine. I literally fell in love with her voice. Her dulcet tone on the telephone would entice the clients and calm me when I was being irrational. But her beauty did not stop at her voice. She had blonde hair, blue eyes and was tall with long, athletic, sexy legs, which she put down to climbing the hills in her native Wales.

Lila, a great ambassador for my hairdressing, spread the word, so we had a few clients on our first day – but not enough to keep us busy. I called not just a close friend, but somebody I considered a sister – an East End girl named Lillian Klot. She had changed her name to Georgia Brown, and three years later played Nancy, the female lead in Lionel Bart's *Oliver!*, which was a smash hit in London and on Broadway. But at that moment she was starring in Brecht's *The Threepenny Opera*. A girl with wondrous talent, we had remained close since we were both young teenagers. I remember taking her to the Stork Club when she was thirteen for the Sunday evening amateur contest night. Her unique melodic sound and the vivacious personality that burst through as she sang captivated the judges and audience alike, and she won first prize.

I said, 'Georgia, I've just opened up in Bond Street, and at this point in my life very few people know me. I want to change things and I need clients who will understand and appreciate what I'm trying to do.'

She said, 'No worries, Vid. I'll send in Annie Ross and Cherry Wainer and word of mouth will spread.' Annie Ross was another great singer. With the Count Basie Band in the States, Dave Lambert, Jon Hendricks and Annie Ross had created a new sound. Europe, which had already surrendered to Count Basie, could not get enough of it. Cherry Wainer played an extremely fine jazz organ and she was in demand in clubs all over Britain. Both Annie and Cherry became clients.

To pay the rent and the salaries and all the other expenses, I decided my rather racy Alpine sports car was a luxury I could do without. So I sold the old banger and took the bus. That was tough, but my first real lesson in survival came three days after we opened. A postman climbed the stairs inquisitive to see what was on the third floor. He held a letter in his hand and as a few of us were gathered around the reception area, said, "Ere, which one of you lot's Fiffal Faffoon?' Without opening the letter, I immediately ran down the stairs to the street level followed by the sound of hilarious laughter coming from the third floor. I looked at the sign and thought, *How could I have been such a fucking idiot?* The S's did look like F's. Obviously the postman had a Cockney sense of humour and purposely mispronounced my first name, too, to make the joke even funnier. To me, however, it was no joke. I called the sign writer immediately, who saw the serious as well as the funny side of my predicament. He came over almost at once and rewrote the name in very bold lettering. It has remained that way to this day.

The cost of a haircut by my very able crimpers was sixteen shillings. If the clients wanted me the price was one pound. The first week the salon took forty pounds, which paid the wages and the thirteen pounds a week rent but nothing else. I had only been open seven days and was already in debt. But word of mouth did the trick and within three months we were paying our way. I was working on clients during the day and training staff during the evenings. Fortunately I had a very high energy level but knew I would need help imminently; the pace we were keeping up was taking its toll – not only on me, but on my very loyal staff.

Suddenly I had two other stylists. Mike Cornell joined me from Freddy French. Mike learned my way of cutting and, coupled with the great techniques that he had studied with Freddy, became an invaluable addition to the team. Then came Robert Edele, a gem of a man who wore a handlebar moustache and sideburns down to the lobes of his ears. Robert had the air of a great manager. He loved to teach, and even in those early days he would say to me, 'One day we'll do something very daring and different.' He was truly the man you'd want beside you in the trenches and we are still very close to this day. Robert soon had his own set of keys and apart from our practice evenings, which I cut down to two days a week – many of our staff told me that there *were* other things to do in London – he would often be there alone, working on models. Both Mike and Robert built extraordinary clienteles, and to my amazement we quickly found ourselves paying all our bills very comfortably.

I was then joined by a very special talent. I could see immediately by the way his hands wove through the hair and how he manipulated shape that he was different. He was trained by Rose Evansky, without question the top female stylist in the country and the equal of any man. His name was Leonard Lewis. Leonard would learn my methods and would add a certain panache of his own to the work. Some years later this brilliant man would not only take a great house in Grosvenor Street and turn it into an extraordinary salon, but with his superb techniques trained many of the leading names in hairdressing today.

In the days before modern technology, prior to the production of many fine hair products, we were in the Dark Ages. We would make our own shampoo in buckets. Laurance was always bemoaning the very limited range of hair colours; creating extraordinary colour with what was available was almost impossible.

One day a client walked into the salon for her nine o'clock appointment with Laurance. He looked at her roots, put his hands through her hair, and asked, 'Is there a certain look you would like?'

She said, 'Laurance, I want to be grey-white.'

The roots of her hair were dark, not ashen. He should have said, 'Can't be done,' but instead he gave it a go. She lived on four cups of tea and a pack of digestive biscuits that day. Her sole concentration was on Laurance and his work. Eight and half hours later, she looked up at Laurance and said, 'I've been here all day and I'm still not grey-white.'

Out of total frustration he answered, 'Madam, when you see the bill you will be.'

As Laurance grew in stature, he trained many fine colourists and abandoned his more extreme outfits, instead wearing pin-striped suits from Savile Row. One day, with a big grin on his face, he came over to me and returned the safety pin.

From the beginning, I had laid down one important rule. There would be no hairdressing in the old-fashioned sense. We would strive to put all our artistry into the cut, and although at the beginning we were setting hair and using small rollers to give the hair a wild look, we were slowly but surely simplifying the way hair looked. One day a flamboyant client entered in a flurry of mink and dripping with jewels. We unwrapped the fur and she sat down. I put a gown over her and picked up a brush.

'One minute, young man,' she said, 'I haven't given you your instructions yet. I want a large "Ann Sheridan" fringe in the front and a duck's tail with a razor cut at the back.' If she had spent a year dreaming up a style that I hated more, she could scarcely have had greater success.

I swallowed and said gently, 'But, madam—'

She interrupted me. 'But nothing. You heard me. That's what I want.'

Suddenly the salon went quiet. For months the staff had been listening to me laying down the law about clients who refused to play by my rules where their hair was concerned, and now I was facing the moment of truth. As firmly as possible I said, 'I'm sorry, madam. We do not style hair that way here.'

For a moment she was silent, jowls heaving. Then she rasped, 'Do as you're told!'

I knew I had to take control of the situation. 'I'm sorry, madam. Perhaps you'd better go elsewhere.'

She shot to her feet. Seeing my opportunity, I whipped off the gown. Hugh retrieved her mink and handed it to her.

'Young man,' she said, 'you're a fool. I will make it my business to pass this outrageous folly on to my friends.'

As she stormed out of the salon, I fell into the chair she had just vacated, flung my feet up on the dressing table and howled with laughter. I had lost a client but I could tell by the way my staff looked at me that I had won a major victory.

Word started to get around about the crazy hairdresser who wouldn't backcomb, tease or lacquer hair. Back in those early days, women would bring in photographs of the latest movie star – often someone they bore no likeness to at all – whose hairstyle they wanted to imitate. I'd say, 'You look nothing like her.' Then I'd explain how the hair must suit the bone structure, and also the client's figure. I'd make them stand up, look in the mirror, and I'd explain exactly what I was going to do. The photograph went into the rubbish bin unless the client wanted to take it home. Most of the time I got my way, but for those whom I couldn't convince, there was always a taxi downstairs that would take them to a salon that would happily grant their wishes.

In the weeks that followed I handled many clients in the same way. Gradually the message got across town that the clientele had to accept our type of work if they came to us. We could not be proud of anything else and we wanted so much to be proud of something.

Our reputation was spreading in the profession and many young people wanted to join us. Stephen Way, a good-natured giant, joined as a junior. He was with me for years and later had his own salon in Bond Street. Gary Berman studied and worked with us for some time but later decided that his talent was better used in cutting men's hair. A chap called Nigel Davis came to see me and confused me from the outset by introducing himself as 'Christian'. I was concerned from the start because he didn't seem cut out for the long hours of training involved for hairdressing, but, boy, was he a dresser! Bright red linings to his suits, fob watches and the sort of beautifully tailored shirts that no one else in the salon could afford at the time. It had me wondering how he'd earned a living before he honoured me with his presence. Still, he was always laughing – and always good for a laugh.

One day, when I told him what I wanted him to do for a client, he began to giggle. When I reassured him again of what I wanted, he vanished! That was the day I'd had my fill of Christian alias Nigel, and I fired both of them. Even though I liked the pair I'd had enough. He disappeared into a London mist. The next time I saw him he was Justin de Villeneuve, manager of Twiggy Enterprises, Ltd.

Soon, we had been joined by Raphael, an Italian stylist, Carlos and Ronny Gilbert. Within a year we had six stylists and eight apprentices, two of whom were helping Laurance with colouring. Robert Edele was quickly developing his skill in helping the crimpers teach their juniors, as twice a week after the salon closed each stylist trained their own apprentice. But though they were all talented and worked hard, some of our stylists had rather overactive libidos and were dating their clients – even the married ones. I held a staff meeting and suggested that not only should we have high values regarding hair, but that it was not quite ethical to seduce a married client – to which Raphael answered in his broken English, 'Nobody cares. They think we're all homosexuals anyway.'

✧

After close to a year of working together, I found it impossible to ignore the feelings I had for Elaine, our beautiful receptionist. It was not only her voice. Just being near her stirred something within me. I tried to suppress the feelings. I was only twenty-seven and had promised myself ten years of total freedom from any responsibilities apart from looking after my family and building an international career. I knew I needed this freedom before I settled down. But Elaine's elegance, self-assurance and beauty wore me down, and I found myself asking her out to dinner again and again. I was in love, for the first time, and had no defences against it. Elaine responded in kind, and it was not long before I was introducing her to my mother, Nathan G and Ivor.

We were very different characters. She loved to spend weekends at home with her mother, who lived in North London, and had difficulty coming to terms with my wild career ambitions.

But we were in love and decided to get married. She introduced me to her elder brother, a man of sound education but whose opinions could be faulted. He wanted to see me alone. The first thing out of his mouth was, 'You're Jewish, aren't you?' My thoughts went, *Uh-oh, here we go again*. And then the shock came. He said, 'That's fine, as long as you're not a damn Papist.' I reeled slightly, but obviously wasn't getting into that argument.

After several Friday-night visits and a Passover at Mother's that she found fascinating, Elaine decided she would like to change her religion. She was very sincere about this decision and for nine months took instruction in the Jewish faith from a progressive young Czechoslovakian rabbi. She seemed to relish learning and at the end of her studies she knew more about Judaism than I did. She was examined by the Beth Din, a Jewish governing body, and was accepted as a Jew. We married in the synagogue at Upper Berkeley Street and went to Paris for a week's romantic honeymoon. My first mistake was to take her to a football match, which she didn't appreciate too much. Otherwise, with the restaurants, the entertainment and the art galleries, we learned a lot – not just about what the City of Lights had to offer, but what we had to offer one another.

Elaine continued working at the salon for a while. But we soon felt it wouldn't help the marriage to be together twenty-four hours a day, so we decided it would be better if she left her job – even though I realized that I wouldn't find another receptionist like her and would miss her calming voice and presence in the salon.

Not long after we were married, in 1956, I was invited to tour Europe and Elaine and I spent three weeks visiting Lisbon, Madrid, Rome, Paris, Brussels, Copenhagen, Stockholm and Istanbul. We met some of the top European hairdressers and in each city I would create a look of the day, working in different locations wherever we went. In Stockholm, we used the zoo as a salon. As strange as it may seem, there I was out in the open cutting hair while ducks ran under the feet of the models and peacocks strutted by. I said to myself, *Why am I doing this?* Elaine, with much more conviction, said, 'Why are you doing this?' She played her part beautifully, looking stunning on each occasion while charming all those fashion people we met. But I knew she would much rather be at her mother's home in London, a place she still found enormously comforting. We had only been married a matter of weeks when I found myself wondering if Elaine's needs and my ambitions were entirely compatible.

5

There's Something About Mary

A year after we opened I did one hair show that took tremendous preparation and created all sorts of expectations for the team. I had recently been to Madrid and had been fascinated by the way that Spain was steeped in its own culture – the bullfights, the flamenco dancing, the castanets, the gypsy singing all really inspired me. I decided to give the show a Spanish theme. One model even had horns made of hair. I am embarrassed even as I write this. Very few of the beauty press came, I'm happy to say, but one paper mentioned that 'Vidal Sassoon's first show was based on a Spanish theme. Unfortunately I have to report it was a lot of bull.'

I was crushed but quickly realized the mistake I had made. The weekend after the show was a time to be alone and reappraise my stupidity. The following Monday I had a staff meeting and we decided there would be no more themes – just great shapes, subtle colour and superb haircuts. The show had been a small setback but my belief in where we were going was unwavering. Our second year of business was one of extraordinary growth. I told Lila that within another year we would need larger premises and a meeting with the Burkemans was arranged.

It went badly from the outset. My heart sank as my partners told me they thought I would never make it in the fashion world – how could I compare to Alexandre, Raymond, René or Freddy French? They felt that the real money was in conquering suburbia and in opening salons in country towns around England. I told them this was not acceptable to me, that I was sorry that their faith in me had lapsed, and I would happily find backers who would buy them out. Lila was distraught; she did not agree with her husband and brother-in-law's decision. Even after the partnership was dissolved, she still came to us for her hair. To this day I remain eternally grateful to her for getting me on that first rung of the ladder. Where would I have been without her?

One day, when Elaine and I had been married for about six months, she called me, very excited about a small flat she had found in a gorgeous Georgian house in Curzon Place, Mayfair. The whole building, which had once belonged to a grand family, had been converted into twelve apartments. The ground-floor and second-floor flats had exquisite high ceilings, but Flat 10 at 9 Curzon Place was the original servants' quarters. We loved it. The ceilings were lower, but it had an amazing ambience. They had to have been very special servants.

We took the flat. It had a bedroom and a living room, a separate bathroom and toilet, a small built-in area where we could play our music, and a kitchen. It also had shelves for our books. Most importantly it came with a delightful lady, Janet Salisbury, who kept the place incredibly spic and span. I was extremely happy there. I could walk to the salon in Bond Street in ten minutes, browsing through Shepherd's Market as I went. It was a lovely neighbourhood.

Living just across the hall in Flat 9 was a Lloyd's underwriter by the name of John Riseley Pritchard. His main home was in Oxfordshire but he needed a small place in town for business. He had all the smooth charm that an Oxbridge education bestows; we were certainly not two peas in a pod but nevertheless developed a fine friendship.

Early one evening there was a knock on our door. It was John – not to borrow the proverbial pint of milk but a bottle of vodka, which he said he would replace the following day. I invited him in and we got talking about the growth of our respective businesses. His was macro; mine was micro. Lloyd's was having a smashing year. He seemed interested in what I was doing and I told him of the philosophical differences I had with my partners even though the business was growing in such a healthy manner. He was intrigued and wanted to know more. I explained to him that unless we created a space large enough to fulfil our commitments to our clients, the business would not advance. He took the bottle of vodka and left. I wondered for a moment why I had given him so much information and then turned my thoughts elsewhere.

A few days later John called, saying he would like to talk to me about my plans for expansion. He'd decided he'd like to have a wager on my future. He spent much of his spare time racing cars at Brands Hatch, so he was no stranger to risky situations. He'd buy out the Burkemans and we'd go international and have a lot of fun doing it. Then he added, 'Actually the family is already international. We own a piece of the Carlton Hotel in Cannes.'

His way of thinking suited my own. Instead of hard-nosed businessmen with their analysts and spreadsheets, here in front of me was an adventurer, a kindred spirit, both of us knowing that only hard work breeds success. I used to tell my staff often that the only time success comes before work is in the dictionary.

I was extremely happy at the thought of having John as a partner. The deal was done, the Burkemans were bought out at a nice profit, and my next-door neighbour had a 50 per cent stake in Vidal Sassoon, which allowed him the right to call for a bottle of vodka at any time.

I introduced John to the team at a staff meeting and he charmed everybody, wanting to know how quickly we could open in Rio, one of his favourite cities. I don't know whether he'd ever been to Brazil, but the international flavour of his talk was just what my staff needed at that moment.

My business had reached a watershed and so, it seems, had the country – 1957 was proving to be a very different kind of year. Slowly but surely traditional English thinking and habits were changing. John Osborne's *Look Back in Anger* created an enormous stir, as did, a year later, Harold Pinter's *The Birthday Party*. The first play in Arnold Wesker's brilliant trilogy, *Chicken Soup with Barley*, opened in Coventry in 1958 and would later open at the Royal Court Theatre. All three were iconoclastic, angry and irreverent about the past. I thought they were wonderful. Some people found these 'angry young men' offensive; they wanted Britain to stay as it was. But the movement for change was powerful and I was right there in its midst, revelling in the beat that came from the heart of London. Britain was finding a new voice. The old one had served it well but the time had come for a change and I was eager to help make it happen.

One magical afternoon, two of the most sought-after people in London arrived at 108 New Bond Street. One was Mary Quant, whose revolutionary vision was changing the fashion world; the other was her husband, Alexander Plunket Greene, a man of discerning taste – debonair, with just a touch of Bohemian spirit.

Mary had come in for a haircut. She was tiny; she must have weighed seven stone at most. She had such a lovely face, perfect bone structure and a very gentle, soft demeanour. When I asked her how she wanted her hair she just said, 'I'm leaving it to you. You know what to do.' She had gorgeous, glossy dark hair. At that time I was taking the bob higher in the back and cutting it to allow the front to fall forward into movement. I then worked on her fringe, leaving it heavy, just above the line of sight. I was so excited to be cutting Mary's hair! But the coup de grâce was not what I hoped it would be. I was dancing around the chair as was my custom, scissors in one hand, comb in the other, when I inadvertently nipped her ear with the scissors. Blood started to flow. Alexander leaned across and said dryly, 'Do you charge extra for that?' As we stemmed the flow of blood with a tissue, Mary asked me if I would do her next show. Even before she finished the sentence, I said, 'Yes. When?' It seemed as if we had become blood brother and sister.

The night before Mary's show was turbo-charged. Everyone's adrenalin was sky high. Mary and her staff were giving the girls their last fittings, and my staff and I actually cut the girls' hair that evening so they would not be seen before the show, as we were giving a very different twist to the bob, with one side shorter than the other.

The following morning, my team and I finished developing the shapes. Seeing the girls wearing a completely new look – something that no one in fashion had done before – brought a smile to my face. They wore tight, skinny-rib sweaters in stripes and bold checks, with knee-high, white, patent, plastic, lace-up boots that had come to epitomize the London look. The hair gave a dynamite finish to Mary's brilliant designs. The press was there in force. The show was at Mary's emporium – called Bazaar – in the King's Road, and to get all the people in who needed to be there was a feat of body manoeuvring. The atmosphere was beyond electric and as these gauche, leggy waifs seduced the audience, with their hair bouncing just as I'd imagined it would, I dared to think – for the first time – *Success. Success!*

We waited with bated breath for the papers to come out the following day. What would they have made of the show? Many of the older journalists didn't quite get it, but the younger fashion and beauty writers understood there was a revolution going on. I suddenly realized it was the first time that I had had such positive coverage. Mary had even better reviews. The press raved about the show and our partnership was born. I did her shows, she dressed mine, and at the after-show dinners Alexander Plunket Greene told marvellous stories with a wicked eye for detail. After one or two drinks, the stories became even more fascinatingly risqué.

The following week, not one but two of the most powerful ladies in fashion called at the salon. One was Clare Rendlesham, the fashion editor at *Vogue*. The other was Felicity Green of the *Daily Mirror*. Clare wanted me to do a fashion shoot at *Vogue* that week, with Jean Shrimpton modelling, and Felicity did an article on the growth of the business from our opening in 1954 until the Quant show. Both ladies were delightful and they became firm allies. They loved the sense of freedom my haircuts gave, they loved my new way of looking at hair, and they both helped make us an integral part of the London fashion scene in the late fifties and early sixties. At last we were moving in the right direction.

❖

One rainy day in 1957, my old pal Georgia Brown came into the salon. It was her opening night in a club that evening and she wanted to feel and look her best. As I started cutting her hair, she began to talk animatedly to me about the benefits of the elocution lessons she was taking. Georgia and I had known each other since our days in the Stepney Youth Club and we had both shared the same Cockney drawl as kids, but now I noticed how much more velvety her voice sounded. Georgia told me that she had been studying with Iris Warren, one of the best voice teachers in London. She suggested I should go to Iris, too, saying it would help me as I built my career, just as it had helped her. Knowing that she pronounced her vowels properly had boosted her confidence considerably. Now, it was very unusual for me to have a conversation with anybody while cutting their hair. If people started to talk, I usually said, 'Do you want conversation or a good haircut?' That way, I could concentrate fully on the cut. But as Georgia and I were chatting, I suddenly realized that I had cut more than I had intended. I was nervous of her reaction, but the new cut gave her an interesting gamine look that I rather liked. I put my scissors down, and waited for her response.

She looked in the mirror, burst into tears and declared loudly, 'Vid, you've ruined my career!' and ran out of the salon crying hysterically.

I didn't go to her opening that night but she called me the following morning. 'Darling, *everybody* loved my hair. I'm sorry I created such a fuss.'

I laughed – I knew she'd come round to it eventually.

The drama was forgotten, but I kept thinking about our conversation. I loved hearing English spoken properly as it was on the stage. Georgia's suggestion had hit a nerve, so late one evening when everyone had left I called Iris Warren and made an appointment to see her at her studio in the West End. When we met, the first words out of her mouth were, 'Georgia Brown has recommended you. I normally do not work with hairdressers; I work with actors.' She looked me up and down critically. 'Be at the Old Vic at two o'clock on Thursday.' There was no 'can you be?' – just 'be' in a clipped, precise tone. I went back to the salon and rearranged my schedule, passing clients over to other stylists.

On Thursday at two o'clock, I arrived at the Old Vic, slightly giddy at the thought of going backstage at this theatre with its glorious past. I was put in a sort of green room where the most extraordinary mellifluous voice was being piped through the speakers – a voice that was obviously rehearsing something rather grand. When all was quiet, I was ushered into the main theatre, where Ms Warren said to me, 'Did you hear the voice?'

'Yes,' I said, 'and with great pleasure.'

'Who was it?'

'I recognize it but I can't put a name to it,' I said lamely.

'Can't put a name to it?' she said. 'That was Laurence Olivier!'

Her incredulous attitude did little for my self-esteem. She looked at me with disdain, and said, 'On the podium. Enunciate.'

I went to the dais as instructed, looked down at the sheet of paper filled with random words she had given me and enunciated my heart out. After a couple of minutes, she said, 'Stop. It's bloody awful, but I think I can do something with you.'

For the next five years, when I wasn't out of town doing shows, I would look forward to my sessions with the inimitable Iris Warren. I was beginning to enjoy speaking the Queen's English and, just as Georgia had predicted, it did boost my confidence.

❖

My energy level was higher than ever and I was thrilled to be working with the fashion magazines and newspapers. John, my new partner, was a real breath of fresh air. He was prepared to invest £30,000 in a new building at 171 New Bond Street, which was at present being leased by José Pou. A noted Mayfair hairdresser for many years, José Pou was leaving Britain for what he hoped would be greener pastures. Apart from paying him £10,000 for the twenty-one years left on the lease, we would rip out the existing salon and build three new floors including a mezzanine. At least, that was the plan. But that July, the *Andrea Doria*, a large luxury passenger ship, had tragically gone down and many people's lives were lost.

I had never seen John so frazzled and out of sorts as when he told me that the *Andrea Doria* had been insured by his syndicate at Lloyd's and that as a result he would have to plough money back into the company. It would be impossible for him to dish out £30,000 for a new salon. But almost in the same breath he promised to find me a new partner.

Within a few days, John called and asked me to have dinner in Soho with him and a man he had done business with who he thought would be absolutely perfect for the project at hand. That's when I met Charles Prevost. He had a handshake that I still felt halfway through dinner and an aura of power that I've since discovered only emanates from the extraordinarily rich. He was an Australian wool man with roots in New Zealand. He was built like a bulldog and was obviously determined to have fun out of life; we hit it off immediately.

Charles said, 'John has spoken highly of you and your talent and I've done some research myself. Tell me about the salon that you want to open.'

I began to set out my dream of opening a salon that would

become the centre of a worldwide operation. He seemed to like the idea. As we spoke I realized he was the kind of man who swept bureaucracy under the mat and did it his way. He then said, 'We don't want to talk about hair all night, but I'm sure there will be lots of pretty girls coming to the salon.'

'Yes,' I replied, 'we're developing a clientele of some of the finest models in Britain.'

I saw his eyes twinkle as he said, 'Would you organize a party each time I come to London and invite these ladies?'

I assured him that these lovely ladies came to many of the parties I gave, and having got to the crux of the arrangement we moved on to other things. We laughed and talked about life. He told me of his struggles as he was building his wool empire and said, 'In my business you need two things – guts and luck.' He seemed to have been blessed with both.

Nothing was decided that evening, but the following morning I received a call from a Mr Louis Zucker, the London lawyer for Charles Prevost. We made arrangements to have lunch. Almost the first words out of his mouth were, 'Mr Prevost will take over John's position.' He went on to suggest that as the company grew, we could create shares so that Charles could leave a nice chunk of cash to his two daughters.

While the deal was being finalized, I kept thinking about a French film I'd seen a few years earlier, *Coiffeur Pour Dames*. In it Fernandel played a sheep shearer in the south of France. He discovered he could cut ladies' hair even better than he could shear sheep, so he moved from sheep to people and eventually opened the chicest salon in all of Paris. I'm sure Mr Prevost, the sheep man, had no such aspirations about cutting hair, but for some reason the thought lingered.

I knew that I would need a really good lawyer to handle the

details of my new partnership, but I didn't really know where to find one. No one we knew was so wealthy that they employed such advisers as a matter of course. However, my brother, Ivor, had just qualified as a chartered accountant. I had introduced him to Colin Fisher, my old Palmach buddy, who was also a chartered accountant, and they had immediately decided to set up a business together with me as their first client. Ivor was extraordinarily savvy and when I called him saying that I needed a first-class lawyer, he found someone he thought would fit the bill almost immediately. The deal with Charles was done. As we were placing our last signatures on our contract, I told Charles about Fernandel's sheep-shearing film. The look he gave me is best described as enigmatic.

I lived carefully and invested all profits back into the business. But I was still determined to give my mother the lifestyle that she did not have when she was young. It gave me great joy to be able to help her and Nathan G – I owed them both so much. Some years earlier, when I was still chasing from job to job, Dad had decided he wanted to buy me a business. He had all of £1,700 in his bank account. It was his life savings. But he had found a small salon in the suburbs that he thought would be suitable and was excited for me to see it. I went to look at it as a thank-you for his thoughtfulness. But it really wasn't right for me – my sights were firmly set on the centre of London. I thanked him, and many years later, as I was becoming very much a part of the worldwide fashion scene, Dad and I laughed when recounting his generous offer of a neighbourhood salon in Hampstead Garden Suburb. A man who wanted to put every penny he had into a stepson who could not keep a job was, to say the least, extraordinary.

Mother and Nathan G were now finding the London winters

extremely hard to take, especially because of Dad's heart condition, so for many years I would pack them off to the Canary Islands at the beginning of November, and they would stay until the end of March. Mother's fluent Spanish made the islands the perfect place for them to be.

New doors were opening for me. I had started to mingle with a totally different set of people, and among them I met the designer David Hicks. As I got to know him, I asked David if he would like to design the reception area of the new salon at 171 New Bond Street. I took a gamble on this – he was an increasingly well-known and distinguished designer, married to Lord Mountbatten's daughter. He hobnobbed with the Queen and was very much a part of the aristocracy! What would David Hicks have in common with an East End boy like me? But he was fascinated by the idea. David was an enormous snob, but not when it came to talent. Once he decided you had something creative to offer, he was immensely loyal. He knew how hard it had been for him to get to the top and he was quite fascinated by my progress, so our relationship was a very easy one. The idea of designing the reception area appealed to him immensely, as though he seemed to have his signature on any number of things – from grand houses to carpets and curtains – he had never been involved with a salon before. At that time, most salons were light and feminine in their colour schemes. David created an all-black reception area with gold bars running down the windows. It was eye-poppingly dramatic and a first. The inside was minimalist but had a great working ambience.

David invited Elaine and me to his country house for the weekend, where his mother welcomed us grandly. We talked politics among other things, and suddenly David turned to his mother and said, 'Mother, I don't believe we've ever had a socialist in the house before.'

David was crazy about Elaine and they became the firmest of friends. She asked him if he would decorate our flat in Curzon Place. He did and later put a picture of our living room – which prominently featured two Louis XV chairs – in his very first book.

One day he brought the great artist Francis Bacon up for tea. Francis had a young man with him who wanted to become a hair-dresser. During an enjoyable conversation, I spelled out how long it would take to become really first class as a stylist, but if he was prepared to put in the time and had that added talent, he could make a name for himself. During the dialogue, Francis, at David's invitation, poked around the flat – which took exactly thirty seconds. David asked Francis if he liked what he saw. Francis replied, 'Yes. It must have been difficult to do something this small, but you've got it spot on. I'm curious, though, why have you covered all the books in white paper?'

David sneered. 'If you saw his taste in literature, you'd have done exactly the same thing.'

I looked at David and laughed. We always enjoyed teasing each other. But it wasn't true. I was reading Camus and Dostoevsky and loving them.

When opening night finally came, a painting by Denis Wirth-Miller arrived. David Hicks told a couple of the workmen to hang it in the reception area. They did – upside down. But it was so abstract that nobody noticed. David, however, was furi-ous as Wirth-Miller, who was a great friend of his and Francis Bacon, was coming to the opening night bash. As he entered the reception area, Wirth-Miller looked at his painting and, to the relief of all of us, said, 'I believe it looks better that way.'

Naturally, all my fellow workers came and by this time we had built a solid team. Robert Edele came over, gave me a big hug and said, 'It looks like one of us is going to make it.'

I said, 'We will *all* make it in our different ways.'

Robert had taken over my first salon, a stone's throw away down Bond Street. When he heard about my plan for expansion, he told me about his own plan to make it on his own. I was disappointed to lose him but could only stand back and admire his ambition. It was sad losing him but it wasn't for long.

When we announced our plans to open 171 New Bond Street, I told José Pou's staff that if they would care to learn our methods of cutting and the disciplines that we had instilled, they were welcome to apply for a job. On that Monday morning when we opened there was just one of José Pou's staff waiting outside the salon. It was Annie Humphries, a pint-sized blonde with glasses and a lovely bubbly personality. Annie was a colourist, and under Laurance's guidance it became obvious that not only was she good, she was *very* good. Although she was tiny, she had a very forceful way about her and eventually, under her rule, the colour department was run like an army barracks.

As time went on it became clear that she was as dedicated to pushing the boundaries of colour as we were to cut. She developed new ways of highlighting and lowlighting hair and she eventually became the chief colourist in the Vidal Sassoon organization. She had a great eye, knew exactly where to place the colour, and as the manufacturers improved their formulas, Annie would mix Clairol, L'Oréal and any other brand of colour that she thought would do the job – a highly unorthodox approach.

One morning three months after the opening, I was awakened at about 2.30 by a ringing telephone. It was the police. 'There's been a flood above your premises in Bond Street. Your top-floor ceiling has caved in and we cannot turn on the electricity, but we're obliged to call you. Can you come round immediately?'

Elaine and I hurriedly threw some clothes on and rushed over to the new salon. Nothing could have prepared us for what we saw. It was total devastation. As the police said, the ceiling on the third floor had collapsed under the sheer power of the water above. Mirrors had broken and chairs were floating towards the reception. I could not bear the sight of my brand-new, avant-garde salon totally ruined, and went into a corner by myself and sobbed, until Elaine's gentle hand caressed my shoulder. I could not remember the last time I had cried, but I was faced with a disaster, enormous debts, all those hard-working people I had trained and a clientele that had been so delighted with the new salon. *What could we do with them all?* And suddenly I had a magical thought. Although it was well past three in the morning, I telephoned Robert Edele and told him what had happened. I said, 'Robert, would you like to be a shareholder in a company called Vidal Sassoon?'

His response knocked me out. 'I never wanted to leave you in the first place.'

'Robert, I need my old salon for a few months.' I asked him if he'd help organize a two-shift system at 108 New Bond Street, where half the staff would start at eight in the morning and finish at two, and the others would come in at two and finish at ten. This way I believed we could keep all our staff and all our clients until we had put the chaos behind us.

It was a crisis but no one complained. Everybody cooperated. Stylists were given either morning or afternoon shifts, the same with the apprentices and the colour and perm staff. Clients were informed, although they didn't have to be. The press had sent photographers and the national papers printed the sad story of the utter destruction of our brand-new salon. The insurance company was informed immediately and the work of rebuilding the salon started at once. It took three and a half months before we were fully reinstalled in 171 New Bond Street. To get the work done, the builders also worked double shifts, starting at eight and finishing at ten at night. It seemed that I was spending all my time at the salon; I simply never went home. It must have been an intensely difficult period for Elaine.

Charles Prevost, who heard of our slight inconvenience, asked if we needed a little more money to tide us over.

Ivor said, 'Five thousand wouldn't hurt.'

He sent a cheque but we never had to use it, thank goodness. It went back to him with a big thank-you and because of this Charles and I became even closer.

There was no party for the second opening. The painting in the reception was hung right-side-up, I think, and my fellow crimpers were all happy to be together again.

It was a disaster that gave strength to our backbone. If we could conquer the flood, nothing would hold us back.

These were wonderful days. Hair excited me. As the old ways – backcombing, rollers and rigidity – went out of the window, I started to feel the possibilities in front of my eyes. Without wanting to elevate our profession above its station in life, I was beginning to see what we did more and more as a modern art form. The passion, the excitement of creativity, and knowing that we as a team were constructively helping to change a whole craft, fed my adrenalin and my curiosity.

The salon at 171 New Bond Street generated a buzz that spread far beyond its front doors. Outside in the street, there were hairdressers from all over armed with cameras to take pictures of our latest cuts as our clients left the salon. A haircut would normally take between half an hour and three-quarters of an hour, but with a new client it could easily take an hour. Round about three o'clock in the afternoon, most of our hairdressers were behind schedule. I was one of the worst offenders.

One Friday morning David Hicks called me up and said, 'Make sure my wife gets out on time, as we are dining with her father tonight.' Pamela Hicks's dad was, of course, Lord Louis Mountbatten.

I said, 'David, it's Friday. Pamela could come to us at any time, but please not late on a Friday.' Friday was always the craziest day of the week.

But she did and when I approached Lady Pamela, I was already three-quarters of an hour behind schedule. David called once more to remind me that time was of the essence. But I couldn't catch up. It was way past seven o'clock when I finished Pamela's hair. Just as I put down my scissors, the receptionist blushingly said, 'Mr Hicks is on the phone.'

'Again?' I said incredulously.

David was furious, complaining bitterly that I was keeping Lord Louis waiting for his dinner.

I said, 'Not to worry, David. You can always warm up the chicken soup.'

He slammed the phone down and for two months we did not speak. I thought, *Well, that's the end of a great friendship.* But then one day as I was walking up Bond Street, I suddenly saw David coming towards me. We both burst out laughing and had a big hug – not David's usual way of greeting people. I did like David Hicks.

That was 171 New Bond Street – the epitome of London in the sixties – with many clients not caring that they had to spend extra time with us, as one well-known face after another graced the salon.

✧

About a year after we opened, Leonard, Raphael, Carlos and Ronny Gilbert all left my salon at 171 New Bond Street the same Saturday afternoon at one o'clock, never to return. Raphael partnered with Leonard in their new salon, and when they parted company it was renamed the House of Leonard. Carlos and Ronny Gilbert went their own ways. I needed a new team, but this time I knew I had to do it differently. I decided to offer shares to the next team of talent that I'd train. I wanted a team that would be with me for their whole careers, and I wanted them to feel it was their business as well as mine. That's when I met Roger Thompson.

Apparently he had applied for a job with me on two previous occasions. Whoever interviewed and rejected him should have been fired, but I never found out who it had been! It was undoubtedly our mistake, but this time his timing was perfect. Roger was tall, dark and very good-looking, and instantly became an object of desire for many of the salon's clients. Apart from that, he was the only hairdresser I knew who was ambidextrous. He could cut hair with either hand. He learned quickly and eventually his brilliance shone through. He went on to create many of our most famous looks, interpreting and softening my original ideas, cutting long tendrils at the sides of the strong geometric shape. I had enormous respect for his talent. For many years he was my right hand.

Christopher Brooker was a whole different kettle of fish. He applied for a job at much the same time as Roger but had an altogether different approach. He argued line with me right from the beginning and I liked that. He didn't argue to be controversial; he argued because he had great vision and a different point of view. He was a thinker – a chess player of some note – with extraordinary avant-garde ideas. He later created some very innovative looks, including the 'Brush' in which the hair was cut to the same length all over and then brushed into shape. I could see that if we didn't run with it and adopt it as one of our 'looks' we would be holding Christopher back – and perhaps holding back the development of new styles. We went with it. It was absolutely the right decision; it was very good for Christopher's confidence and marked the start of true democracy within the company. He would soon become my left hand.

Roger and Christopher were truly great stylists and they helped change the face of hairdressing. They had immense influence on the other young hairdressers who joined us, training them and guiding their careers. We were a formidable trio.

Every hairdressing salon needs a mother, someone to look after the housekeeping, and our Katie was *very* special. When she joined us, at 108 New Bond Street, she was a woman of about forty with a strong rural accent. When we moved to Number 171, Katie came too. She had a maternal instinct towards everyone – staff and clients – and earned everybody's respect as she practically ran the salon. Katie would make the tea, boil the green shampoo, wash the gowns and towels, and generally see that the stylists were well looked after. And while she was definitely not one of the cleaning ladies, some days she'd come in early to see that they had done their job properly. Her loyalty was touching, and if there was a gloomy moment in the staff room, Katie's wonderful sense of humour would see us through. She was such an expert at what she did that she never seemed to be in anybody's way. She stayed with us until she retired – by which time she had been with me for over twenty-five years.

Although professionally things were going from strength to strength, it didn't take more than a year of marriage before both Elaine and I realized we had made a mistake. I was working all hours. I left the house at eight in the morning and was rarely back before ten at night. Elaine had gone from a busy, lively job at the salon to twiddling her fingers playing at being a house-wife. And when I was at home, we had very different ideas of what we wanted to do. At first, I went with her on weekend visits to her mother, but badly needed the exercise I craved. I joined the Ruislip Water Ski Club, which was run by David Nations, who was the British water ski champion at the time. David taught me first to ski on two skis, and then to slalom, also to make a jump start from the pier into the water on one ski from a moving boat. I would sometimes scream with elation in the middle of the lake. I loved the fresh air, the exercise and the total freedom that skiing gave me.

Elaine eventually decided to come along, despite saying, 'I can't even swim. How do you expect me to ski?' She didn't, but she did have an instant rapport with David Nations. That rapport turned into a romance. As for me, I thought it was far better for two people to be happy than three unhappy. Our marriage ended cordially and Elaine went on to marry David. Believe it or not, it took place in the same synagogue with the same rabbi offici-ating as at our wedding. Understandably I was not invited, but I still skied at the club and marvelled that three people who understood their own needs were never embarrassed to meet, as we often did at Ruislip. Members of the club enjoyed the whole drama and some even went to Elaine and David's wedding.

Elaine moved in with David, which gave her at least three times as much space. And as was her way, as she was the one who made the final decision regarding our divorce, she said graciously, 'You keep the flat at Curzon Place. And if you need money at the end of the month to pay the rent, don't come to David.' It was the only divorce I went through that had a sense of humour attached to it. We are still friends to this day and we talk often.

Having a bachelor pad in Curzon Place enticed the ladies and I had very little trouble adjusting to life as a free soul, but it would be bad manners to talk about that now. Once again I promised myself ten years of total freedom from the responsibility of marriage – even if I found someone as beguiling as Elaine. Work took up so much of my time. There were constant ups and downs depending on how well the work was going. Because so much of what I wanted to do was totally different from what anyone else had done, there was no one I could discuss my problems with. If the work was going poorly in the salon or an idea I had wasn't working, my moodiness would take over. I would quietly put my brush and scissors down and take a long walk. Once I got to St James's Park, I would let out a big scream. I am ashamed to admit this happened on more than one occasion. The harassed receptionist would then have to try to fit my poor abandoned client into the already-tight schedules of other hairdressers.

At the end of the day, when all was quiet and the clients and stylists had left, I would sit and listen to music. Miles Davis's *Kind of Blue* generally suited my mood. On other occasions, Mahler's Eighth, the symphony of 1,000 which needs an orchestra of 200 and nearly 800 in the chorus, seemed more appropriate. I still love that extraordinary piece and hum the melodies – *Er kommt zurück ... Er kommt zurück*: 'He comes back ... He comes back.'

✧

Wella, like many other hair-product companies, was vying for the number one spot in the British market and approached me to do a national tour taking in ten cities. The strategy of touring so boldly to promote products was brand new in the hairdressing world and Wella proposed to do it with great style. The man in charge of it all was Phil Wren. He was very English, rather literary, and given to quoting poetry during shows. His vision for the tour got my interest. 'We'll hire the Eric Delaney Orchestra' – the big swing band of its day – 'only use top models, and bring with you a team that can not only cut hair, but has showbiz personalities.' I immediately thought of Ricky Burns, one of our top stylists, an outrageous extrovert who was wonderful on stage. I also took the rest of my best show team. We had more than our share of top models by this point, but they decided that, since a tour of Britain was hardly Paris or Milan, they were going to have enormous fun on this trip.

One girl, Jackie, had a boyfriend who had been rather naughty and was serving time in Broadmoor, a maximum-security prison. He was a second-storey man who would climb the drainpipes of big houses to get into open windows and take away a few goodies like jewellery, money and paintings. Inevitably, he had got caught and was doing five years for breaking and entering. But he had a bit of cash and knew how to work the system. After shows in Edinburgh, Manchester and Leeds, we were on our way to Wales and the West Country. I believe

Cardiff was the next stop. During the journey – I have no knowledge of how – our bus was met by a prison van carrying Jackie's boyfriend. She jumped in the back of the van rather quickly and was there for a good hour while we rested by the side of the road. Eventually she reappeared, totally dishevelled, and joined us. Everybody's eyes were on her, including our bus driver's. With a devilish look, I asked her, 'How did things go?'

She said, 'Well, to tell you the truth, I've never been fucked by a guy wearing hob-nailed boots before.'

Yes, the models were having fun. And so were quite a few of the stylists.

The tour was a sell-out. In fact, in Glasgow they oversold tickets and we had to do two nights. While the second night was supposed to be part of our day of rest, the team was doing such good work they didn't want a night off and were totally energized for the second show. The shows were a sensation and controversial enough to provide a talking point. Young hairdressers packed the audience and were keen to learn about our new styles and techniques. Phil Wren was a very happy man. Nothing quite like this had taken place in Britain before and the success of our shows built his reputation enormously. He deserved every credit for his visionary enterprise.

❖

In 1961, Larry Gelb, the founder of Clairol, while passing through London on his way to Paris, telephoned me: would I meet him for breakfast at the Savoy? It seemed Clairol wanted to get in on the act, too. I had heard rumours that when he started his company, he had to walk across the States peddling his products from a knapsack, so I was quite familiar with his tough reputation. We met and with great excitement in his voice, he told me of the grand plan he had of taking Alexandre, Maurice Frank – another very artistic and accomplished French hair designer – and me on a tour of the east coast of the United States, taking in New York, Philadelphia, Washington and Miami. He asked me if I was interested. I had never been to America and I was *very* interested. His negotiations in Paris obviously didn't go quite as well, as in the event I would find myself touring solo.

My first visit to New York was as near disaster as was possible. They had booked me into an enormous hair event, working in a booth alongside hundreds of other hairdressers in their booths, all screaming at the top of their voices to command an audience. I bit my lip and said nothing until after the show – which by the way took several hours – and then approached the man who was running things for Clairol. I said point blank, 'If this is the way it's going to be through the rest of the tour, I'm jumping on a plane to London tonight.'

'Absolutely not,' he said. 'The show will be the total opposite of what you've encountered in New York. You will be working in halls with audiences of a thousand or more hairdressers, but you can't go anyway because *Vogue* has booked you with Richard Avedon tomorrow.'

This thrilled me. This absolutely *thrilled* me. I knew Avedon's photographic work, of course, but very recently Suzy Parker, the actress and top model, had been in London filming. She'd become both a client and a great friend. She had told me of her deep affection for Avedon, who was a close friend of hers, and that she would like me to meet him. Little did she know that I would be meeting him the following day. And little did I know that in America hairdressers were almost treated with disdain. They were seen as pretty useless types, mostly off-the-wall zombies who couldn't do anything worthwhile and therefore became hairdressers.

When I arrived at Avedon's studio, I was totally awestruck. On my first visit to America I was going to be working with one of the greatest photographers of our times. I was shown where I was to work and was introduced to the models.

China Machado, a gorgeous model who was part-Asian and had a very unique look, came over to me and said, 'Suzy's been telling me all about you. She said you were a whizz with the scissors. Would you please shape the sides of my hair?'

I said I'd love to, got my scissors and began to cut. I had not realized the speed and intensity of Avedon's work. He came almost running into the dressing room and demanded to know what I was doing.

'Well, China asked me to shape her hair,' I explained.

He was not interested one bit in what China wanted, or in what I might be trying to do, and barked, 'I want those girls out and I want them out now.'

I saw red. 'You'll get them out when I'm ready,' I replied.

Everybody was taken aback. Hairdressers didn't talk to Mr Avedon that way. But I wasn't going to be bullied and stood my ground. I got the girls out as fast as I could, and though Avedon looked at me quizzically a couple of times, he said nothing. The session went on, with great music, models who moved beautifully, and hair that swung quite nicely – considering I hadn't had much time to use my scissors.

By the end of the day, we were not bosom pals, but a mutual respect was born. I would work with Avedon again, not long afterwards, when Rudi Gernreich – for me, one of America's greatest designers – asked me if I could be in New York to do a session at Richard's studio. He brought with him Peggy Moffitt, a quite extraordinary model who after her haircut would pose theatrically in front of the mirror, almost acting out the clothes before being photographed. She would get up, shake her hair and dance. Music going, hair swinging, nobody moved like Peggy. It was a wonderful shoot.

As was the session I did with the great Irving Penn. Penn's work was as instantly recognizable as Richard Avedon's, yet they were so different. The quietness of his studio was what hit me first. I felt the powerful sense of what he was doing. Penn was gentle and yet brilliant. He had a technique that so many photographers tried to copy. He met and married the exquisite Lisa Fonssagrives, who was a model with classic looks, and when people in fashion spoke of the great photographers, Penn was always mentioned – either first or second on the list. Penn lent a calmness to the razzle-dazzle of the Sixties.

The Clairol shows in Philadelphia, Washington and Miami were done with very much more style than the original New York session – a day I have tried to forget for many a year. But I'm not sure that the American hairdressers who came to the shows really understood my work. I had to explain my techniques in detail, and the idea of forgoing backcombing (or teasing, as they call it) was foreign to them. In the end, though, I think I won them over with my British accent.

In Miami, Mr Gelb arrived and after the show, took me for a late supper with some of his people, and announced that I had to go to Los Angeles immediately. I patiently explained to him that I had a week's work booked in London and that I *did* have to get back.

He convinced me that Los Angeles would be a marvellous venue to show off my talents, so I called London and said I would be in the States for another week. I flew to Los Angeles and was met by a Clairol executive, who immediately pounced on me, saying, 'Had we known three months ago, we could have organized something, but Mr Gelb has put us in a terrible position.' He said, 'Let me take you to the Hotel Roosevelt, where you will be staying and where the show will be.' I could see he was very nervous.

After I dropped my baggage in my room, I was taken to the ballroom to meet the 'models'. When I saw them, I immediately knew it was going to go horribly wrong. These were not the highly professional girls I had become used to; they were badly bleached blondes with hair like straw. I had to do something. I told the Clairol people, 'I can't express the type of work I want to show with these girls.' There was nothing for it but to find my own models.

The show was the following night. They had been in a panic since I first met them and now I was in one, too. I left the hotel on Hollywood Boulevard and walked the street in a daze. On the corner was a delightful-looking girl with a great bone structure and hair to her shoulders. I took a chance, walked up to her, told her of my dilemma and asked, 'Would you care to model for me?'

She appeared to think it over for ages. Finally she said, 'Yes, but hairdresser or no hairdresser it will still cost you a hundred bucks.' She smiled. It turned out she was a prostitute. I thought of Peggy at Mac & George and I smiled too.

I had a restless night wondering whether she would turn up or not, but she did. She met me in the lobby and I took her into the ballroom. It was empty – scary for me, and a very new experience. As I was brushing the model's hair waiting for *anybody* to arrive, a tall, good-looking man with great style entered the ballroom. He introduced himself as Gene Shacove, *the* master hairdresser of Los Angeles. He had come with twelve of his staff, and that was the total audience for the night.

I was well aware of Gene's reputation in the business and I was also well aware of the huge empty auditorium. I decided we needed more intimacy, so I asked him and his hairdressers to come up on stage and have some fun while I was cutting this girl's hair. I cut it into an asymmetric bob with a light fringe – which in America they call 'bangs' – creating a look that really suited her bone structure. Gene had his own method of cutting and argued with me during the whole session. We agreed to disagree but we got into that hairdressing mood and talked shape and design. He encouraged the stylists that were with him to ask questions; they wouldn't stop.

My friend from Hollywood Boulevard with the marvellous bone structure was absolutely delighted with the result – especially when I gave her two hundred dollars instead of the one hundred she normally charged for a rather different evening's work. Without her my scissors would have been silent. She made the evening for Gene, his staff and me. What could have been a total disaster turned out to be quite an innovative success and Gene and I became buddies for life.

From that point on, Gene would stay with me when he was in London and I would stay with him in Los Angeles. He had quite a way with the women and Robert Towne, the screenwriter, spent a lot of time studying his lifestyle. Hardly surprising then that his hit movie *Shampoo*, starring Warren Beatty, was widely believed to have been about the antics of Gene Shacove.

Being a great hairdresser in LA, Gene had a film-star clientele and our friendship meant we soon had a very good thing going. He would call me when someone special was coming to London and ask me to look after them, and I did the same for him when any of my acting clients were going to Los Angeles and needed looking after – meaning their hair, of course.

✧

My visit to the United States had given me much food for thought. Its architecture had made an extraordinary mark on the way I felt about cities. Great structures like Mies van der Rohe's Seagram Building and Marcel Breuer's Whitney Museum of American Art, both in New York City, made it clear that modern architecture led the way. My work was fed by architectural shapes and I found fashion second in its influence. In hair we needed a revolution – an explosion – and there were many people in other art forms who felt as I did. Was hair just an accessory to clothes? Of course not. It was your clothes that you took off at night. We had to find a way to create angles and shape to the living bone structure, as architects had done with great cities.

In London, I went with some friends to a restaurant for dinner. I was beckoned from another table. A developer, whose wife was a client of mine, was sitting with his guests and he introduced me to them. One was Marcel Breuer.

I looked at him and said, '*The* Marcel Breuer?' and he laughed. I said, 'Excuse me. I'll be right back.' I went to my table and explained that I needed at least twenty minutes and to carry on and order.

I returned to Marcel Breuer's table and a waiter placed a chair for me next to him. Breuer was a thoroughbred. He not only knew his own subject matter so well but studied the reasoning of ideas in other fields, and shared with me his view that the newness of form was impacting on art worldwide. What blew me away was that he knew *my* work, and we talked shapes and bone structure and angles and how much I was influenced by architecture. Fifty years or so on, I can still remember the conversation in perfect detail.

With the Clairol jamboree over, it was time to catch up with the girl I then adored. Her name was Maggie London and we were together for well over three years. A knockout redhead with a personality to match, she was also one of my models. Our relationship was enormously volatile but also enormously compatible as she, too, craved a certain amount of freedom and kept her own flat. She was popular, vivacious and kind, and was on everybody's party list. She gave a wonderful party for my homecoming. Michael Caine, Georgia Brown and Terence Stamp were there, as well as many of the gorgeous girls that Maggie modelled with.

Maggie's parties were legendary and one she gave – at my flat – was probably the craziest scene I'd ever attended. She had said, 'Darling, don't worry. It will just be an intimate affair.' But a flood of alcohol and the fact that the actor Stanley Baker was giving another party in the White Elephant restaurant down the street soon saw things turning a little riotous. Just who owned which guests I'll never know. I remember at one time or another seeing Albert Finney, Steve McQueen, Robert Wagner, Alma Cogan, Christopher Plummer, Pat Lewis, Sean Connery and Diane Cilento all squeezed into my little flat. Terence Donovan, that wild and wonderful photographer, made a bet with a beautiful model: giving her a head start, they both had to run from the flat around the Dorchester Hotel, back along Park Lane and into Curzon Place, and if by then Terry had her knickers in his hand, he had won. Maureen was her name and they didn't come any gamer. Many of the guests went down into the street to see if the dirty deed could actually be done. Suddenly there he was

– Terry Donovan – galloping into Curzon Place, triumph written all over his face, returning with Maureen's panties. He waved them around his head and bellowed, 'Another blow for the equality of the sexes!'

Christopher Plummer opened a wardrobe, only to say, 'Who the hell has stolen the elevator?' I'm sure he got home safely but I have no idea how.

A crisis arose when a well-known actor and his girlfriend, consumed no doubt by an overwhelming desire to examine the plumbing system, got locked in the lavatory together. Others were waiting their turn impatiently. I dashed across the corridor to my neighbour. Naturally enough he was wide awake. So, I imagine, were most other people in the neighbourhood. With no time to apologize, I gasped, 'May we borrow your lavatory?'

With a sigh he said, 'Certainly, and I suppose I might as well borrow your party. There seems to be a law against sleep tonight.'

When I surfaced, very late the following day, *I* felt there should be a law against parties. Chairs were overturned, pictures hung askew, and a couple of bodies lay snoring in armchairs. I picked up a beautiful Chinese lacquered box that David Hicks had given me. It had been crushed under somebody's heel. Before even a cup of tea, I called the brilliant interior decorator Eugene Howe, who had also been at the party. 'Eugene, I've just taken a look at the flat and I've decided to go away for a while. Do you think you could give it a complete facelift? New York beckons. I have stuff to do there. You have three months to complete the job.'

He arrived an hour later and winced at the sight. Much later I winced at the bill. His taste was superb but came at a price.

Dear Maggie – what a lovely party that girl could make! I

still adore her to this day and have many beautiful memories of our time together. But there is one memory that isn't so beautiful. In fact, it became a total embarrassment. For three years, nobody else came into our thoughts, but then we started to have an 'open' relationship; we both saw other people. This was the sixties after all. I thought we were being very cool with that. Even though we were still emotionally involved, I knew she was seeing a young actor. I also knew where the spare key to her flat was hidden. One day, I went round and let myself in. And there was Maggie with her new lover. I hit him and he fell across the room. He did not fight back, but what he said shamed me. 'I don't fight over women. A girl should be allowed to choose her own boyfriend.'

Maggie's Irish temper flared and she threw me out. I was totally in the wrong and had no way of putting it right. It was the end of a long and beautiful affair.

In the fifties and early sixties, sex was easier to get in London than a good meal. If a problem came your way, penicillin cured everything. It truly was a golden age and I rose to the occasion. One evening a girl called, said she had been given my number by a friend and asked if she could come up and see me. Curious, I said yes. She was an exquisite beauty and it turned into a night of wild lovemaking. In the morning we had breakfast together but hardly a word was said. Afterwards, she got dressed and then pulled out a notebook. I saw her cross my name off a list and asked, 'What are you doing?'

'I'm going to screw half the West End of London and each man on my list only gets one shot.' As she left, she giggled and said, 'It was nice meeting you.'

6

Me and Mr Jones

In the autumn of 1961, a gentleman walked into our salon in
Bond Street and asked to see me. I finished my client and made
my way to the reception area. Introducing himself as Mr Jones,
he explained that he was the manager of the Grosvenor House
Hotel in Park Lane, and he was planning to open a salon there.
It would be on the ground floor, would be easily seen from the
street and was I interested? I told him I would like to see the
space, and we agreed to meet at the hotel the next day.

I asked Mr Jones what motivated him to come to me. He said,
'I've walked all around Mayfair. There are many busy salons, but
yours is the only one that is as busy on Mondays as it is on
Saturdays, and it strikes me you must have more clients than you
can deal with in just one salon.' I felt that I had to explain that we
were not hotel hairdressers and that there would be some people
who didn't care for our modern, radical looks. He'd need a
smaller space in another area to deal with those clients, otherwise
we would have no choice but to turn some people away.

He didn't seem concerned, and in fact agreed that it would
be a very practical solution. He went on to say that they would

build the salon using our architect to our design, and would only take a percentage of the profits, giving the salon time to grow. At this point, I began to be very interested. When he rounded off by saying that because our name was becoming so popular in Britain, it would be very good for the hotel, I saw that this was not just an interesting proposition, it was extremely appealing and I kept thinking, *Boy, has this come just at the right time.*

Obviously I didn't say yes on the spot, but it was clear from the outset that it was perfect for our needs. We had so many new clients that 171 New Bond Street was bursting at the seams. I contacted Gordon Bowyer, an architect whose work I admired, and when he saw the space and described the possibilities it conjured up to him, I hired him on the spot.

I called Roger Thompson. 'Are you busy, or can we have dinner tonight?'

We did – in a little Italian restaurant close to the salon – and I asked him a very simple question. 'Tell me,' I said, 'if you were in my shoes, who would you pick to run the salon at Grosvenor House?'

He thought hard and began slowly to reel off a few names. I kept telling him he was way off beam, until in exasperation he said, 'OK, then, who would *you* pick?'

I finished my glass of wine slowly. I was enjoying this. 'Do you know a character called Roger Thompson? I'd pick him. I'm going to put *his* name outside the salon in large letters. It will be called "Roger at Vidal Sassoon".'

He gulped. Then he began trying to talk his way out of the job. He was too young. Hadn't enough experience. Wasn't as good as so-and-so and so-and-so. Roger might have been only twenty-one, but I knew he had the talent and imagination and I was sure he was ready for the responsibility.

He was dumbfounded. 'But no one has ever done this before,' he said.

I told Roger I had made a promise to myself after leaving Raymond that I would not only build an international team, but also do my best to build their names as well. He deserved the opportunity. The rest of the staff loved the idea. They already knew that they could get a named credit in newspapers or magazines when they had created Sassoon styles for the models. But giving one of them their own salon was in a different league. It was a huge gesture, but one I was happy to make. I've always believed in teamwork. Giving Roger his name above the door showed everyone, not just my own staff but throughout the craft itself, how far one could go when a team was working together really well.

Grosvenor House had a magic all of its own. Gordon Bowyer did not let us down and built a superb salon that was both minimalist and very beautiful. Roger and I also explored many innovative ideas for our exciting new venture. I'd been going to various health resorts since the days of 108, my first salon, and I thought we should put certain contemporary health principles into practice in the salon. I personally kept to a strict fitness routine of swimming and stretching, and a diet that was rich in fruit, nuts and vegetables with the occasional one-pound beefsteak and, luckily, my weight never altered. Now, I said to Roger, 'Let's be revolutionary, not only with hair.' He gave me a look as if to say, *What have I got myself into*?

We hired a nurse to give vitamin B and C injections to boost the energy levels of any clients who wanted them. It was all the rage then and many of our hairdressers, including me, also pulled down their pants for a quick shot – in the privacy of a cubicle, of course. We had a health-food bar too, where the person who served the protein drinks and various other fruit and vegetable concoctions also gave tips on exercise and losing or gaining weight as was needed. In the early sixties, this was a revelation and I was enjoying myself thoroughly. Roger, on the other hand, thought I was stark raving mad and he would often say, 'Let's stick to hair.' But it wasn't hard to convince him that having a great hairstyle was only one part of an overall feeling of vitality and beauty.

When the health authorities got to hear of what we were up to at the salon in Grosvenor House, they went completely bonkers. They sent along a very irate health official, who explained to us in no uncertain terms that vitamin injections could not be given without a doctor's orders, and said doctor would therefore have to be with us on the premises. As we did not intend to open a clinic, Roger's common sense won the day. 'The nurse has to go or they will close us down,' he said. There were no more vitamin injections, but the health drinks remained.

Of course, the goings-on in Grosvenor House soon spread around the hairdressing community. The general reaction was, 'Oh, that nut Vidal is at it again.' Everybody knew that Roger was sane.

There was no doubt in my mind that Roger would make a huge success of the new salon. He had his own rather large clientele, and they followed him there, as did Herta Keller, a very beautiful young German girl who had been with us for some time and who would later become a key member of the international artistic team. She had actually been trained by Roger and was now quite brilliant in her own right. The international artistic team was formed once we were on more than one continent. It was not easy to become a member of the team. First you had to prove yourself as top stylist in a salon to be made artistic director there. Then if your ideas were fresh and innovative, you would become a member of the artistic team in the continent in which you were working. Roger and Herta taught and worked with an extraordinary group of young crimpers, and before long the Grosvenor House salon was as busy as 171 New Bond Street.

I thought I'd capitalize on our success – and the many visits I had to make to the salon – and start using the superb swimming pool at Grosvenor House. How wrong I was! I was told very definitely by an executive member of the hotel staff that the clientele wouldn't want to be seen swimming with their hairdresser. Then the RAC, an excellent club in the West End, also turned me down. Apparently I didn't have the right make of car! It might have been Swinging London, but certain institutions were still bedrocks of the old-school system. Did it affect me? Of course; even hairdressers have feelings. Eventually Mr Jones heard about the hotel's folly and made me a member immediately. I was then allowed to taint the water of the exclusive Grosvenor House Hotel pool as often as I liked. The times, as they said, were definitely a-changing.

✧

That same year, *Lawrence of Arabia*, starring Peter O'Toole and Omar Sharif, was in production with Columbia Pictures. The studio heads decided that although O'Toole was naturally blond, they wanted him white-blond. Laurance, our master colourist, was called and asked if he would perform this task. For him, it was an easy assignment.

Much to the excitement of our staff, Peter came to the salon at 171 New Bond Street. He strode in, an imposing figure at six foot three and his personal magnetism ensured the atmosphere was highly charged that afternoon. I tucked him away in a corner, where Laurance masterfully executed the colour change, after which he was given a haircut by one of our top people.

Around 7.30 his wife, the actress Siân Phillips, escorted him from the salon to the Ivy restaurant, where they were to meet John Gielgud for dinner. At that time the O'Tooles were *the* couple in London and heads would turn wherever they went. As they approached Mr Gielgud's table, he looked up and, observing this beautiful God-like figure standing before him, said admiringly, 'Any prettier, Peter, and they'd have to call it *Florence of Arabia.'*

I can't remember how I first met the actor Terence Stamp but we hit it off instantly and for a while were as thick as thieves. I know he'd just finished making *Billy Budd* and his performance was the talk of the town. He wasn't exactly a social secretary but he did seem to know everybody. Terry and I used to swim together at Grosvenor House and occasionally visited health spas together. Once with Terence Donovan and Colin Fisher we spent four days at Grayshott Hall Spa in Surrey, where I drove them absolutely nuts with my fitness programme.

Not long after Terry and I met, I was out of town on a three-month working tour. While I was away I lent my flat to Terence and Michael Caine. When I first met him, Michael was earning thirty pounds a week in a West End play, but very soon he was offered the part of a beautifully spoken British officer in the film *Zulu*, an extraordinary role for a Cockney. I remember the opening of *Zulu* well. Michael obviously had his four tickets, and he and Terry Stamp took two delightful girls. He had another two tickets spare, which he gave to Maggie London and me. *Zulu* created much excitement and Michael, who acted with extraordinary aplomb, never looked back. Like me, Michael was interested in architecture and on occasion the conversation would turn away from the movies to other subjects, like architects whose structures we admired. Terence, Michael and I were three kids from the wrong side of the tracks trying to make our way.

Michael and Terry vacated my flat as soon as I returned, but they left behind some interesting mementoes of their stay. There were some rather unusual smells that lingered. My mattress sagged somewhat and never seemed to recover. It seemed as if pretty girls had been specially invented for Terence and Michael, and both naturally took full advantage. I was a positive saint by comparison.

Terence was so thrilled to have had free rein at my flat that he took me straight to his tailor, Dougie Hayward, who at that time worked from a place in Putney. Terry insisted that Dougie should make me a white suit, which with a deep tan looked rather special. It was the sixties after all.

Not long after this, the Duchess of Bedford was in the salon having her once-a-month trim, and just as I finished cutting her hair, the Duke walked in, as he always did. After making his usual glib remark about how I had once again succeeded in making his wife look like a lesbian, he said, 'I'm a little bored. Can you bring up a dozen people for lunch on Sunday? I'd like to meet some of your friends.'

Great, lunch in the country, I thought. *I'll bring him a crowd he won't easily forget.* I called Mary Quant and Alexander Plunket Greene and, although I had only given them four days' notice, they were very happy to come. Two other old friends, Lionel and Joyce Blair – then a brother-and-sister TV dance act – the songwriter Hal Shaper, Terence Donovan and five or six other eccentrics were only too happy to accompany me to Woburn Abbey for Sunday lunch. After introductions all round, we were shown into a spacious dining room hung with lovely scenes of Venice by the eighteenth-century Italian artist Canaletto. We ate a scrumptious lunch, and out of the blue Alexander turned to the Duke and said, 'We are related.' After a rather lengthy discussion about exactly how they could be, it was established that the Plunket Greenes *were* related to the Duke of Bedford. The Duchess, who was French and the Duke's third wife, was delighted to hear the news. Alexander and Mary were given a standing invitation to visit whenever they desired.

Hal vied with Terence in telling the most outrageous stories, which seemed doubly funny as various liveried staff came and went and gondoliers looked down on us from the priceless paintings. It was one of the most splendid afternoons I remember from those days, but it says something about the times that such an extravagant and eccentric lunch party seemed quite normal. The Duchess's last words were, 'Please don't send flowers. I've got far more than I can handle growing all around me. But do come again.' And in jest she added to the others, 'Just don't bring Vidal.'

❖

Early in 1963, I got a call from a Mr John Krish of Seven Arts Studio. He was directing *The Wild Affair*, which was being filmed in London and starred Nancy Kwan. Three years before with William Holden, Nancy had made a smash-hit movie called *The World of Suzie Wong* and she hadn't stopped working from then on. She was definitely the girl of the moment. Now, John Krish wanted me to cut her hair for her role in her new picture. I said yes immediately.

As we made plans for the following day, John told me that apart from himself, Nancy's manager, agents, photographers and their various assistants would also join us at 171 New Bond Street. It was clear we needed to pull out all the stops at our end and I knew just the man for the job. Joshua Galvin was the Roger Thompson of the Vidal Sassoon management side – and he was also Roger's brother-in-law. The warmth and easy collaboration between these two simplified my life more than a wee bit. Joshua was a great hairdresser in his own right but I also realized he had the potential to be a formidable manager. He was the man who had gone to Paris to find me a pair of five-and-a-half-inch shears because I had wanted something tiny that would be like an extension of my hand. Joshua was a stickler for detail and could organize us to perfection.

I asked Joshua to arrange a space on the second floor to accommodate a small army of people, and the next day at the appointed time I walked down to the reception. I saw Nancy and stopped dead in my tracks. I can't remember ever seeing such an exquisitely beautiful face, framed by a curtain of inky-black shiny hair, and I must have studied her for at least half a minute. She wasn't very tall, about five foot two in fact, and rather demure in her manner.

John Krish stepped forward and introduced himself. He said that he wanted me to give Nancy a short classic look. How he managed to persuade her to give up four feet of hair I'll never know. I took them all to the part of the salon that had been set up for their benefit. I asked Nancy to stand in front of the mirror while I combed her silk-like tresses, which reached way beyond her waistline to the curve of her bottom. She could sit on it. She had marvellous hair, which made me want to be at my very best.

Quickly, I chopped off three feet of hair. Nancy looked down, showing no emotion. *How cool*, I thought. She had *my* admiration. Her manager asked for a small table, which was promptly fetched. He sat by the table, brought out a chess set, and for the next hour, as I was creating the look, he and Nancy played chess. The two of them were playing a fairly serious game as her hair was cut shorter, then shorter, and still shorter, into the newest bob. Being Chinese and Caucasian, her hair had both strength and thickness, and it seemed to dance as my scissors worked through it. As the shape developed, I became totally immersed. The top layers in the back were shorter, being cut layer by layer into long sides. Nancy Kwan had the perfect head of hair for what I had been working towards for so long. She was a gift.

I hadn't planned it, but I was beginning to realize that this was – for me, at least – a seminal moment. The cut was almost there and the adrenalin was working overtime. I asked my assistant to get Terence Donovan on the phone. When I heard Terry's voice on the end of the line I asked him excitedly, 'Can we work tonight? I think I've got something!'

He said, 'What have you got?'

'Nancy Kwan. I've just cut her hair into the new bob.'

I didn't have to twist his arm. 'Let's work!' was his reply.

I went back to Nancy and suddenly realized I had forgotten to ask her whether she was free or not. Fortunately she was.

I then called Max Maxwell, the art director of *Vogue*, and told him about the afternoon's drama, and that Terry Donovan would be photographing Nancy that evening. He said, 'I want to see the proofs first thing in the morning.' Everything had to happen immediately and, if possible, sooner.

I called all the stylists up to the second floor to see the cut. They were buzzing with excitement. I had told Roger that Nancy was coming in when we spoke the evening before and he popped over from Grosvenor House. The moment he viewed Nancy's hair, he gave me a giant hug. I looked at him and saw that he had a radiant smile on his face. He knew immediately that something very different was happening. Nancy's manager put away the chess board, and then he and John Krish left, along with the rest of the entourage. I ordered a soft drink for Nancy, although a stiff drink might have been more appropriate. She kept looking in the mirror and shaking her head. I wasn't sure whether she liked it or not, but I could feel in my bones that once Terence photographed the shape and immortalized it in print, it would become the classic bob – for ever. And that's what happened.

Nancy and I went to Donovan's studio and he was really switched on, ready for action. There was an instant rapport between them and they got to work right away. I was completely fascinated by this encounter between Donovan, a wild, way-out character, and the cool, cool Kwan. The session took two hours and there was no clash of temperaments. Instead, they worked almost in silence like a well-trained team. Here were a couple of pros, with Nancy reacting instinctively to Terry's mood and seldom having to be told what he wanted.

Afterwards the three of us went for a meal in a Chinese restaurant. Naturally, we asked Nancy to choose the food, and as we talked I realized that behind her shyness, there was gentleness, warmth and a sharp intellect. And even though she'd had a long, long day, Nancy still made for delightful company.

Terry was an enormous man. He was also a grand master in martial arts and could have easily been a sumo wrestler. Dinner with Terence Donovan was always an extraordinary experience. Generous and expansive, he had a way with the English language that was mind-boggling. What started as a dialogue often finished as a monologue, but I never thought of interrupting him in the midst of a diatribe as he was so amusing. Yet on this occasion, he listened intently while Nancy expressed her thoughts, only interjecting occasionally to make a point.

Terry was brilliant at looking at my work and seeing just how to get the best angles for his photographs. He had such a good eye, always searching for a great shot and he never failed to find it. The following morning he picked me up at the salon with the proofs and we went to Vogue House in Cavendish Square to meet with Max Maxwell. The picture that the three of us chose was an obvious one. It had the Donovan magic written all over it. Max was so impressed that he cut the lead time by two months, and the photo appeared in the very next issue of *Vogue*, before being syndicated right around the world. Fashion had suddenly become very important to me and it was exhilarating to be part of a team that was creating it.

Days after the shoot, I got a call from Nancy. She was ecstatic because the cut had not only shocked her friends, but they had loved the fact that she was wearing something so new and different. She had relatives who lived just opposite the Berkeley Hotel in Knightsbridge, and asked me if I'd like to join her, her family and some of her friends for dim sum the following Sunday. We went to an enormous Chinese restaurant in Limehouse, right out by the docks. The food was absolutely delicious, and with the encouragement of Nancy and her group, I devoured dish after dish with gusto. It gave me great pleasure to become an honorary Chinese citizen for the day.

The Nancy Kwan bob was a turning point for me. Suddenly the visionaries in the world of fashion and the arts had woken up to the fact that we were doing what they were doing, and sometimes we were doing it first. I started to get regular calls from fashion editors who wanted to discuss a session rather than dictate one, and being consulted in this way boosted confidence. Roger Thompson and Christopher Brooker were commanding the same respect. We were one hell of a team.

I was often at Vogue Studios, and one day I was called to do a session with David Bailey and a new model. Bailey, with his extraordinary pictures of Jean Shrimpton, was the new dashing young blade of the photography world and he had an outrageous sense of humour. I loved working with him. The feeling was mutual, though you would not have thought so if you had over-heard some of our verbal battles.

I turned up at the appointed hour and Bailey was nowhere to be seen. I walked through the studio and noticed a youngish-looking girl sitting agitated in the rafters. She had tears streaming down her face and I asked, 'What are you doing up there?'

'David Bailey put me up here,' she answered nervously.

I said, 'You've been crying, and he can't photograph you like that, so come down and have your makeup retouched.' I helped her down and asked her name.

'Twiggy,' she said quietly.

Moments later, David stormed into the studio. 'Twiggy, what are you doing down here? I put you up *there*!'

'Don't be frightened of Bailey,' I said, winking at her. 'He likes having fun with people.' Twiggy was a client of Leonard's, so there wasn't very much for me to do hairdressing-wise. He had cut a beautiful shape less than a month before. I literally just had to cut her fringe and clean up the neckline a bit. Her makeup was redone, and Bailey did a superb shoot. I don't think any of us realized at that moment that Twiggy would become one of the biggest names in fashion. Boy, did she make her mark. In fact, at one time, *nobody* was bigger – not only in Britain, but globally. With all her fame, she never lost her originality or charm, and still recounts the story of how we met much more dramatically than I do.

Unlike Terry Donovan, David Bailey wasn't too crazy about my geometric cuts. We argued once in a session how the hair should look. Finally, in utter frustration I said, 'OK, David. You do the hair and I'll take the shot!' Without skipping a beat, he set up the camera for me and proceeded to run his fingers through the model's hair. It was *not* his forte. I took the shot, and believe it or not, the picture was published – though I wasn't too thrilled with the hair and told him so.

After one of our sessions with Jean Shrimpton, he wanted more fullness. So I put my hands through the hair and just let it go wild. He said, 'Now *that's* what I want!'

I'd given up arguing with him and once, in total agitation, said, 'At least I've made my mark in my craft.'

He retorted, 'Made a mark? You've made a bloody scar.'

Despite our creative differences, we worked together often and there were actually days when he photographed my geometrics with a certain amount of relish – although I know he much preferred the tousled look of a woman who had just rolled out of bed, preferably with him.

There was one style, though, that Bailey and I did agree on – Suzy Parker's wild and curly look. It used to take me about half an hour to set Suzy's hair. I'd take her downstairs into a private room to do this. It was the old-fashioned way of working, but with a modern twist. I set her with small rollers mixed with pin-curls and then put her under one of the old bonnet-style hairdryers. When her hair was dry and ready to be brushed out, the whole look would be done with fingers. The result of running the fingers from the back of her head to the front to the sides to the top was Suzy's signature look and I got a great charge out of it. She was known for this style and her fans expected it. It looked free and untamed, but it was underpinned by a serious haircut every bit as precise as my sleeker styles.

Suzy, who had made a movie with Cary Grant called *Kiss Them for Me*, was the supermodel of her day – her fees were twice as high as any other international model. Her sister, Dorian Leigh, had one of the largest modelling agencies in Paris, and Dorian sometimes came over to London for photo shoots with Suzy.

Once, I got an urgent call from Suzy. 'Dorian and I have a two-day session with a top French magazine to be shot in London. I want you to do the hair.'

I said, 'Suzy, they don't pay hairdressers. They think we work for the credits.'

'Vidal, ask for a thousand pounds.'

'OK, Suzy – but they'll think I'm nuts.'

I called the agency representing the magazine, and after being given dates and times, we talked about the fee. The man at the end of the line said, 'You'll get credits and a hundred pounds.'

'I think you're talking to the wrong person,' I said. 'My fee is a thousand pounds for the two days.'

'You're crazy!' The phone was slammed down in my ear.

I phoned Suzy and related the incident to her. She said, 'I'll call you back in five.'

Within minutes the agency was on the phone again. 'You'll get your thousand pounds – thanks to Miss Parker.'

She had apparently called them to say, 'No Vidal, no shoot.'

Trying to educate the model agencies and the fashion editors that hairdressers had to be paid for their skills and knowledge was an important part of my strategy for the future. And getting a little bonus was always nice.

Terence Donovan and David Bailey were part of a threesome. The third member of the group was Brian Duffy, another brilliant photographer. Duffy and I once did a Paris show for *Elle* magazine and subsequently we worked together often. The three of them had an enormous influence on the Sixties, and when we all hung out together it was usually a very wild time.

One night, the three photographers, Clare Rendlesham, Mary Quant and Alexander Plunket Greene, Max Maxwell and his girlfriend and Maggie and I were eating at a restaurant in Chelsea. We had a raucous time, and as we left the restaurant we were still talking up a storm. Suddenly a window opened three floors above us and a woman angrily shouted, 'Piss off!' as she poured a pot of urine onto us. Max then wore a beautifully shaped beard. However, at that moment it was dripping with pee. It had been a long time since I had had a laugh that came truly from the belly. Happily for Max, none of our photographer friends had their cameras on hand to capture the anguished look on his face. It was priceless, and would have made a great cover for *Vogue*.

In 1963, the shock of the Profumo Affair took many of us by surprise, not least of all me because Christine Keeler and Mandy Rice-Davies were regular clients at the salon. John Profumo was the Minister for War in the Macmillan government and was having an affair with Christine Keeler, who, it turned out, was a call-girl. She, in turn, was sleeping with Yevgeny Ivanov, a Soviet naval attaché. She and her closest friend, Mandy Rice-Davies, also a call-girl, were under the spell of Stephen Ward, a well-known London osteopath who on occasion had given me treatments. An enormous scandal broke out about secrets being passed across the pillow to Ivanov.

As the scandal escalated it became impossible to protect Christine and Mandy from the waiting photographers. It was also impossible to protect them from some of our clients. I was called to the reception area one afternoon, where two clients berated me for allowing the girls to come to the salon and mix with 'decent' people. I answered that I was not a judge, and that as long as they acted like ladies in the salon, I would treat them as such and certainly wouldn't ask them to leave. The clients who took exception to my stance cancelled their appointments there and then – and they never came back. Despite my attempts to stand up for them, it soon became impossible for Christine and Mandy to visit us; the paparazzi were everywhere. The girls did allow my very good friend the photographer Terry O'Neill to shoot some excellent complementary pictures of them. But the coverage of the Profumo Affair was getting uglier by the minute, so I called the girls and asked them if we could send the stylists to their homes to save them from the embarrassment. They agreed.

John Profumo, who had lied to Parliament about his relationship with Christine Keeler, resigned. Stephen Ward, who was accused in the scandal of living off immoral earnings, committed suicide. And I, who knew many of the players in this, was deeply saddened.

There were downs to the ups of life in the fast lane.

7

Suddenly It Happened

Looking back, I realize how much the years between 1954 and 1967 were the time when everything really happened for me creatively. I had been on a mission to make my mark ever since my rather chequered beginnings on the competition circuit and it was all coming together. The 'Five Point Cut' was the epitome of my work. It was the hardest of the geometric cuts to achieve and yet, when I first tried it, it seemed to come quite naturally. It was as if it was a culmination of all the earlier architectural shapes that the team and I had created over the previous ten years.

It happened quite by accident. Rudi Gernreich was being given the *Sunday Times* Award for Designer of the Year. There was to be a special show in London and he'd asked me to do the models' hair. As he was based in California, we talked about the look of the show over the phone. I was as excited to be designing the hair as he was about designing the clothes. Nobody deserved the award more than Rudi. His passion, vision and leadership made him an absolute powerhouse.

As one of the key press people, Clare Rendlesham was going to be one of the guests of honour and she also asked me to do her hair for it, too. It is very hard for me to explain, but as I was cutting Clare's reddish-blonde hair, *it happened*. The creative excitement of working with Gernreich had inspired me in some profound way; a sort of cross-fertilization of ideas. I don't think it was only cerebral; it came from my gut. When you are collaborating with the Gernreichs, the Quants and photographers of the quality of Bailey, Donovan and Duffy, the creative juices work overtime. Suddenly, the 'Five Point Cut' was there!

I felt it immediately and so did Clare. She looked at me and said, 'I think you've done it, dear heart. Let's give it to Grace Coddington and have it photographed for the magazine.'

Gernreich's evening was a smash hit, with rave reviews everywhere. The British papers were quick to point out that even though they were six thousand miles apart, Rudi and Mary Quant shared a similar aesthetic – and yet each was unique in their own way. And Clare's hair raised a few eyebrows, too.

Clare was true to her word. She set up a session with David Montgomery and two days later, we were in his photography studio raring to go. Grace Coddington was an exceptional beauty. She was no Shrimpton or Twiggy, but had a very distinct look, though no particular style, and was only just starting out. But, boy, did she have possibilities. Her high cheekbones were perfect for the very heavy fringe that came all the way down to her ear lobes, creating the first two points, and the three points at the back were cut to follow her natural hair line. I was determined to create a total look that nobody had seen before. I consulted with my makeup artist, who gave Grace an all-white makeup with heavy black eyes, a touch of rouge and a very light red lipstick. What stood out were the hair, the eyes and the bones of a very white face.

Clare gave one picture two pages in *Queen* – the whole

middle section. And now the 'Five Point Cut' had given Grace Coddington the status of an international model. It was a moment of great pride. I still regard it as the finest cut I have ever created – the geometric design in its purest, most classical form. It had taken ten years of stretching, reaching and searching to come to this point.

Hélène Gordon-Lazareff, the majestic editor of *Elle* magazine, was without doubt the most powerful voice in Paris where fashion was concerned. She had complimented our work on many occasions by bringing my team to Paris to work for *Elle* or to do the hair for the Paris collections. But where the French were concerned, it wasn't always easy for me to hold true to my vision. This was especially so when Hélène called me herself one day, saying, 'Vidal, we cannot use you this season as we are doing curls with Thérèse Chardin.'

She'd made it clear on previous occasions that she disliked sycophants and appreciated honesty. I gave it to her: 'Madame Lazareff,' I said, 'it's too early for curls. They will get here, but not this season.'

'Well, what do you have in mind?'

'I'll bring Grace Coddington over to see you,' I said confidently. Grace was working in Paris and many models were trying to copy the look of her hair – but they didn't have the cut.

I flew to Paris on the first available flight that afternoon, and I met Grace the following morning. We walked together into Hélène Lazareff's office, and after a *Bonjour, ça va bien?* and a kiss on both cheeks, I got down to business. I said, 'Grace, run your hands through your hair. Now shake it.' And the 'Five Point Cut' just fell back into place.

Hélène looked at it and for half a minute said nothing. She just walked around Grace feeling her hair, telling Grace to shake it and watching it fall back. Hélène turned to me and said, 'All right. You'll get half the magazine, but you will see curls in the other half.'

Thérèse Chardin and I each got equal space. And strangely enough, the magazine was edited with such skill that our work seemed to complement each other's.

❖

We still worked a five-and-a-half-day week; Saturday was the half-day off. At one o'clock one Saturday, John, a young hairdresser, was drying a lady's hair with a hand dryer. Annie had coloured her hair, and it had been shampooed and conditioned, so she had already been in the salon for quite some time. I saw John using the hand dryer and was curious as to why. He said she was in a hurry to leave. I accepted his explanation without much thought. Then the clock in my head started to tick, so I left the salon and went to Chelsea to see a game of football – just as I always did – and to the theatre that evening. I can't remember what I saw. The only thought in my head was the hand dryer. *Let's use it instead of those big, bulbous bonnets that we stick people under. If the cut creates a great shape, it only needs hand drying.* It was the same on the Sunday and I couldn't wait to get back into the salon. First thing Monday morning, I arranged for a staff meeting to be held that evening.

Roger brought all his people from Grosvenor House over to the Bond Street salon. I explained that this was one of the most important staff meetings that we would ever have; the hand dryer and the bob would soon be inseparable, rendering the old fixed hair dryer obsolete for modern hairdressing. I told them what I had seen John doing on Saturday and how he had given me a very restless weekend. The big hairdryer had to go. We would keep two for the 'Suzy Parker' look, which needed setting; for everything else, we would use the hand dryer. All training sessions for the next month would be cut, hand dryer and brush; cut, hand dryer and brush.

Not long after this, I gave an interview to a newspaper about how we first started using the hand dryer. Days later I received a letter from top stylist Rose Evansky, who had read the article, saying that *she* discovered the hand dryer and had the newspaper articles to prove it. I had some wonderful competition at the time. There was Edward Morris ('magic hands'), the artistic director of André Bernard, who, to his credit, had invented the word 'crimper' and had innovation written all over his work. And then there was Rose, who was a wonderful hairdresser. Leonard had served his apprenticeship with her. Knowing how talented she was, I would not dispute her claim. She was such an inspiration and provided a role model to the many young girls and women working in the craft. I called her straight away and told her all about John and his one o'clock accident. Laughing, we both agreed that every modern stylist would be hand drying before the year was out. As I put the phone down I thought to myself how lucky I was to have such friendly competitors – even if they tried to beat me to the punch on every occasion.

❖

Before and during the Mary Quant era, there were about a dozen top designers who made clothes for the very rich. Among them were people like Norman Hartnell, John Cavanagh and Hardy Amies, all of whom did beautiful work. One day I got a call out of the blue telling me that the Queen Mother and Princess Margaret wanted to hold a reception for great British designers, many of whom they knew quite well, and also two hairdressers.

The first-choice crimper was René – a blond, blue-eyed athlete who was startlingly good-looking and adored by London's female society. The other hairdresser was yours truly. I was a little taken aback by the invitation as I knew that many people thought my work too avant-garde.

The reception was held in a beautiful private home. It had a large palatial room where, on the appointed day and hour, we were asked to stand in line and wait for the Royals to arrive. An hour later, they did – the Queen Mother even apologized for their lateness – and she and Princess Margaret came down the line mouthing well-rehearsed lines to us. It was all very pleasant, and Princess Margaret stopped for two or three minutes to chat with René, as she was not only a client at his salon, he actually did her hair and made Princess Margaret, without doubt, the most fashionable member of the Royal Family. When it was my turn, she gave me a very agreeable look and a 'Glad you're here' before moving on.

Back home in Kilburn, *I* was treated like royalty. Mother was pleased beyond all reason. She wanted to know every last detail. She was always being told that she looked like the Queen Mum and for her, this little incident was far more important than my creative work. Forget the 'Five Point Cut'!

While we had been waiting for the Queen Mother, René and I started chatting. It felt rather improper – we should have been solemnly preparing for our meeting with Her Majesty – but we had so much common ground, it seemed too good an opportunity to pass up. We quickly agreed that he would bring his wife and I would bring my girlfriend to dinner at the White Elephant, truly *the* restaurant of the sixties. It was in Curzon Street, seventy-five yards from my flat, and anybody you would care to meet would be there at one time or another. It was one of the few restaurants in town that served late, so it got the post-theatre crowd. The likes of Sammy Davis Jr, Tony Newley and Albert Finney were all served under the careful eye of the delightful proprietors, Stella Richman and Victor Brusa, who were husband and wife.

There were two toilets in the basement of the White Elephant: one for men and one for women. On the door outside the men's it just said, 'Gentlemen.' But on the door outside the women's, it had a picture of Grace Coddington wearing my 'Five Point Cut'. I wasn't asked if they could use it, but I was thrilled that they did.

During the dinner with René, there was much storytelling between us. Why not? There was much to tell. From his days in Paris, René had the most elegant of clienteles but he preferred to talk about his career as a footballer, when he was a goalkeeper with Racing de Paris. They're no longer in existence but I'm convinced this was not René's fault. I was so impressed. He had actually played for a professional team while I, on the other hand, only had fantasies about playing for Chelsea – although they were beautiful fantasies. Eventually we got back to hairdressing and talked about the different ways we carefully built our clientele, creating exactly the atmosphere we wanted in our salons.

René's was unquestionably the first choice of many of the most elegant women in London and Paris. My clientele tended to be much more eclectic, much more mixed. Yet I was as proud of the shop girls and nurses who saved a few shillings a week and had one blow-out haircut every couple of months as I was of the *Vogue* cover-girls. We were a melting-pot of class and race and money, or so I told myself. One day I found the Duchess of Bedford sitting on the stairs dictating a letter to her secretary.

They were both waiting for a chair and a haircut. There were absolutely no spare seats, which made for a wonderful atmosphere. Society ladies, the fashion crowd – with lots of beautiful models, editors and writers – were all in the salon at the same time and all treated with great respect, especially the young working girls, who we treated like princesses.

Frances Shand Kydd was, without question, my most elegant client. Even in later years she would not be eclipsed by the beauty of her daughter, Lady Diana Spencer, as her innate style never left her. I hadn't a clue at the time she was officially Viscountess Althorp, as she never used the formal address with us. I looked after her personally and she always had a smile or a kind word. She would come in quite often and each time, about fifteen minutes before I finished her hair, a very distinguished general would call for her. He would come into the salon to have a look around – he was quite fascinated by its ambience – and would ask me pertinent questions relating to hair. He was always in mufti – a distinctive Savile Row suit, bowler hat and cane. He had a great air of authority about him. I found his inquisitiveness rather fascinating and we would talk each time he came to the salon. One particular day I walked them from the salon into Bond Street, and then it happened. A raven-haired guy poked his head out of the taxi cab he was driving and shouted, 'Wotcha, Vid! How's your bum?'

The general turned to me. 'I say, do you know that man?'

'Yes, he's an old friend from the East End.'

There was a rather long pause while he chewed this over, so I hurriedly filled the gap. 'His name is Monty Valance.' As though that made it any better.

He said, 'How extraordinary! I shall dine on this for a month.'

Mrs Shand Kydd and the general walked up Bond Street to the Ritz Hotel for lunch, giggling.

When she arrived at the salon the following week, she told me that half the general's staff now knew Monty Valance by name.

About the same time, a new client started coming to the salon. She was not a model; she was a businesswoman. Tall and beautiful, her hair was a joy to cut. She had an exquisite bone structure and I always looked forward to her visits. Then she got married. Her husband, who was extremely wealthy, objected to her working and so she did what most women in 1963 did when they married; she became a housewife. She was so bored that in the course of just one year she gained nearly three stone. Her bone structure, which had always drawn me to her, had disappeared. She looked troubled and asked if we could speak privately. I took her to my office and she told me of her faded dreams. Her marriage was on the rocks as she could not convince her husband that she was an active, vital person who needed challenges. We talked and I put a proposition to her. 'I would like to send you to Weight Watchers and to Mary Quant – and forget about me cutting your hair until I can see that marvellous facial structure again.'

She agreed. I called Mary, told her the story of my client's woes and asked her to make something that would fit her in three months, after she'd lost the three stone. Mary enjoyed a challenge and met her. It suddenly hit me that I was wandering way beyond the boundaries of just hairdressing. My client would come in on occasion asking me whether she was ready for a haircut and I'd say, 'No, but you will be.'

She stuck to her guns and within three months in walked this gorgeous figure in a Mary Quant creation, which showed off her exquisite long legs. I took an hour giving her an asymmetric bob. As I finished the cut, I touched her cheekbones and we smiled at one another through the mirror. She left the salon with the eyes of half my staff following her through the door. For me, this was a first. But it didn't end there.

Two weeks later I was called to the reception and a gentleman asked if I was Vidal. 'Yes,' I replied and he introduced himself. He then went on: 'I need to thank you. Because of you, I lost my wife – and found my old girlfriend.' He'd finally understood that he had come close to destroying her sense of identity, and she went back to work with his blessing.

Out of all the personalities and big names that I've had the pleasure of working with and meeting, this is the story I most cherish. Saving marriages was *not* my forte, but making women look and feel as good as they possibly could was.

❖

In January 1964, Clare Rendlesham asked me to come to Paris and work with her and the notable fashion photographer Norman Parkinson. Norman was a giant of a man, mentally and physically. He wore a walrus moustache and had the look of a man who one skipped very gently around. His authority was laid down in the first minute of meeting him and never questioned.

During one of her scouting missions to New York, Clare had found triplets – the Dee sisters. Singly they were very good-looking girls, brunettes and quite well built. None of them would ever be mistaken for a Twiggy. But as a threesome, they were the find of the season. Even though they looked alike, they were exquisitely different, and they were the models I was to use for this session. I remember giving each of them her own distinctive geometric hair look. As soon as I put my scissors down, Clare, who never held back if she thought the work could be improved, said, 'OK. Let's shoot!' Norman was pleased and when the work was finished, asked me if I would do one more shot – this time outside. We took just one of the girls and drove about thirty minutes until we reached a field of flowers that filled our nostrils with the sweet scent of the French countryside. Norman turned to me and said, 'I want you to take the hair back and make a shape on the head out of the flowers.'

'Norman, that's not my kind of work.'

'Do it for me, dear boy,' he said, in a very commanding voice.

I kept putting flowers in her hair and Norman would say, 'More, add more,' until the whole crown of her head was covered. Only one side showed any resemblance to the haircut I had given. He loved it, took his pictures with glee, and my last words to him were, 'Norman, you owe me one. Just make sure my name isn't credited on this picture.'

Damn it, it made the cover of *Vogue*. My name was there as the session stylist and hairdressing friends called to see if I'd gone soft in the head.

The Paris collections were fast and furious. One year I went with Roger Thompson and a super young crimper from Manchester, Christopher Pluck. He was a key member of our artistic team and his marvellous Mancunian accent went down a treat in Bond Street. You needed stamina to work the collections in Paris. I chose Christopher not just for his skill but for his resilience. Most shows were afternoon and evening, so the dresses coming in from different fashion houses arrived at different times, from late afternoon to the wee hours of the night. As in the photography studios, we worked on each fashion house individually, so timing was indeed important. Fortunately, Brian Duffy was taking the pictures, and he had the stamina of an ox.

One of those crazy nights at three in the morning, when we were all fairly exhausted, the last collection of the day finally came in. Roger and Chris were snoozing on the floor; I'd thought that if I joined them, I would never get up. I nudged them awake and gently whispered, 'Saint Laurent's collection has arrived.' They suddenly sprang expectantly to life, as Yves was the way forward with so many new ideas. Looking at his clothes on the models inspired and invigorated us all. He had a way of making his collections stand out. From the Mondrian to the Rive Gauche, he was the master. Some of our best work that night was accomplished between 3 and 4.30 a.m., when the session was finally finished.

We crept back to our hotel and I was almost asleep even before I hit the bed. I remember sleeping until two in the afternoon. Then it was back to the studios. Fortunately, the last collection came in at ten that night, and we were through by eleven. Afterwards we went to Castel, then one of the great clubs in Paris. For two hours, we let it all hang out.

On the plane ride back to London, I said to Roger with a half-smile, 'I'll see you in the salon in the morning.'

His wife, Shirley, called me at the salon early the following morning to tell me that Roger was totally out of it and needed a couple of days' sleep. There was apparently no question of him coming in. I wasn't surprised. It happened after every collection.

Even I was no stranger to the feeling of total burn-out. As I was greeting the stylists, emotionally I was already on my way to detox and purify myself from the inside out at my favourite health farm in Surrey.

Grayshott Hall was a grand, old country estate that had been turned into a health farm. They believed in a total cleanse of the system and were fairly serious about it. The first morning began with an enema and then every day you had colonic irrigation massage and all kinds of exotic treatments from various far-flung parts of the world. You spent four days fasting, followed by a diet of just fruit and vegetables. My body reacted so well to this treatment I did it twice a year. It was the only way I could recover from the terrible beatings I was giving it.

Most people would arrive at Grayshott Hall on a Sunday as I did, and their first treatment was at eight o'clock on Monday morning after they had tried to get a good night's rest. Monday morning at 7.50, I was in the treatment area waiting to be called.

After a few minutes I was duly summoned: 'Mr Vidal, your treatment is ready.'

In the London salons, I was never called 'Mr Sassoon'; it was always 'Vidal', so I hardly registered the odd form of address. I made my way for my first treatment, and about twenty minutes later I heard a loud voice outside the room that sounded American, saying, 'Are you always late this early in the morning? My appointment was for eight.' Although I was in a separate treatment room, his voice was irate enough to carry through to me.

The manager was called and I heard him apologizing profusely. 'We're extremely sorry, Mr Vidal, there appears to have been a mix-up.' As I lay there with little else but a towel covering my modesty, it suddenly dawned on me that there could actually be a real Mr Vidal whose turn I had taken. When they sorted out the problem, it became apparent that they were giving me Gore Vidal's enema. It was an inauspicious way to meet one of the great men of letters.

It was a wonderfully relaxing week. I spotted a very beautiful girl, and as I was alone and single, I introduced myself. After a pleasant chat, she gave me her room number and asked me to come by. I obviously was in a daze and took down the wrong number or was given a fictitious one because at eleven that night, I knocked on the door that I thought was hers, and a woman's voice growled, 'Who's there?'

'Vidal,' I said and immediately realized that this wasn't the voice of the divine young creature and I'd got the wrong room. I quickly scarpered.

The following morning, Gore Vidal was called into the manager's office and asked not to bother the female guests at night. By the end of the week, I think he'd had enough of me – he had come for a restful, quiet time and through no fault of his own, it was becoming rather hazardous. He was charming about it, though, and we walked to the neighbouring village one day to take tea together. On leaving Grayshott, his last words to me were, 'One of us has to change his name.'

Even though I had worked in Paris for many magazines and had done the hair for many top designers, I had never yet created the hair for an entire collection for any one designer. One day, the receptionist in Bond Street came over to enquire whether I could find space for a lady from Paris who would fly over if I could possibly squeeze her in. Her name was Emmanuelle Khanh.

I had always kept a space open each day – I hated telling people that I couldn't work on them for three weeks. 'Give her the appointment,' I said.

When I saw Emmanuelle walk in, a big grin came over my face. I had met her in Paris, although we had never worked together. I kissed her on both cheeks and said how lovely it was to see her. 'What are you doing here?' I asked.

She said, 'I want you to cut my hair.'

My fellow stylists were very excited when they found out

Emmanuelle Khanh was in our salon. She was all the rage in Paris, in every magazine. Emmanuelle was about five foot six, slim and exotic – the epitome of why men loved French girls. I was really touched that the designer would fly from Paris just for a haircut. But it wasn't just for a haircut. She asked if I would do her next collection. My toes began to tingle as I thought of the possibilities. A show in Paris with Emmanuelle Khanh would be an enormous breakthrough, as the French had their own home-grown hairdressers who always did their shows and were historically rather snooty about British hairdressing. I hadn't realized at the time that she had also asked James Wedge, a British milliner, to create hats that would go with my haircuts.

The day came. James Wedge was in Paris with his hats. I was there with Roger, Christopher Brooker and a couple of other crimpers from my top team. Emmanuelle came over to us and said, 'Please don't worry about the hats. We're going to surprise the press.' Normally hairdressers and milliners have a natural animosity towards one another but I didn't fret, as James and I had collaborated before and his hats always complemented our cuts superbly.

The clothes looked futuristic, as was Emmanuelle's way, and James's hats fitted snugly on the models' heads. The girls first came out individually, and after three changes of clothes they all came out together. As they pranced around the podium, with one bold movement of hand to head, the hats were gone. The girls shook their hair, put their hands through it, shook their hair again, and the cuts fell into place beautifully. There was a gasp – even among the French press, who were used to surprises. French hairdressing was brilliant – world-renowned – but it wasn't architectural. Looking at the audience from the curtains at the side of the stage, I observed people talking excitedly to one another. Emmanuelle had pulled off another coup with her stunning show. She took her bow, then invited James and me to join her on the runway. James held a hat in his hand so the audience would know that he was he and I was me.

That evening was probably one of the happiest I'd spent in Paris. Emmanuelle had booked a restaurant. Quasar, her husband, came too. The models, James Wedge, Christopher, Roger, the rest of our team and I all enjoyed a sumptuous meal. The press, both French and international, gave Emmanuelle, James and the Sassoon team a warm reception in the days that followed. Everywhere we went we were fêted; we were truly the flavour of the month. We were *'futuriste'*, *'avant-garde'*, *'extraordinaire'*. It was almost enough to turn an East End lad's head.

8

Sassoonery Goes Stateside

The press came to us now. We no longer had to court media attention. And the warm glow of working with cutting-edge designers of the calibre of Mary Quant, Rudi Gernreich and Emmanuelle Khanh showed no signs of wearing off. Then someone came into my life who would change it for ever. His name was John Addey and I was introduced to him through a friend, John Kennedy, who managed the actor and singer Tommy Steele. We met at the Connaught Hotel, a brief meeting where nothing of vital importance was said. But a week later, I was at Les Ambassadeurs, one of the few private clubs that would allow me to cross the threshold. Les Ambassadeurs was in a magnificent house on Park Lane. The restaurant had very good food and an excellent ambience, and the club also had a small casino for those who wished to try their luck. In the basement area, there was a rather convivial sauna, and a masseur with a magic touch.

There were about six people in the sauna when I joined them. And one of them, sitting across the way from me, was John Addey. After a brief hello, he pronounced, 'If I handle you, you will become international.' I did not necessarily want to be handled in the sauna, but as he left John said, 'I'll leave my card for you at the desk.'

We arranged to meet at the Connaught the next morning. Breakfast lasted two hours and we clicked. John was very astute and seemed to have an uncanny way of conjuring ideas out of thin air. Unlike me John had had an excellent education on both sides of the Atlantic, going to a very good English public school and then graduating from Harvard Law School, but we thought alike. I left the Connaught feeling that here was a public relations man who really understood what we were trying to do and who would be able to spread the word about us internationally.

A short time later, I received a letter from Intercoiffures, an international organization of top hairdressers, inviting me to do a show with thirteen other hairdressers from thirteen different countries at the Pierre Hotel in New York. I was to be the representative from Britain. It was 1964, and I was ready to unveil everything I'd learned in the past ten years of studying the craft. The Dee sisters, the triplets whom I had worked with in Paris with Norman Parkinson, were available, and John Addey recognized it as a great PR opportunity, saying, 'I'm coming with you. We can make so much of this.'

We arrived in New York and I checked into the Elysée, a small hotel on East 54th Street owned by Leon Quain and recommended to me by my dear friend Arthur King, a superb New York jeweller. John meanwhile checked into the prestigious Harvard Club and got to work. All press interviews for me had to be arranged through him. The New York press was aghast that they were expected to make arrangements with a crimper through a publicist staying at the Harvard Club. As I've already said, hairdressers were not held in too high esteem in New York in the early sixties.

The show at the Pierre was a Sunday afternoon event, and, even though it was a weekend, the beauty press turned out in force. The other thirteen hairdressers did lovely work and I was thrilled to be a part of such a top-level international show. I cut three different versions of my geometric styles on the triplets. They looked stunning. Other stylists came over and most had a positive reaction, though I distinctly recall one looking at my work and saying, 'It will never happen.' The press were photographing what everyone had done, but I couldn't help noticing how much time they seemed to be lavishing on my three girls.

Five New York newspapers reported the show in their beauty pages the following day. I had got much of the coverage. Priscilla Tucker of the *New York Herald Tribune* really loved what she saw and gave me what could only be described as a dashing headline: VIDAL SASSOON THE VISIONARY: HAIR WILL NEVER BE THE SAME.

Priscilla and I became great friends. I wonder why.

But it wasn't just the press who were interested. The show also opened the door to another person who would walk into my life and make me an offer I simply couldn't refuse.

Richard Salomon was a man of great style and business acumen. He was chairman and chief executive officer of the perfumery and cosmetics company Lanvin-Charles of the Ritz. His great coup was not only to bring the Yves Saint Laurent fragrance 'Rive Gauche' to New York, but to get Yves himself to New York to publicize it. Mr Salomon had asked two of his trusted lieutenants, Natalie Donay and Dan Olian, to attend the Sunday afternoon show and find out what all the fuss was about. The next morning, with great excitement, they tried to explain what they'd seen.

That done, Natalie called me. 'Mr Salomon would like to meet you.'

The following day I walked into his office. He stood up to greet me and we shook hands, but instead of retreating back behind his desk, we sat in two armchairs in front of it – the gesture of a man who obviously wanted to make me feel comfortable. He asked his secretary to hold his calls and for the next two hours he concentrated solely on me. Towards the end of our meeting he announced thoughtfully, 'Vidal, I don't know who arranges your schedule but I like your style. If I buy a building on Madison Avenue, will you go back to London, send me your architect, train a team for New York, and we will open a year from today?'

It was phrased as a question but it wasn't one I needed to chew over for long. I accepted. We shook hands and he said to me, 'I'll make sure the lawyers make this an easy one.' I left his office and went straight to the Museum of Modern Art, where I sat in the sculpture garden, reflecting on how lucky I was. I loved New York; it had so much to offer.

A note came from Mr Salomon the following day that he would let me know when he had purchased the building and we must keep in touch on a regular basis.

After the first wave of publicity generated by the show at the Pierre, John Addey went to work with a vengeance. Each night there would be a note under my door with my appointments for the following day. It was a marathon and over the two weeks we remained in New York, I must have done at least a dozen television shows, including *The Tonight Show Starring Johnny Carson*, *The Dick Cavett Show* and *The Mike Douglas Show*, which we travelled to Philadelphia to do, and a slew of radio interviews. All the magazines wanted to photograph me with the

Dee triplets. I even found myself discussing existentialism on American television! The pioneering talk-show host David Susskind did something quite out of the ordinary – by taking me seriously and trying to find out what made me tick. Somehow we got on to the French writer Camus and the loneliness of being ahead of the game, an innovator constantly having to prove oneself. It was wonderfully stimulating. As the taping of the hour-long show came to an end David said, 'I want more. Can we do another hour?' And before I knew it, we were taping another episode.

When John and I boarded our British Airways flight to return to London, we had the sense of a job truly well done. I couldn't thank him enough for the expert way he had handled everything. We drank a glass of red wine together and looked forward to more adventures in the future.

Soon after we got back, I went to see John in his offices in Mayfair for a catch-up about our trip. I had a large briefcase under my arm and stepped off the curb looking the wrong way. After being in the States for weeks, I instinctively looked in the wrong direction for any oncoming traffic. The next thing I knew – or rather *didn't* know – I was up in the air and then flat on my back. A taxi had hit me sideways on. I was shocked, but not unconscious and as I regained my senses I saw a familiar figure standing over me saying, 'Are you OK, Vid? Are you OK?' It was my old mate Michael Caine. He helped me up. I felt my body and nothing seemed to be broken. I said, 'Yes, I think I am.'

He said, 'Good because I've got an appointment,' and took off.

The taxi had stopped ten yards away and the driver was slumped across the steering wheel. Michael had asked somebody to call an ambulance, which came. The taxi driver had had a heart attack and was immediately taken to St George's Hospital at Hyde Park Corner. The paramedic looked at me and said, 'You'd better come along too and have some X-rays.'

I climbed in the back, where this poor man was truly in a bad way. I held his hand and said, 'I'm sorry I made you run me over.'

I was given some X-rays and released. I had never once looked at my briefcase, although it stayed with me during this whole encounter. When I did, I saw a gaping hole in the leather. The briefcase had saved me. It was such a strange story that the papers ran it and the following day I got a call from Terence Stamp, who was in the south of France. 'Are you sure there's nothing wrong with you?'

'No, I'm absolutely fine.'

'That's a shame because I wanted to use your Chelsea season ticket next Saturday.'

✧

Back in the salon, a near disaster became one of our biggest hits. I was working with Danae Brook, a favourite model of mine, one evening at the Grosvenor House salon. A fashion photographer, Vic Singh, was with us. Danae had been wearing her hair in a long bob for ages, but I was giving her a short geometric cut. I had just completed the cut on the left side of her hair when, with a gasp of horror, she grabbed on tightly to the side that was still long and yelled, 'I've changed my mind!'

I studied her for a full minute while she clung for dear life to what was left of her hair. 'Danae,' I said, 'I've changed my mind, too. You have just helped design our next look – the "Asymmetric" – one side long, one side short. We'll leave one side longer, but the hair will be gradually cut from the fringes into that long side. It will be a completely new look and you, Danae, will be the first to wear it – and Vic Singh is here to photograph you as you make history.'

Unconvinced, she panicked, and kept a firm grip on the side of her hair I hadn't touched, while Vic, who was a good buddy, snapped away wildly. I went through it with her once again, explaining the possibilities of wearing something so new and exciting, and the horror began to ebb from her face. Her grip loosened. I gently took her hand from her hair and put it in her lap. Then my scissors went to work. Slowly but surely, the cut came to life. When Danae's blood pressure had returned to normal, she shook her head, and grinning, said, 'You know, I think I'm going to like this.' How quickly a girl can change her mind.

John Addey sent the pictures out to the press and I got a call from Deirdre McSharry, the fashion editor of the *Daily Express*. She said, 'I like the feel of what you're doing, but how's this going to look once it becomes wet and dishevelled?'

I said, 'Easy. It will fall right back into place.'

'Can you prove it?'

'The only way I can convince you, Deirdre, is to put Danae's head in a bucket of water and let the hair fall into line in front of you.'

'I've got a better idea,' Deirdre said. 'Meet me tomorrow morning at the Oasis Swimming Pool in High Holborn. Bring Danae with you.'

Danae, who was game to try almost anything – work-wise, that is – got into the carnival mood immediately. Naturally, I took my swimming trunks. What a great way to have a workout, presided over by the *Daily Express*. Deirdre brought along a staff photographer. Danae and I jumped into the pool, swam a few lengths, and returned to the side of the pool. I asked an assistant for a towel. Dabbing the top layer of water from Danae's hair, I then asked Danae to push it back into shape. Deirdre and I were both smiling as Danae's hair fell beautifully where it was supposed to, while I asked Deirdre if the next time I created a look, would she want me to walk through fire to please her?

'I'll give it some thought,' she said.

The *Express* used four pictures the next day: a beauty by Vic Singh taken in the salon, and three at the Oasis Pool. Apparently we made quite a splash.

The water stories didn't end there. That summer, Emmanuelle Khanh's husband, Quasar, who was a qualified engineer, had the wackiest idea for a range of products he was launching. He was born in Vietnam where he had done much of his studying in architecture and furniture design. He had gone to Paris and met Emmanuelle there. They were a perfect pair, as Quasar matched Emmanuelle in crazy ideas, which often became a part of pop culture.

My love affair with Maggie London was over, but my respect for her never ceased and we remained close. We saw one another from time to time, so I invited her to join me with the Khanhs in St-Tropez for a long weekend, along with other assorted friends of theirs. We were simply told to bring our swimwear. From the beach, on the horizon, I saw what looked like floating plastic blow-up furniture – and *was*. It was all very surreal. Quasar had created a living- and dining-room space 150 yards off shore, anchoring each piece of floatable furniture into a semi-livable 'room' in the middle of the ocean. I asked him where we were going to have lunch.

'Out at sea,' he said, and with that two speedboats came along and delivered fourteen of us to the new Khanh residence on the water. We took our places in the 'dining room' and were served a mixture of French and Vietnamese dishes.

The Khanhs weren't fools. They had arranged the whole thing as a publicity stunt, and suddenly we were surrounded by photographers in speedboats feverishly taking pictures of this bikini-clad affair in the ocean off St-Tropez. It was a ridiculous piece of theatre but it had verve and worked miraculously. We wined and dined till the sun went down. Music played throughout lunch, and afterwards Quasar invited all who cared to, to join him in the 'living room', where a waiter was serving what was left of the Dom Pérignon. The French papers were full of it the next day, calling it a zany farce and clearly thinking it had been a great idea. To us, it was just how things were in the Sixties.

9

Passing the Yankee Test

New York was a very hard nut to crack, but the opening night party for our Madison Avenue salon in June 1965 was such a star-studded event that you would never have guessed the uphill struggle that lay ahead. The guest list didn't mean a thing. People seemed to be popping in from everywhere, and I can still remember some of the faces that flashed by me. There was Sybil Burton, who had fallen out with Richard and was now Sybil Christopher, Mrs Oscar Hammerstein, Joan Collins, Mary Quant and Alexander Plunket Greene, Emmanuelle and Quasar Khanh, Terence Stamp and his brother Chris, the comedian Buddy Hackett and his wife, Sherry, Beverly Todd, star of the Broadway musical *No Strings*, and the husband-and-wife musical duo Steve Lawrence and Eydie Gorme, to mention a few. My brother, Ivor, and Charles Prevost, the wool baron, flew in. Ivor's jetlag vanished as soon as he took in the scene. He gave me a big hug, then looked for a beautiful girl to talk to. Charles took it all in his stride; this was exactly the sort of evening he had envisaged when he made his initial investment.

Richard Salomon had invited the cream of New York society.

John Addey had invited important press not only from New York, but from around the world. Apart from his public relations duties, John seemed to take over the job of maître d' for the evening and had arranged that people ate on separate levels. There was a British floor serving fish and chips and where the beer flowed freely all night. On another floor were served caviar, lobster and all the seafood delicacies that were then so much more available in America than in England. A slightly inebriated guest announced in a loud voice, 'There hasn't been a party as good as this in New York since last week.' Photographers took pictures of models sitting under a vast Venini chandelier, which cascaded down through two storeys. It had been designed and made especially for us in Italy, and the enormous picture window through which it was displayed had taken an army of workmen to install. *Life* magazine not only took pictures of the gala affair, they also ran a fabulous story about the evening.

The cleaners came in at about 1.30 in the morning, which was a cue for the stragglers to leave. I was on such a high that I knew if I went back to the hotel I wouldn't sleep. An African-American friend took Ivor and me to a quiet jazz club in Harlem, where I slowly unwound from what had been a truly amazing day. *Was I dreaming, or did it really happen?* We left the club in the small hours, so I had very little sleep that night. The salon opened at nine the next day and I needed to be there first to welcome everyone.

Despite the party being such a huge success, very few of the people who were there became clients. Getting our message across to the ladies who lunched was very difficult. The prevailing style in New York was the 'old money' look, conservative and rigid – just as it had been in London before I attacked it. Backcombing and high hair were very much the look and it took about a year before the New York salon had that wild Bond Street feeling.

During this slow period, I had a call from Amy Greene, beauty editor of *Glamour*. She wanted me to have lunch with her and Kathleen Casey, the magazine's editor. The conversation was an edgy one right from the start. Kathleen suggested that as I was getting so much publicity, *Glamour* would like to utilize my services. Then she added a caveat: 'But your work is far too angular for America. If you could soften it and make it more like Kenneth's, we'd be happy to use you.' Kenneth Battelle was hairdresser to Jackie Kennedy and the Manhattan elite; I had no ambitions to step on his patch.

No one was more aware than me that we needed clients, but to take this insult lying down was not in my nature. I took a gamble.

'Mrs Casey, when the Seagram Building was first finished, many New Yorkers could not understand its great shape and simplicity. I often think that it takes a year or two for the eye to get used to a new shape, so with all due respect, I cannot accept your offer – as you already have a Kenneth and my name is Vidal.'

Amy Greene was disappointed that Kathleen Casey and I were not on the same wavelength, but she was absolutely furious that I had told her editor that it would take her eye a year or two to understand my work.

Close to a year later, I got a call from Amy. 'You've won,' she said. 'Mrs Casey wants you to do a whole session your way.'

John Addey started seeing Grace Mirabella, who worked closely with the legendary Diana Vreeland, the doyenne of *Vogue*. I thought something fascinating might happen between them but it didn't – they just remained very affectionate and we all became dear friends. Not long afterwards, however, Grace asked me to come and meet Diana Vreeland. As I walked into her office, Mrs Vreeland, with an air of stern authority, said, 'Many of my friends are talking about you but are scared to death of your scissors.'

'With good cause,' I said. 'My team has been waiting to give New Yorkers the London look. It *will* happen in time.'

Then she pointed to a girl sitting across the room and said, 'Cut her hair in one of your classics.'

I put my hands and a brush through her hair, looked at her hair line and realized that this was not the girl on whom to demonstrate a textbook geometric cut. I looked straight at Mrs Vreeland and said, 'Her neckline grows up at the back, and since her hair is so fine, there would be no weight to hold the cut in place. I could cut her hair and fake it, but in the morning she'd hate me. Also, as a model I can see the versatility of her current style – she can throw her hair back into a knot quite easily at the moment. This is the wrong head of hair to demonstrate my work.'

Mrs Vreeland said, 'Interesting. Sit down.'

She turned on a tape recorder and we talked fashion, art, architecture and about the people we admired. She let her hair down in a way that was so unexpected that I was tempted to suggest I cut it. Again, just like Hélène Gordon-Lazareff at *Elle*, Diana Vreeland respected honesty. And I got to know what an extraordinary, gutsy lady she actually was.

The team we took to New York had an average age of twenty-two. These young hairdressers were exhilarated to be given the opportunity to start a new life in America. In their different ways, they were all looking for an adventure and had left behind families and friends and the way of life they were used to in Britain. They were my kids and I was proud of them. Without them the American adventure might never have happened, so they deserve to have their names mentioned here: Susan Davidson, Ian Harrington, Adam Hewison, Harvey Kaye, Peter Green, Charles Booth, Lynda Riches, Lynda Berman, Raymond Prudhoe, Suzette Newman, Jane Crafts and the man who had done so many shows with me in Europe, Christopher Pluck, who became head stylist. Knowing that Americans love hearing a British accent, Dan Olian suggested we also hire British girls as receptionists, so two of our best girls from the London reception team, Ann Bradley and Caryl Wilkie, travelled with us. The anchorman, however, was Laurance Taylor, who years earlier had conned me into giving him a job by kidding me that he was a fully experienced colourist. And I counted my lucky stars on a daily basis that I had been so easily deceived. In whichever position he worked within our organization, he created an exciting atmosphere that encouraged innovation.

The American chapter had been perilously close to being over before it started. All had been going to plan; our architect had been duly sent out to New York to work with Richard Salomon's people and staff in our London salons had been approached with an offer many felt was hard to refuse. In New York, the Quain family, who owned the Hotel Elysée, had adopted me and always had a room available for my frequent commute between Madison Avenue and Bond Street. And then bureaucracy caught up with me. Apparently, in the States, all hairdressers, whether Americans or foreigners, needed to pass a test before they were allowed to touch a hair on anyone's head. We would have to sit an exam. No one was exempt.

Grace Coddington modelling the 'Five Point Cut'.

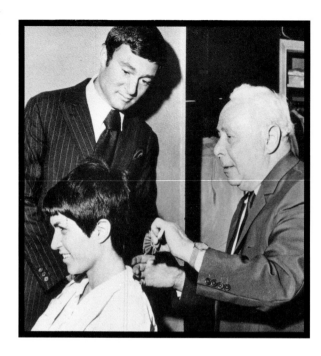

With
Adolph Cohen,
watching him
give a model
one of my
geometric cuts.

Styling
Suzy Parker's
hair.

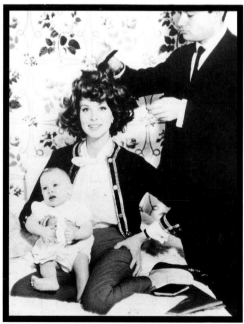

With Grace
Coddington
in my flat,
which was
decorated by
David Hicks.

Rudy Gernreich and
Peggy Moffitt.

Cutting Mary Quant's hair.

With Danae Brook.

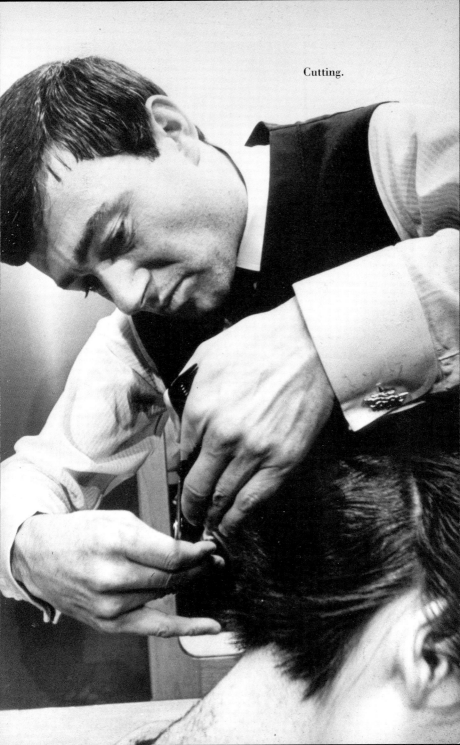

Cutting.

Kari Ann Jagger
modelling a
geometric cut
created for
Ungaro's first show.

Peggy Moffitt wearing a
trademark asymmetrical cut.

Clemence Bettany
modelling 'The Shape'.

Maggie London,
wearing a long
Sassoon bob.

Jill St John sporting a
geometric bob with curls on top.

Square curls.

The Nancy Kwan bob.

It was a travesty. The work one was expected to do to pass the New York State Board of Cosmetology hairdressing test was not only out of fashion; it was never *in* fashion. I was not surprised that two of my top people, Raymond Prudhoe and Lynda Riches, failed the test. But I was very angry. Lynda had been one of my top stylists for twelve years. And the stories from the other stylists who managed to limp through and get their licence were horrifying.

On the morning that I went for my test, Christopher Pluck warned me how bad it was. Apparently it was everything I had taught them *not* to do. I arrived at the salon that the New York State Board used to humiliate thousands of hairdressers, and as I watched what was going on, that old feeling of rebellion came to the fore. They had a system of cutting where you backcombed the hair to the roots, and whatever was left in your hand you cut off. That was their way of thinning hair. I looked around the room, truly aghast at what I saw – the sheer absence of style, the lack of any form of modernism (I could go on) – then an instructor came over and asked when I was going to start. The girl they had given me had obviously never had a good haircut in her life, but was expecting one.

I said to the instructor, 'Excuse me, but what is that form of thinning hair called?'

'Effilating,' he replied.

I could not resist retorting, 'Oh, I thought that was something you did in bed.'

After a humourless pause he said, 'Are you going to take the test or not?'

I replied that I could not do hair the way they wanted and therefore I would not take the test. After saying goodbye to the would-be model, I quietly left the salon and then phoned

Priscilla Tucker, my beauty-journalist friend. I explained what had happened, knowing that the State Board would not let me work unless I took the nonsense they called a test and passed it. Priscilla could always smell a good story and wrote about my predicament in the *New York Herald Tribune*. Priscilla also had gone to see Judge Lomenzo, the Secretary of State for New York, whose office ran the Cosmetology Department. He gave her a quote that added weight to the story – and dug his own grave: 'We're not going to be told what to do by these damn foreigners, especially those limeys. Over there you can't tell the difference between the boys and the girls.' Suddenly it became a cause célèbre, written about in several newspapers and magazines and talked about on television. I thought of writing to the judge personally to thank him.

Richard Salomon understood my reasons for not taking the test, but the publicity did not rest easy with him. He was not happy that a month after we had opened, I still couldn't cut hair in the expensive, avant-garde salon we had built together. Although I was constantly in the salon encouraging the stylists to do the work they did in Britain – the sole reason for our being in America – this wasn't how he had imagined our collaboration. But then the American hairdressers got in on the act and started to complain about the very old-fashioned methods of examination. The State Board became increasingly concerned as the situation seemed to be getting a little out of hand.

A month later I received a telephone call from an official at the State Board. I was asked to bring a model, do the test, and receive the licence to work. I was put in a corner away from the main body of hairdressers, so just to tickle their fancy I did a far-out geometric. I think the examiners were told to be courteous and gentle with me, as the authorities wanted no further trouble from *this* limey. My work wasn't examined. I was just told that I had passed and would never have to darken their doors again. I asked myself why I had gone through so much angst. Was it to raise standards within the craft or was it just my ego? Suddenly a memory came to me of that RAF officer who had remarked, 'You and trouble seem to have a sound relationship.' Perhaps he had a point. But that said, the nicest thing that happened during this ugly period was receiving a note from Irving Penn. All it said was: 'Vidal, congratulations. Never give in. Never give in.'

A month later, Lynda and Raymond both passed their second exam with ease. Enormous changes were taking place within the organization. Roger Thompson, who had visited us regularly since we opened, now decided that he would bring his family and work in New York. Suddenly the salon grew a great deal busier, as Roger had an international name and a ready-made clientele. So many Americans who had stayed at the Grosvenor House Hotel had begged Roger to come to New York to cut their hair, and now their wish had come true. His name was carefully removed from the outside of the building in London but we photographed it for posterity.

Another draw was the arrival of Paul Mitchell, one of our top stylists in the London salon. Prior to this we had been asked to do a fashion show on the *Queen Elizabeth* during a luxury cruise from Southampton to New York. Paul captained the team and captured a great many clients along the way. He joined our Madison Avenue salon and as our business continued to grow, many New Yorkers who had been nervous for months at last plucked up the courage to visit us. After having their hair cut, they looked at themselves in the mirror, shook their heads, watched as the cut fell back into place beautifully and became loyal clients on the spot. The atmosphere was now really buzzing and the team was doing some of the most inspired work I'd ever seen.

Socially I was still finding my way on the west side of the Atlantic, but all that was about to change. Bobby Freedman was *the* host of New York; his legendary parties were a veritable who's who of fashionable society. He was an art connoisseur who had one of the finest collections in New York – Monet, Mondrian, Degas, to name just a few. To add to his collection of pretty things, he made it his personal mission to keep a check on which gorgeous girls were in town and which were out of town. His radar for the zeitgeist was precise and unfailing. Nancy Kwan's haircut had gone over big in New York and Bobby was well aware of it. Nancy and I had remained friends and whether in London or New York, we occasionally went out to dinner. Through his many connections, Bobby found out where she was staying and called her. Eventually the conversation turned to me, and he came right out with it. 'I'd like you to join our group. I hear you've been running around town with a hairdresser. No harm meant, but he must be gay.'

'Actually he's not – and he's just a friend. I'm married to an Austrian ski instructor and we have a small child.'

'What are you doing tonight?' Bobby asked.

'Having dinner with Vidal.'

'Can I join you?'

The three of us had a hilarious dinner, and I got a call from Bobby the next day, who was having a few friends over that afternoon, asking if I would like to join them.

Bobby had an extraordinary house on the Upper East Side, perfect for entertaining. He surrounded himself with an eclectic group of people – designers, models, writers, athletes. That night

I met one of his closest friends, Dick Savitt, who had won the Men's Singles Championship at Wimbledon in 1951. Oleg Cassini, who was also there, had designed superb clothes for Jackie Kennedy when she was the First Lady. Oleg had a quirky sense of humour and I enjoyed getting to know him.

Gradually Bobby and I became really good friends and he announced that as part of my initiation into society, he would introduce me to American football. He decided that I should accompany him to a New York Giants game, when they were playing the Cleveland Browns. We took the subway, ate a hot dog, had a beer, and suddenly I was inside this enormous stadium, watching gladiators intent on mayhem. About fifteen minutes into the game, I said to Bobby, 'This game is fixed, isn't it?'

'Fixed?' he said. 'What *are* you talking about?'

'Well, there's a guy down there with thirty-two on his back who's running through the New York team like a knife through butter.'

Bobby said, 'That's the great Jim Brown.'

I made no other comment, but saw a hysterical, wild crowd become rather docile as Brown and Cleveland gave New York a well-deserved thrashing. Although I was thrilled at Bobby's invitation, I wasn't really won over to the game, not on this or subsequent occasions – give me Chelsea versus Manchester United any day.

My frequent flights across the Atlantic were becoming second nature. I carried only a briefcase and a book. At each end I would arrive to find my clothes pressed and my shoes polished. What more could an East End kid ask for? One Thursday evening, I flew into New York from London, checked into my usual room at the Elysée and called Bobby.

He said, 'Come right over! And wear a jacket. I've got a dinner party going on.'

It was a beautiful evening and I walked to Bobby's house. I was let in by James, his valet. Bobby came to greet me and showed me through to the kitchen. He poured two glasses of red wine and said, 'People are dining right now but we'll join them for coffee.'

He had left his dinner guests and stayed with me until we joined them. Sitting there in the main dining room were Senator Jacob Javits and his wife, Marion, with five other guests. The conversation went from politics to politics. It was riveting.

I didn't only meet bigwig politicians and socialites, though. My friend Walter Fontaine was a very well-known hairdresser in New York. I liked him a lot. He had a wonderful sense of humour, a great fashion look of his own, and, being African-American himself, he invented brilliant ways of working with black hair. Even though he had a mixed clientele, both white and black, he was best known for giving some of the big names in entertainment their own distinctive look. He invited me to join him at a musician friend's opening night in a Harlem club. Beverly Todd would be there as well, he told me. She too was African-American. Just as we were sitting at our table, a bouncer came over and demanded, 'Who's whitey?'

Beverly said, 'He's with me, and he's a very dear friend.'

'OK. But if he goes to the toilet, make sure someone escorts him.'

Twice that evening I had to use the rest room, and each time I was escorted by Walter and one of his friends. At first I found this amusing, but I soon realized that segregation was at the heart of it, which saddened me. There were palpable racial tensions in certain areas of New York then. I quickly learned that if

I wanted to go to Harlem in those years, I would need to go with black friends – which I did fairly often. Harlem and jazz were synonymous. It's there that I saw so many superb artists perform – musicians like Billy Eckstine, Miles Davis, Dinah Washington and 'Cannonball' Adderley. Sammy Davis Jr had introduced me to Nancy Wilson, who, one night, after she finished singing, came over to the table to say hello. Sitting there with this exquisite beauty at a club in Harlem, I really felt that I'd *arrived*.

✧

Despite a few good moments, Paris proved another tough nut to crack. The Parisians loved home-grown talent – and I was a London boy through and through. Emmanuelle Khanh had made it easier for me to work in Paris and yet live outside France, but it was my regular work with *Elle* magazine that really opened the gates. Hélène Lazareff was the last word in fashion and felt she had partly discovered me for Paris – which she had. She also felt that French hairdressing needed a kick up the arse.

In 1965 the designer Emanuel Ungaro had his first show. Ungaro had trained with the renowned Balenciaga and knew instinctively what he wanted. He called me directly and asked if I would like to create the hair for his show. I was thrilled to be asked but I told him that I did have one condition. I wasn't going to tell him how to design the clothes so I hoped that he wouldn't tell me how to design the hair.

He said, 'That's why I've called you. Hélène Lazareff feels we should work together. We will make a good team. Let's get together and discuss ideas.'

We met. I liked his sense of purpose and we both grew excited about the prospect of collaborating. True to his word, he did not tell me how to design the hair; he just asked what I had in mind. I told him I would work on it and let him know closer to the date.

I'd never seen our team as invigorated as they were by the prospect of a major debut show in Paris. Although there would be time to cut the hair of four or five models, we would be working with so many girls we would have to create a look from wigs. Fortunately we had done this many, many times.

Suddenly, Paris Fashion Week was upon us. Roger Thompson, Christopher Pluck and two of our apprentices accompanied me. We settled in and the team decided to get something to eat in the hotel restaurant. Many of our friends from the British press were also staying at the hotel and the first person we bumped into was my old friend Felicity Green of the *Daily Mirror*, who asked, 'Vidal, what are you boys doing tonight?'

I explained that we would be going to the Ungaro atelier, taking a look at some of the finished clothes and preparing the models for the following day.

She said, 'Darling, you've got yourself a new shampoo girl.'

I knew instinctively where she was coming from. 'Felicity, it's not possible. Our two apprentices are half your age and Ungaro would spot that something was up immediately.'

Very convincingly she said, 'You'd be *amazed* how young I can look when I try.' There was no arguing with Felicity. She was going to be at Ungaro's that evening whether I said yes or not. She travelled with us from the hotel and, dressed in high boots and a short skirt, was soon shampooing heads. I wish I'd had a camera, but these were completely banned before a collection was shown. Felicity played her part beautifully, although Ungaro did look at her quizzically a couple of times. I couldn't help thinking he would see her at the show the next day and would never trust me again! But, apart from having a marvellous sense of adventure, Felicity was a true professional and knew that she couldn't release her story in the *Daily Mirror* before the other fashion writers had filed theirs.

The look I decided on was a fringe that started from the ear lobe and went three-quarters of the way across the forehead, to a long side. It framed the face and threw out the cheekbones. Roger and Christopher were at their very best. Looking at their work, I realized how lucky I was to have such a talented team. And as Felicity had dressed more like herself for the show the following afternoon, Ungaro either didn't spot her or was much too busy to ask why one of our shampoo girls was sitting in the front row. It was one of the great fashion larks of all time. Felicity's story duly appeared the following day and it was a classic. How did she get all that information?

Ungaro was thrilled and his first show was a smash. All the magazines and newspapers had a field day and *Paris Match* wanted to do a cover in the street outside his atelier. I had no idea that the cover of *Paris Match* was such a big deal, but soon learned that it was seen by millions – and our hair was very much in the picture. But though the clothes were a hit, the hair was more controversial. One elderly member of the French press said, 'The girls look like boys. It is not natural. The French will never wear architectural shapes. It destroys their femininity.' However, it didn't stop Ungaro inviting us to do the hair for his second collection six months later – without our celebrity shampooist. She was greatly missed.

Not long after the show, but many years after we had left Israel in 1949, my old comrade Colin Fisher and I took a trip back there. Israel had rarely been out of mind but actually seeing it for real again brought back so many memories. We visited Nir

Am, Dorot and Beeri, places that were very close to our hearts, as these were the *kibbutzim* that we had defended. The majestic beauty of Jerusalem had a powerful effect on both of us and nowhere more so than in the Holocaust Museum. We then spent a week in Tel Aviv, the other city that never sleeps. We visited the concert hall, where the big argument was should the orchestra play Wagner or not. That night we listened to Bruckner's Ninth Symphony with great joy, then went to a club near the shore. In Tel Aviv, you never seemed to get home until three in the morning. We had a blast. While driving from Tel Aviv to Haifa, Colin and I sang Palmach songs and wondered what our lives would have been like had we had the opportunity to stay in Israel. It would be the first of many trips back to that country.

On one trip, I introduced my good friend Hal Shaper to Israel. Hal and I had been close friends for many years. A white South African lawyer, he had come to Britain to get away from apartheid, which he loathed. His true love was music and writing song lyrics and the apartheid system had prevented him from working with talented black artists. One of his lyrics – 'Softly as I Leave You' – became a hit for Frank Sinatra, Matt Monro and Elvis.

After he arrived in London, Hal opened a music publishing business and tried desperately to compete with companies that had been well established in Britain for half a century or more. Even for a man with enormous self-confidence and a large personality, it became too much to handle. He called me one day, saying, 'Vid, I'm going broke.' When I asked him why, he said, 'I can't compete. What should I do?'

'Well, how much money do you have, Hal?' I asked.

'A hundred pounds.'

'Hal,' I said, 'the best thing you can do is to gather ten of the people that you most admire. Wine and dine them and let them all enjoy your last hundred pounds.'

'Good idea, Vid. You'll be there.'

It was a great evening. Hal's fellow South African and close buddy Herbie Kretzmer, a well-known critic, writer and a formidable lyricist himself, was there, joining an extraordinary group of people who took great pleasure in toasting to Hal's demise. Even if Hal ended up homeless, we all agreed that we would take turns putting him up for a night. This last-ditch celebration turned out to be a master-stroke for Hal, as the next morning he called and said, 'You'll never believe this. Completely out of the blue I've just received the offer of a large contract, which I have, of course, accepted. So your idea of celebrating my future poverty has worked beautifully.'

He never looked back. Over the years, I would frequently tell Hal about the wonders of Israel and eventually he decided to see for himself. When he asked if I would be his tour guide, I was delighted.

We stayed first at the Hilton Hotel in Tel Aviv, then visited Jerusalem, where we had lunch with Teddy Kollek, the mayor. Teddy was an extraordinary man whose passion for his first love, Jerusalem, never wavered. Eventually we arrived at Eilat, the winter holiday resort by the Red Sea. We stayed at the Queen of Sheba, a small, intimate hotel, where we swam and water skied to our hearts' content and in the evenings visited Eilat's one nightclub – called the End of the World. The owner had lost an eye during the war and would laughingly say, 'Israel is so small. You only need one eye.'

Unfortunately, there was another guest there, a lady who knew me by reputation. She wasn't a client of mine but kept demanding that I cut her hair. Hal got so pissed off with her constant demands that he told her that my doctor said I mustn't pick up a pair of scissors for at least a month, to give my hands a rest. On the last day of our trip, he also informed her that he was my assistant and would happily shape her hair. After shampooing her on the beach, Hal cut her hair with all the aplomb of an artist. Several people stopped to watch. He finished his performance by applying conditioner, telling her to leave it on for at least four hours. She was thrilled to have got her way, but there was no way of knowing how much damage Hal had done. We left before we – and the unfortunate lady – found out. Hal, I realized far too late, was dangerous to be around.

While we were in Eilat, the Hilton management had called and expressed a desire to meet with me regarding a salon they were building at their new hotel in Tel Aviv, which was currently under construction. Despite my frequent visits, I'd so far been unable to combine my two great passions – Israel and hairdressing. A sun-filled salon overlooking the ocean in Tel Aviv would be a dream come true. Hal was keen to come along for the ride so at an appointed time, he and I both met the manager of the new hotel. Before we met with the management team, he wanted to show me exactly where the salon would be. He asked us to be careful as we climbed some rickety wooden stairs. As we got to a mezzanine landing, he said, 'Through here a salon will be built and we'd like to talk to you about the possibility—' and as he got to 'possibility', my adrenalin started working overtime and I skipped to the area where the salon would be. I heard a loud cry of 'No!' but it was too late. I was up to my knees in wet cement.

After Hal and the manager pulled me out, Hal said, 'We'd better get those trousers off. If they dry on you, mate, you're in big trouble.'

'But I've got a meeting with the Hilton management group in ten minutes!' Nevertheless, the trousers had to come off.

Ten minutes later, I was sitting with the manager and the rest of the Hilton team round a large, formal boardroom table. From the waist up, I was dressed in the latest London fashion. From the waist down, I had no shoes, no socks and no trousers; I was sitting there in my underwear. During the meeting I noticed that nobody was looking at me directly. Only respect for my unfortunate situation stopped them bursting into raucous laughter. I said to them, 'Laugh. Get it out of your system.' They did. I laughed with them.

At various intervals, Hal came through the door with the latest news of my trousers, the last time to say, 'We've got most of the cement out of the left leg, but the right is doomed, never to be worn again.'

Fortunately, the Hilton management team thought that anyone who could sit through an important meeting of this kind without his trousers deserved a salon. But I'd had second thoughts. It was so tempting, but opening in a new country takes time and a lot of hard work. You need to pick your team, train them and build up a loyal clientele. It was too risky; my time was divided between two cities, London and New York, as it was. A third would be too much. And I didn't want to fail – especially not in Tel Aviv. With enormous regret, I told them that while I truly appreciated their offer, I could not accept.

All I had now to do was get out of there with no trousers. Our hotel was only a couple of hundred yards from the Hilton, so Hal volunteered to pop back to my room to retrieve another pair of trousers, shoes and socks. I didn't want to lose what little dignity I had left by walking down a very busy Tel Aviv street half naked. However, when he got to the front desk, Hal was told he couldn't enter my room without reception first getting permission from me. It took him at least an hour to persuade them. No one believed that anybody would be so stupid as to walk into wet cement. Would they?

10

Movie Stars, Mia and Me

Back in London, business was thriving. When Roger Thompson went to run our New York salon, Christopher Brooker became the artistic director of Vidal Sassoon in Great Britain and Europe. And just as British hairdressers now wanted to work in the States, many of the American hairdressers we had trained in New York begged to come to London. They wanted to be part of where it all began.

On the strength of all this movement across the Atlantic, Christopher, together with Joshua Galvin, who was running the London salons, developed a training programme that was even more effective than the one we had been using. Christopher was fizzing with ideas and general creativity and Joshua was the man to turn his dreams into reality. Between them, they were determined to keep our London standards high. They were damned if Roger in New York was going to get all the glory, and would regularly call him to tell him how well they were doing without him. He was always very laid-back, saying, 'Great, my shares will be worth all the more.' The camaraderie between these three and the great loyalty the team showed to one another gave me much to be thankful for. And by the late sixties we had a very powerful team in place in London – conveniently, as a new opportunity was about to present itself.

I'd known Gerard Austin for many years, since he'd worked with me early on in his career. Although you wouldn't call him the most handsome chap you'd ever met, he had an extraordinary way with women and always seemed to have a beauty in his bed. He was intelligent and ambitious and, unusually for those days, looked beyond the narrow confines of Britain and brought the Carita sisters over from Paris. Maria and Rosy Carita were world-renowned. They had opened their first salon in the forties and were still at the top of the profession, running one of the most exotic hair salons in Paris. Gerard's gift of the gab served him well and he pulled off a marvellous coup. He persuaded the girls that they could work one week in London and one week in Paris, thereby maintaining their clientele while he created a beautiful new salon for them in Knightsbridge, at the top of Sloane Street. They were welcomed with open arms.

It did not last. Soon after the glamour of their tremendous opening had worn off, the Parisian sisters found it physically impossible to continue to fly Paris–London, London–Paris every other week. Gerard had spent a considerable sum of money on the salon and grew very concerned about his investment. Mayfair had always been the location for the best hairdressing, and opening in Knightsbridge was risky. Without the Carita sisters the salon would be in serious trouble. But with Mary Quant and others making Chelsea and the King's Road the fashionable place to be, I sensed people were spreading their wings – and I saw a great opportunity to spread mine. Gerard and I did a deal. No cash changed hands, but the Sassoon organization would take over the Sloane Street salon and Gerard would have shares in our business. The arrangement suited us both.

The Carita sisters flew back to Paris for the last time, their wonderful reputation still intact. Their style was definitely very French, very Parisian. They were well aware that London was developing its *own* look and we were at the forefront.

The Sloane Street salon, opposite the Carlton Towers Hotel, was too far from the King's Road for our new clients to wear Mary Quant's clothes or even see the Mary Quant effect. The salon was frequented by Knightsbridge ladies who were very resistant to our ways. I kept thinking, *How are we going to change them?* I asked my friend the actress Adrienne Corri to come in and cheer the place up. She arrived with a thespian friend, looked around, and in that deep, dark theatrical voice said disdainfully, 'Darling, do you think any of these old dears fuck?' Not what I had in mind at all. Inevitably, lots of the original old dears went to other salons, but the move to Knightsbridge was still fortuitous for us. The stylists who moved to Sloane Street brought their clients with them from Bond Street, so it was not long before the new salon was grooving.

One Sunday morning three months later, on my way back to London from a two-week stay in Barbados, I dropped my bags at my flat and decided to walk to our three salons, despite the fact that they were closed. Bond Street looked pristine but cool from the outside. Grosvenor House was equally impressive. But as I arrived at the Sloane Street salon I saw an enormous workman's ladder in the window. I was infuriated. Who would be sloppy enough to leave a scruffy ladder on show for the whole weekend?

The Barbados trip had given me a deep tan. I was extremely dark, and at nine o'clock on Monday morning I was at Sloane

Street, tearing a strip off the manager at the same time as clients were coming through the salon's reception area. One of them said to her hairdresser, 'Do you know there's a mad Pakistani in reception screaming about a ladder?' News of this hilarious incident travelled around the salons with great speed, and for a week I was known by staff and clients alike as the mad Pakistani.

Sloane Street soon developed its own personality and the hairdressers enjoyed the challenge of changing the local style. I was always keen for a stunt and, being a Chelsea football fan and season-ticket holder, came up with a brilliant one. The Chelsea team were all invited in to have haircuts at the Sloane Street salon – but there was a catch: they had to wear their playing gear. Amazingly, the club agreed. I was given star fullback Eddie McCreadie's kit, which I wore while cutting the great centre forward Peter Osgood's hair. Of course the press was there for this bit of madness. Next day, Peter Osgood, legs and all, was in every major newspaper across Europe – with yours truly cutting his hair.

We had a great day, which made it doubly unfortunate that the following Saturday our boys in blue lost to Arsenal in the semi-final of the FA Cup. In fact that was bad news however you looked at it.

We kept quiet about our celebrity clientele at the time – there was no kiss 'n' tell back then – but looking back, in any given week we'd see the likes of Mia Farrow, Margaret Leighton, Ava Gardner, society ladies like Viscountess Althorp and the Duchess of Bedford, and Fleur Cowles (who gave legendary tea parties at the Albany, where she lived), and nearly all the top models. Peter O'Toole had been a regular since we'd done his hair for *Lawrence of Arabia*. He said he couldn't go back to a barbershop having experienced the pleasure of a ladies' salon. In 1960 I'd even gone up to Stratford-upon-Avon to give Dorothy Tutin a haircut. She was starring in the RSC's production of *Troilus and Cressida*, wearing a heavy wig. I waited in her dressing room until the interval. Off came the wig and I cut half of her hair. The wig went back on for the second act and I finished the haircut when the performance was over and the cheers had died down. Our clients included many, many actresses – Jill Bennett, Adrienne Corri and, when they were in town, Carol Burnett, Carol Channing, Dionne Warwick, Georgia Brown, Annie Ross and Rita Hayworth. If I named them all it would take a page. Adrienne was a rather special friend and not just because of her winning ways with the grand dames of Knightsbridge. She was an actress of some notoriety, famous for the fiery and flamboyant characters she played. Born and raised in Scotland with some Italian thrown into the mix, she starred in many West End plays and had the most vivacious personality. Her red hair and green eyes gave her a distinctive look and audiences found her captivating. We had become friends in the early sixties when she took to breezing into the salon with about five minutes' notice. Sometime in 1966, Adrienne called and said, 'Vidal, Albie is opening at the Old Vic in a Feydeau farce called *A Flea in Her Ear* and you simply have to come with me.'

'I'd be delighted,' I said. I was an Albert Finney fan and had seen him in John Osborne's play *Luther* three times. I also knew him socially; he was one of the young actors who had ventured to some of my parties.

On Wednesday evening I had a car fetch Adrienne. Even though she'd been off filming and I hadn't seen her for months, I always felt so comfortable in her company. She had a delightful sense of the ridiculous and told me in her best thespian voice to prepare myself to be shocked by the play, because it was about infidelity and impotence. As it happened, the play was a riot. The curtain came down and Adrienne said, 'Let's go backstage and congratulate Albie.'

As Adrienne and I walked into the dressing room, Albert kissed her, turned to me and said, 'Hello, Vid. Meet Larry.'

I looked up. It was Laurence Olivier. *The* Laurence Olivier. He looked me over and said, 'Did he call you "Vid"? What's your real name?'

'Vidal Sassoon.'

A sigh came from Olivier. 'Ohhhh, so *you're* that barber.'

❖

In 1966, the American actress Beverly Adams came to London to make a new film. She had made two movies with Dean Martin and was gradually climbing the ladder to stardom. One Saturday morning, I was sitting upstairs on the fourth floor in my office at 171 New Bond Street, dealing with paperwork. The office and I did not get along – my natural tendency was to be in the salon, where the action was. There was a knock on the door and Joshua Galvin entered, not at all his usual self. He very excitedly said to me, 'There's a girl downstairs who's an absolute knockout. She's here making a movie and I believe you should meet her.'

I told him to bring her up when her hair was finished or to call me and I would come down. Then I told him to calm down – our salon was always full of beautiful women.

I resisted the temptation to follow Joshua downstairs, but an hour later there was another knock on the door and Joshua presented Miss Beverly Adams to me.

I was gazing at the loveliest young movie star I had ever

seen. She had dark hair, blue eyes and a beauty and freshness about her that took my breath away. Tall and slim, she walked towards me with an athlete's grace, all the time smiling broadly. I offered her a seat and a cup of tea and Joshua bowed out gracefully. Beverly and I talked. She had just arrived and didn't know a soul in England.

'I suppose the studio is keeping you busy over the weekend?' I asked.

'No,' she said, 'I'm totally free.'

'Would you care to have dinner tonight?'

'I'd love to. I'm staying at the Hilton Hotel in Park Lane.'

'That's perfect because I'm having a drink with a friend of mine in the bar there at seven o'clock. Please join us.'

Seven o'clock that evening found me sitting at the bar with Sammy Davis Jr when Beverly walked in. Sammy and I gave one another a knowing glance; we both knew we were looking at a stunning woman. Beverly knew Sammy because of the Dean Martin connection and I knew him for the fabulous parties he gave. Maggie London had introduced us some years before.

Sammy excused himself a while later, saying, 'I'm having dinner with Liz and Richard tonight.' I had a reservation for the White Elephant at eight o'clock and when Beverly and I got there, Victor, the owner, sent over a bottle of wine with his compliments, which meant that he approved of my dinner companion. Dinner went well and I took Beverly back to the hotel, where she chastely shook my hand and said goodnight. We arranged to meet on Wednesday evening, filming permitting.

On Wednesday morning, I was in the accounting offices of Fisher Sassoon – Fisher being my wartime buddy and Sassoon being my brother, Ivor. Charles Prevost had joined us, wanting an update on the general direction of the company while at the same time making it clear that he was in no way displeased with the way it was being handled. We four were having a quiet chat when suddenly the loudest groan interrupted the conversation. It was me. The next moment I was on the floor in utter agony.

Ivor quickly called Dr Philip Lebon's office. He came to the phone and when told what had happened said, 'It could be an acute appendicitis. Let's get him over here as quickly as we can.' Nobody wanted to move me, but an ambulance came and within an hour I was in the operating room. Philip was right; it was appendicitis. There was absolutely no way that I could meet Beverly Adams that evening, and it wasn't until two hours after our scheduled date that Dr Lebon called her on my behalf. When told that I was in hospital, she said, 'If he isn't, he will be. Nobody stands *me* up.'

I couldn't stand up at all. Beverly took pity on me, though, and came to visit me in hospital. I must have looked terrible because as she entered the room, she gasped. I didn't feel like talking, and she left soon after she arrived. This romance – if there was to be one – could only get better.

Two telegrams came to the hospital the next day. One was from Terry Stamp. It read: 'Stay where you are. I need your ticket for the Chelsea match.' The other was from Beverly: 'The lengths some people will go to get out of a date.'

I was in hospital for four days, and every night Beverly came to see me. By the time I was discharged, the two girls I had been previously romantically entangled with were suddenly out of my life.

Instead of going back to my own flat, I went to my mum's in Kilburn to convalesce. I was there for three days and she pumped me with enough lokshen soup to feed the British and Israeli armies. It worked too; my insides healed up with amazing speed. Every night Beverly called and both Mum and Nathan G took to her immediately. Dad nicknamed her 'Sunshine'. The pair of them could see, I think, that this was no ordinary girl-friend.

As I recuperated, I spent most of the time concentrating on the new look that had been on my mind when I collapsed. What I wanted was a short cut with a perm, but so far I had not been able to marry those two simple elements into a shape that bore my signature. I took a risk and tried it out on Beverly. I gave her a soft perm, which she was delighted with, but which I knew was not quite spot on.

We had done so much with straight hair over the years, curly hair had hardly got a look in. All that would change one week-end in 1967 when the second part of our hairdressing revolution took place. This time nothing was left to chance – it was no happy 'accident' like the asymmetric cut, it was a carefully planned manoeuvre. I took three rooms at the Grosvenor House Hotel and asked Roger, Christopher and Annie if they would mind working the whole weekend at our salon there, resting when they needed to in their rooms at the hotel. Jenny Fussell and Jane Johns were the models; their faces were perfect for the cut I was visualizing. The photographer was Stephen Bobroff. I knew what I was looking for, having spent so much time walking through Harlem when I was in New York, where I would see great head shapes full of closely cut but defined curl. I was so envious of this look, which I saw everywhere on black Americans, and was determined to see if I could get the same look with Asians and Caucasians. By sheer bad luck, I could only master-mind the operation – I wasn't allowed to work so soon after having had my appendix out. Roger and Christopher did the cutting while I explained in depth what I was looking for. We looked at lots of photographs together. It had to be more than new; it had to be revolutionary.

We started on Friday evening, cutting and perming. We worked through Saturday, but didn't come up with anything special. Then on Sunday afternoon something magical happened. Roger had cut a head of hair, following the principles of our geometric looks, and Annie had permed it. Usually at this point a perm would be set in pin-curls and rollers and put under a dryer. But on this occasion it was just cut and permed. When Annie had finished rinsing out the perming solution, Roger put the finishing touches to the cut, ran his fingers through the hair, and suddenly there it was! I remember shouting like a madman: 'Roger, that's it! Let Stephen photograph it.' We were like Chelsea after they'd scored a winning goal, hugging one another and slapping each other on the back. We knew it was the breakthrough we'd been looking for; people could now have curly hair that they could wash at home and the shape of the cut would still fall in beautifully. Nobody had *ever* cut and permed hair without setting it before. This indeed was the new look we'd been waiting for and I couldn't wait to see Stephen's pictures.

They were sent over first thing Monday morning, after we'd all been home for a few hours' sleep. I called Felicity Green and told her about our experiment over the weekend and the result, which was dynamite. She took the pictures immediately and used three or four different angles in the next day's *Daily Mirror*, calling the cut the 'New Revolution'. The following day Carol Phillips, the beauty editor of *American Vogue*, called. She'd seen Felicity's article and thought it was an astonishing breakthrough. Please could I send her pictures of the people we'd given it to, immediately.

I said, 'Carol, we just did it two days ago on the models. We haven't yet given it to a client.'

She said, 'Well, hurry up. I want to use it first in America.'

About a month later she had her pictures.

I wanted to call the new look 'Harlem', but there was so much racial tension at that time that I decided on my second choice – the 'Greek Goddess'.

Overnight the practice of setting hair went out of the window and a whole swathe of women were liberated from their weekly appointment with the hood hairdryer. The 'Greek Goddess' needed no explaining, or training the eye to see. It was an instant hit. It made sense from day one. These days nearly all modern hairdressers simply cut and judge how much curl they want in their permanent wave for each individual client. It is now commonplace worldwide.

Soon after this epiphany, I took Beverly to Grayshott Hall. John Addey came too. Ostensibly he came for a thorough detox but inwardly he suspected that I was about to do something drastic. When I told him I was thinking of getting married, he said, 'Damn good choice. Public relations will have a marvellous time with this.'

Beverly, who was only twenty-one, had to tell her parents that she was marrying a thirty-nine-year-old hairdresser – from London, no less. Her mother was in a dreadful state of shock and her father, who in his younger days had been a pitcher for the St Louis Cardinals, wasn't too happy either. Back in the States, Beverly had been dating the Los Angeles Dodgers' baseball legend Sandy Koufax. Her father's only comment was, 'How could you choose an English hairdresser over an American hero?'

My stepfather and Beverly soon developed a very good relationship. My mother, on the other hand, found it hard to adjust to the idea and was quick to remind me that movie actresses, in her opinion, were rather flighty. She was far more impressed with Ivor's choice of mate, Deborah. She was the niece of Sir Isaac Wolfson, had a very good education, spoke French without a trace of an English accent, and played the piano beautifully. In Mother's eyes, Ivor was definitely the smarter one. Mother was also convinced that no woman I chose was going to be good enough for her and that she should do the choosing. I tried to persuade her that while Beverly was very glamorous it was actually her zest for life and craving for adventure that most attracted me. Eventually, once Mum realized that Beverly was going to be part of the family, she softened towards her.

Beverly and I figured the easiest way out for both of us was to elope to Las Vegas. A quick call to LA later and my old hairdressing buddy Gene Shacove became the saint who put it all together. He called the comedian Buddy Hackett, whom I had also got to know, and told him we were getting married. As he was working Vegas perhaps he could arrange something?

A few days later, on 16 February 1967, a select group gathered together in Buddy's suite at the Sahara Hotel, with a gentleman who had a licence to marry people. Amazingly, Buddy refrained from cracking any jokes during the short ceremony, but we were all invited to watch his act that evening downstairs in the main room. Buddy was bantering with the audience when he noticed somebody with a haircut that was reminiscent of one of ours. He asked her where she had it done and she replied: 'Vidal Sassoon.'

Buddy said, 'You think you're sporting the newest Sassoon? You're not. *She's* sitting right over there with him. I just married them up in my suite. Beverly, Vidal, take a bow.' Buddy, the marvellous storytelling comedian, was a friend indeed that night. He even asked a fellow entertainer, Tommy Leonetti, to come on stage and serenade us with 'I Love You Truly'.

After the cabaret we made our way to Puerto Vallarta in Mexico for our honeymoon, for twelve magnificent days. The beauty of Puerto Vallarta left us breathless. So did passion, and life was good. Back in London, there were so many people I wanted Beverly to meet there seemed scarcely enough days in the week. And for a young girl from Burbank, California, she adapted very well to London in the Swinging Sixties. In fact I'd say she thrived on it.

But no sooner had we settled down to married life than I got an invitation from one of cinema's rising stars and suddenly my new bride and I were off to Hollywood.

A couple of years earlier, Roman Polanski had dropped into the Bond Street salon to say hello. We had met through a mutual friend, Bernie Cornfeld, a European businessman, and had immediately hit it off. Roman was in town making a movie called *Repulsion* with Catherine Deneuve. It was good to see his twinkling eyes sizing up the salon. He sauntered around, climbed the stairs to the balcony, all the time casting about with his director's eye. I suspected there was something else on his mind as it seemed unlikely he had walked all the way down Bond Street to wish me a good summer.

Once he had taken a look around, he came to the point very quickly. 'I want to film here this weekend with Catherine. I'd need to use the whole balcony, so that would be out of action. But we won't interfere at all with the clients on the floor below.'

Roman did not stay just one weekend. The filming lasted a

week. It was a total madhouse and our clients loved it. It was real-life theatre at its best. You could feel the excitement the second you came through the door.

As Roman left the salon on the last day of shooting, he said goodbye to me with a slightly guilty look on his face; he was concerned about having outstayed his original invitation. He needn't have worried. There was no fee; he was a friend in dire need of a balcony and I had one. To have built something similar for the shoot would have cost a fortune. But fortunately my liaison with Roman did not stop there.

In early spring 1967, quite soon after Beverly and I were married, a call came from California. It was Roman. 'Vidal, can you come to Los Angeles to cut Mia Farrow's hair for a film I'm directing called *Rosemary's Baby*?'

I asked when he needed it done by.

'Within the next two weeks.'

'But, Roman, I only cut it six weeks ago and I had to take it very short because something had gone on at home and Mia had taken a pair of shears to her own head. I've never seen such a mess.'

'Well, you could take half an inch off, couldn't you? Mia would like that.'

I was rather warming to the idea and told him I thought I could do better than that.

He said, 'Let's do it. I've seen you dance around the chair and it will make for great theatre. Bring Beverly. Everything will be first class. And would a five-thousand-dollar fee be OK?'

Beverly and I flew out to Hollywood and made our way to Stage 13 Paramount Studios. Roman's production team had created a makeshift 'salon' in a boxing ring, surrounded by seats for the press and the audience – the whole thing was going to be broadcast live on American television. When we arrived, Beverly was escorted to her seat and I was taken to Mia's dressing room. Mia gave me a hug but I could tell she was somewhat distanced from the day's events. I led her into the large studio space. The press were not allowed into the ring but could photograph from the surrounding edges while I was working. This segregation lasted about two minutes. Then they were all over us. There was one young photographer on the floor underneath the chair, shooting upwards. He got a mouthful of Mia's hair as it fell from my scissors. It was like a zany scene out of a silent movie. There was no way I was dancing anywhere, though. I had to carefully step over the photographers' bodies to do my job.

It soon became obvious that Mia wasn't happy. Her heart wasn't in what was really a publicity stunt for the movie. So she decided to use the press conference for her own ends. Instead of answering questions about her role in *Rosemary's Baby*, she started lecturing the press about the American Indian population and how miserably they were treated. Instead of photographing something as trivial as her haircut, she said, they should be out there on the reservations taking photographs that would educate the American public and show them how badly they treated their native population. She spoke passionately about this cause, which she truly believed in, but I couldn't help wondering if this was really the right forum for it. But Mia's sincerity paid off and both the journalists and the invited audience seemed to be enjoying themselves. And once Mia got her message across, she visibly relaxed and was, once again, happy to be the centre of it all, a fun-loving girl enjoying her success. But little did I expect her haircut to be copied by so many young women worldwide. After all, the style itself was very simple. All

I did was follow the contours of her admittedly lovely head with my cut, leaving the sides and front slightly longer.

Afterwards Roman wined and dined us all. Mia had to leave early to meet her husband, Frank Sinatra. Beverly and I left shortly after her and went back to our hotel. Just as we were settling down for the night, the telephone rang. It was Lainie Kazan, an old friend who had just taken the lead role in the musical *Funny Girl*. 'I've just been watching television. Did you really get five thousand dollars for a haircut?'

'Yes.'

'Good. I'm coming over right now and you're doing mine for nothing.'

She was true to her word. The three of us had a very good laugh while I cut Lainie's hair. It was the perfect ending to a perfectly extraordinary day.

Beverly stayed in LA for a few days with her parents and I flew back to London. On arrival at Heathrow, I was greeted by a few of the press people who worked the airport. I'll never forget the first question: 'Vidal, that five thousand dollars, was it before or after tax?'

'I don't know,' I retorted. 'You'll have to ask the Chancellor of the Exchequer.'

❖

Within a year, it seemed increasingly obvious that we should make our home in New York. So we packed our bags permanently and moved to the United States.

My friends in New York were immediately crazy about Beverly. Bobby Freedman threw a bash in her honour. It was enormous fun but sedate compared to the London party scene. Bobby introduced us to Huber and Lillian Boscowitz, who seemed to want to adopt us. Huber was a high priest in the Republican Party so we never talked politics, but we went to some delightful dinner parties at their home. Huber insisted that everybody dress for dinner, so a black tie soon became a wardrobe staple.

We met several wonderful people at the Boscowitzes', including Van Johnson, a major film star. Van was known not only for his film work, but also for the red socks that he wore with everything. He grew quite fond of Beverly. At one dinner, sitting next to her – as was his choice – he presented her with a pair of red socks. 'Worn but washed,' was all he said.

Beverly ran around our flat with Van's red socks on for about a month.

By this time New York had acquired the buzz and glamour that London had had throughout the sixties, and many Brits like me were spending as much time in the Big Apple as we were back home. Sybil Burton had opened a club – 'Sybil's' – in midtown Manhattan on the East Side that had captured the vibe and was increasingly popular. Always full of exotic ideas, Sybil approached me about a haircutting competition she wanted to host there. 'None of the people involved will be hairdressers, but the idea is for lots of my acting chums to cut their friends' hair on that day. You will be the judge.'

I did suggest that many of those who began the day as friends might well end it as enemies by the time they'd had their hair cut by a complete amateur, but apart from that I thought it was a splendid idea. I was happy to agree that the first prize would be a year's free service at the Vidal Sassoon Salon on Madison Avenue. The runners-up would get one free appointment – which they would almost certainly need to straighten out the mess that their hair was obviously going to be left in.

Rudi Gernreich, the designer, had flown from Los Angeles to New York that weekend on other business, but when he heard about it, he couldn't resist getting a model and joining the thespians in this one-off competition. A huge crowd of people turned up to watch, and Rudi won the competition hands down and scissors up. Once the winner was announced, there was an enormous uproar among the actors, who protested that Rudi was a fashion designer and shouldn't have been allowed to compete in the first place. Rudi graciously bowed out and I judged the competition for the second time. It would have been much easier voting for the worst cut, but eventually a young actor won. He was overjoyed and for the next year came in once a month for his free haircut.

Sybil's club was not only full of Brits and Americans. The wonderful ambience seemed to attract patrons from all over the world; people seemed to fly into New York just to go there. Rachel Roberts, who was Sybil's dearest friend, was also a very fine actress, with a wonderful sense of humour, which I shared, and I got to know her rather well. One day, we were talking about charisma and how some people have that presence the public adores and others don't, when she said in a very sexy Welsh voice, 'Vidal, look at me. I'm an ugly Welsh cow – but if you look into my eyes, I'm beautiful.' I looked into her eyes and her beauty did indeed shine through – radiantly so. I'm sure she was just being over-dramatic as the rest of her – face and all – had very few flaws and was quite lovely, but it was an interesting lesson in how actors can just switch on their charm at will.

Through my old buddy Gene Shacove I'd become friendly with the actor George Hamilton. One hot summer's day in New York, the telephone rang in our flat. It was George. 'I've got two hours to spare. Can I come up and use your roof?'

Fifteen minutes later there was a knock on the door. It was George. 'I need a couple of towels to cover the lounge chairs and one to rest my head on.' He was wearing shorts, a T-shirt and a pair of sandals, and had a sun visor in his hand. Without another word, George took the towels and vanished for two hours. He was sunbathing on our roof.

He brought the towels back, then left for his appointment. What I found amazing was that he didn't need to take a shower because he wasn't sweating at all. And I'm convinced he used a magic potion, because his skin colour had darkened by about three shades. We assumed he must have been 'getting into character' for an audition, but in fact the sun-kissed look was to become his trademark; in the years to come, George became infamous as the perpetually tanned leading man of both big and small screens.

I met Robert L. Green when we appeared on a television show together. Robert taught at the Fashion Institute of Technology (FIT) in New York and we hit it off immediately. A large man with a mellifluous deep voice, hearing him speak reminded me of my London theatre days, listening to the sounds of English being spoken beautifully. To the envy of us all, Robert was also the fashion editor of *Playboy* magazine. He could not have had much to write about as the girls wore very little, but he certainly had some wonderful storylines. To say that Robert was an extrovert would be a gross understatement. Beverly and I found his company exhilarating and the three of us often had dinner together.

Once when I was in Los Angeles, Robert called and told me he was going to take me to a very special place for a Chinese dinner. He picked me up and the car took us to a delightful-looking house in Beverly Hills that bore no resemblance at all to a Chinese restaurant. With a perfectly straight face, Robert proclaimed, 'This is where we stop.'

I was quite puzzled and told him so.

'Wait,' he said, and rang the doorbell. It was answered by the staff of whoever owned the house, and suddenly we were in the kitchen with another man who had his back to us, as he was busy cooking. Robert turned round to me and said, 'Vidal, have you ever met Danny Kaye? He makes the finest Chinese food in town.'

Danny shook my hand and laughed. *This must be a dream* ... I could not believe that Danny Kaye was preparing *me* a meal. I was a great fan and told him how when I was a kid during wartime, I used to sit in the local cinema in the East End of London, watching him do what he did best – make us all laugh. He was without question one of the most popular entertainers to come to Britain and there was never a seat to spare when he played the Palladium in London.

Danny was a master of the wok – and his gentle manner made me feel I had known him much longer than just one evening. We had a great time, and devoured every last morsel of his delicious Chinese meal – a classic dish that had been embellished by the hugely inventive chef in Danny Kaye.

Beverly and I spent five years in New York having children. Catya, Elan and Eden were all born at the Mount Sinai Medical Center in Manhattan, New York, in 1968, 1970 and 1973 respectively. I made a point of being a thoroughly modern father and was in the room when they were delivered. Nothing can prepare you for the birth of a child, for how miraculous and intensely emotional the whole thing is. Holding them in your arms for the first time is quite simply a wonderful feeling. Forty seemed the perfect age for fatherhood. I had sown my wildest oats and the opportunity for bringing up a family with my new wife was what I wanted to do.

Catya, our first-born, was the most gorgeous little creature. She had dark hair and blue eyes, and even as an infant had a smile that could light up my heart – and did. Later, when she was three or four years old, I could not resist passing my last few clients over to other stylists, whisking Catya from her nursery school and walking with her on my shoulders to the carousel in Central Park. I loved stealing time to spend with my little girl, she was so gutsy and full of energy. She learned quickly how to be irresistible. She'd give everything away. One time I noticed the janitor's children at school wearing clothes that looked very familiar. It turned out that Catya had given them hers.

Elan, our second child, was a very handsome boy. Sharing the same birthday as me – 17 January – how could he *not* be? Even when he was in kindergarten, we'd spend our birthday together. All our staff knew never to book me on 17 January, as Elan would have a day off school and we'd spend our time doing whatever he wanted. Even as a youngster, he was a fine athlete and became a football fanatic like his dad. In one game I proudly watched him score three goals. One weekend, I was doing a show out of town and as I arrived home, Elan jumped into my arms and said, 'Dad, you missed my best game. I scored FIVE goals yesterday!'

He was a terrific young athlete but was always getting into fights. One day I was called to his school and the headmaster said, 'If Elan wants to be a boxer, let him join a gym. But I will have no more fighting in school.' He really did learn from this warning as he had no intention of being expelled. I had told Elan never to hit a girl but some time later, he and a girl had an argument at school. She had bashed Elan in the face, and as she was ready to give him more, he started to run, with the girl chasing after him. He ran all the way home and was embarrassed as his friends had seen the whole incident. But Elan did not hit her back and I was very proud of his restraint.

Eden, our third child, was born in June 1973. She had beautiful blue-green eyes and tiny blonde tendrils of hair, which turned into wonderful long curls as she grew older. What a spirit she had! I remember as a young girl she was very shy and reticent to speak her mind. Once, when she was about four, I picked her up from school and Eden blushed to the roots of her hair as she introduced me to one of her teachers. It seemed to take her quite some time to develop a sense of herself. Catya was the dominant one because of her age and personality, but Eden was a different child, reluctant to come forward. Eden was an athlete like her brother, and when she was about nine, she beat her big sister and her friends in a fifty-yard dash. This helped to build her confidence enormously. She was smart enough to take acting classes in high school – not because she particularly wanted to be an actress, but she knew she needed the ability to express herself with confidence. She was shorter than Catya, but every bit as stunning – and far better in her studies, which later stood her in very good stead.

Life in New York was idyllic. Our home wasn't very grand in itself as all the profits we earned went back into the business, but our cosy condominium on the Upper East Side did have a certain charm. We hung the walls with large black-and-white photographs by Cartier-Bresson, Irving Penn and others.

Coming home to a beautiful wife and three small children under five who had energy to spare was something I looked forward to greatly. Beverly had taken a break from her movie career to look after the babies and create a home and she had thrown all her energy into it. The salon was only ten minutes away by foot, and as I walked home through the New York twilight, I forgot about the demanding clients and the bills to be paid, and felt my energy recharge as I reached our front door. Suddenly I was on the floor, with Catya and Elan crawling all over me. Eden, being under six months, was not yet ready for floor-rolling. There was nothing like it, and sometimes I wished they could stay tiny for a little longer.

11

Crimpers' Academy

By the early seventies, New York was at last waking up to what we had to offer. I had slowly built up a considerable clientele. Princess Lee Radziwill – a regular client – would come in for a haircut, always promising that she would bring her sister, the former First Lady Jacqueline Kennedy, with her the next time. Sadly, it never happened. Kenneth Battelle, who had one of the most elegant salons in New York, looked after Mrs Kennedy with great style. But I couldn't really complain. Carol Channing, Suzy Parker, 'Baby Jane' Holzer, Britt Eckland, Sybil Christopher and Carol Bjorkman often frequented our salon. It seemed full of women from the art world, young actresses, models and society ladies who had decided at long last to let their hair down. As the prices in New York were so much higher than in London, it was difficult to encourage young office girls to become regular clients. It happened, but it took longer. Our stylists, colourists, permists and everybody associated with the New York salon were absolutely thrilled at our growth. And to suddenly see so many of our haircuts walking down Madison Avenue was a reward for the tough time we had all had convincing the locals.

Bolstering us even more was the fact that between 1968 and 1972, we had also opened salons in Toronto, Beverly Hills, San Francisco, Chicago and, back home in England, in Manchester.

The expansion happened very quickly once it started. We tended to go with our instincts rather than what the market analysts might be saying. The first branch we opened in North America was in Toronto in 1968. This truly was not part of my original plan, but I had recently met a rather persuasive character by the name of Richard Wookey. Richard had helped developed Yorkville, a hitherto run-down neighbourhood of Toronto, and wanted us to be part of the project. He invited me to Canada to see where the salon would be. I visited the space and fortunately there was no wet cement to walk into. I liked it immediately. It had a vibrancy and a charming village-like feel, even though it was the new centre stage of a great city.

Wookey knew how to sell an idea and within a month of my return to New York, his lawyers and mine had worked out a deal. It turned out to be a very popular decision back at HQ. A lot of our British staff in London who didn't qualify for visa status to the United States were keen to come to Canada and bring our work north of the border.

Training had always been the key to our success and the reason why a Vidal Sassoon haircut was as good in New York as it was in London. Up till then, it had been a strictly in-house affair, but you can't keep a revolution a secret. We wanted the world to know our methods and the philosophy behind them. So many hairdressers from so many different countries wanted to come and study our techniques that we were eventually persuaded by their enthusiasm – and our own desire – to open a training school. It was a very proud moment for me in 1969 when we opened our first Vidal Sassoon Academy in London. We realized that it would have to have the status of one of our salons, so we didn't hide it away in the backstreets. A large ground-floor space in Knightsbridge, just a stone's throw from Harvey Nichols became our teaching headquarters. The highest-quality materials were used to give it the same look and feel as a Vidal Sassoon salon.

Robert Edele had already proved to be an excellent teacher during practice nights, and when I approached him with the idea of getting the ball rolling with the academy – first in London and then, if it was a success, internationally – he loved the idea. He insisted, though, that all the teachers should be top-notch and they would have to come from our salons. I agreed wholeheartedly. Apart from Robert, the first tutor at the academy was a young man named Jason Peller – who just happened to be my cousin (he was my aunt Katie's grandson). Jason had joined us some years before as an apprentice. He was an excellent stylist who also had a gift for teaching.

Our top team – Robert, Roger, Christopher Brooker, Joshua Galvin and I – developed the curriculum for our first training course. Brand-new students would study for one year. Soon after, we introduced a one-week refresher course, which many hairdressers have taken annually from the beginning. Right from day one the academy was hugely popular. After six months, it was obvious that we needed more teachers – and we needed them immediately. I called a general staff meeting of all the stylists in our London salons and let Robert take the floor. Robert's passion for the company was equal to mine, and his ambition to teach the world our way of hairdressing was positively inspiring. He explained that by teaching in the academy over the last six months, his *own* work had improved. Many years previously I'd felt exactly the same when I was teaching Robert Zackham's staff. Robert Edele made his point so eloquently that within a week four stylists had decided that they would like to join the academy as well. Robert, Jason and the rest of the teaching staff shared their skills with all the students, inspiring them to work hard and develop new ideas in cutting and styling hair. Sometimes the ideas were so good we even used them in our shows. And once we'd opened the academy, the business expanded faster and faster. We were able not only to train people but to give them jobs in new salons, which we could now open at a much faster rate.

✧

My friendship with Gene Shacove frequently took me over to the west coast of America and, having conquered New York, I now set my sights on the rather different city of Los Angeles. Gene Shacove was, without question, the number one hairdresser in Beverly Hills. His eye-catching premises on Rodeo Drive had a nightclub called the Candy Store and a clothing outlet selling Gernreich and the work of other exclusive designers on the ground floor – a lift then took you to the first-floor salon. Having built one of the largest clienteles I had seen anywhere, Gene was crazily busy and needed even more space. When he put the salon on the market, we bought it from him. It was the perfect entrée to LA. Much to the delight of the staff, Henry Fonda came to our opening party with his wife, as did Shirley Jones and her husband, Jack Cassidy, Rudi Gernreich, Martha Raye, Stefanie Powers and Hugh O'Brian, to name just a few.

We started with four stylists – Joseph Solomon, Fernando Romero, Nicholas Kardulias and Bernard Daly – and a colourist, John Carlos. We had to struggle, though. The marvellous buzz that Gene had created in that salon had to be built up all over again; every one of his loyal clients left with him. But within a year, we had created something special. The art crowd and the film crowd were a big part of our clientele, but we still encouraged the housewife and the working girl to come to the salon, as we did not ever want to be elitist. Rita Hayworth had come to me when she was in England. Now, in LA, she was a regular client. I had to hide her in the back room, as she didn't want to be seen, but once we were in there, we told each other stories and had great fun. But Hollywood star or secretary, it was always a source of immense satisfaction to give someone a haircut and change their whole appearance.

In 1971, we opened on Grant Street in San Francisco. The staff was divided between stylists who had trained in America and others who had trained in London. San Francisco took to us immediately and within six months the salon was flourishing. Herb Caen, a Pulitzer Prize-winning columnist, worked for the *San Francisco Chronicle* for over half a century. Herb seemed to like me and more than once mentioned the salon in his column, saying we added style to the ladies of San Francisco. One day, he invited me to lunch and told me that a friend of his would be joining us. The friend turned out to be Joel Grey, who had created the role of the MC in *Cabaret*. Joel was wonderful company and the three of us – a writer, an actor and a hairdresser – swapped stories of our journey to the top of our professions, agreeing how hard it was to stay successful in each of our very different businesses. It was a very memorable lunch.

In 1973, we opened our first academy in the United States on Ellis Street in San Francisco. Tony Beckerman, who had moved to New York two years previously as Director of Training USA, became the very first teacher. Tony had been in my life for ever.

He began as my shampoo boy and junior in 1960 in the Bond Street salon, and I wonder if his ankles have ever recovered from the kicking he got as I danced around the chair. In 1962, he became a stylist and, years later, part of our show team that toured the States. We are in constant touch as I write this book, as his excellent memory of the Sassoon adventures jogs my more hapless one.

✧

Bill Fine, who had been publisher of three top Hearst magazines, decided at the age of forty-two to change his career. His decision to take over as president of the department store Bonwit Teller caused a major stir in the fashion industry. He wanted to make Bonwit *the* speciality shop of New York and quickly did. We had known each other only casually when in the spring of 1971 he asked me to open a barbershop at Bonwit Teller. My immediate response was that we were far more interested in beautifying the other sex but he was having none of it. Everything was possible with Bill. He was very well groomed and elegant-looking himself, and simply said, 'Men need beautifying too.'

I thought it would be unwise to give that line out to the press and told him so. But I said I would go back to Madison Avenue and talk with Roger and Laurance to see if it would be at all possible.

Laurance was all for the idea. Roger, on the other hand, made it clear that I would have an uphill struggle persuading the stylists.

He was right. There were very few volunteers – the general feeling was that women's hairdressing was so much more creative. Eventually we found a few who thought the change might be good for them, and special nights of practising short-back-and-sides and crew cuts were set up. In those days, American men were very much more conservative in their appearance than the Brits.

In the autumn the first Vidal Sassoon Barbershop opened at Bonwit Teller with a fashion show featuring cuts, colour and a couple of 'Beatle' looks thrown in. London was green with envy. There was one scene in the show that I especially liked, where two male models and two girls came to the podium with similar looks. This was a trend that would eventually become very popular. In fact, I wore the 'Mia Farrow' myself for many a year. The men's salon created an enormous interest as men were being introduced not only to precision cutting, but to highlights, tinting and perming, too.

When our Madison Avenue stylists saw what was going on at Bonwit, another three volunteers became part of our barber contingent. I suddenly realized how clever Bill Fine was. Men who might never have shopped at Bonwit Teller before left our salon feeling great and then visited other departments to buy presents for their wives, girlfriends or themselves.

It took a while for British boys to cotton on to the fact that the Yanks were getting something they weren't, but as men on both sides of the Atlantic became more interested in their appearance, so the calls to the Bond Street salon for appointments increased. When it was just the occasional enquiry we would make an exception and slip them in at the back, but by the mid-seventies we were getting a handful of calls a day. To accommodate the growing demand, it seemed only natural to open a salon exclusively for men, and so in 1976 we opened a barbershop – suitably masculine in décor – in Brook Street in the heart of the West End. Given this change of direction, it was clear we needed a spectacular opening. It suddenly came to me that we should hark back to a time when male hairstyles had been even more decorative than ladies' hair. I envisaged something large and powdered and slightly absurd. What I needed now were two personalities who would wear the outrageous, eighteen-inch-high wigs I had in mind and be photographed in them for the opening. I was amazed when, after having their arms gently twisted, two good friends gave their thumbs-up to the idea. One was Mary Quant's husband, Alexander Plunket Greene, who was always game for any adventure whether it made sense or not; the other was Dougie Hayward, the now-legendary tailor, who said, 'As long as I can wear one of my suits, you can do whatever you want with my hair.'

The opening had its usual Sassoon pizzazz. There were male models whose hair was beautifully cut with colour and highlights. Two of them even wore the 'Greek Goddess', which had become an androgynous style by then. But what created the real excitement for the press were Dougie and Alexander, who were well known to them, sitting quietly in their ludicrous wigs, conversing seriously with all the airs and graces of eighteenth-century noblemen. The two of them got so fully into character they even managed to look completely bewildered at the fuss they were creating, which just added to the amusement. A number of guests at the opening were so fascinated by the precious pair that after three or four drinks, they wanted to wear the wigs themselves – but Dougie and Alexander were having none of this, as by that time they were having too much fun.

The following day, every newspaper carried a picture of the two of them in full regalia. The opening was a smashing success and, the following morning, the switchboard lit up with calls for appointments. Nobody asked for a wig – but then you can't win them all. Or can you?

✧

Paula Kent founded the hair-care-product company Redken in 1960. By the time I met her in the late sixties it was on its way to becoming a giant. For someone who had originally wanted to be a movie star, I found her passion for business and her innovative approach to hair care inspiring, to say the least. In the summer of 1967, she hired the Vidal Sassoon team to do trade shows for Redken all across America. In the end we worked together for close to two years. Paula would always be with us and under her arm would be the latest business bestseller. She was a natural entrepreneur. Redken was a small company when we worked with her, but eventually she turned it into a multi-million-dollar business. She was gracious to everyone she came into contact with and her sales patter to the wholesale distributors at the end of our shows was magic, seductive – and well worth watching. She *was* a star in a business where she is deeply respected worldwide to this day.

These tours were far from easy and some weekends we'd work three cities. We'd do a Saturday evening show in one city, sleep over, catch an early plane and do a Sunday afternoon show in another city; then we'd fly to our next rendezvous in another town for a Monday afternoon show before heading home. One weekend, owing to a cancelled flight due to extremely bad weather, we were forced to pile on board a charabanc for an all-night ride to our final destination. We pulled into Atlanta at six in the morning, checked into our hotel and the team only got four or five hours' sleep before rising to create a show that, strangely enough, turned out to be one of our very best. Sometimes when you're gaga from lack of sleep, adrenalin and instinct take over and crazy, unexpected things happen.

I'd wanted to get into products for some time and early in 1971 I'd approached Richard Salomon and desperately tried to convince him that a product line would be a good idea. He told me he would love to back it, but Lanvin-Charles of the Ritz was putting all its resources behind Yves Saint Laurent's 'Rive Gauche' perfume and he couldn't finance the two of us at once. It was perfectly reasonable. But he graciously said, 'Vidal, I won't hold you up. If you can create a product line without us, go ahead.'

Seeing what Paula had done with Redken, I was now even more determined than ever to start a product line – and the perfect opportunity soon came along. Joseph Solomon, a bright young man with enormous potential who had started his career with us in New York, was now managing our Beverly Hills salon. Joseph found Don Sullivan, a chemist based in LA, and I flew from New York to Los Angeles for a breakfast meeting at the Beverly Wilshire Hotel. Don brought his wife, and Joe was there to introduce us. We talked about the direction hairdressing was taking, the new styles we were developing and the need for first-class products to help us keep our clients' hair in perfect condition. Don, who had done some truly innovative work for Paula Kent and Redken, was looking for another project. As the meeting went on it became clear that we had an extraordinarily similar outlook. I couldn't help liking Don. He was in LA, like most other young people from across America, waiting to be the next great movie star. But unlike the other wannabes he had a degree in chemistry.

We agreed on almost everything until I asked when he could

move to New York. He laughed. He wasn't moving anywhere. If I wanted us to work together, apparently I would have to move to Los Angeles.

My thoughts were racing as I left the meeting. Beverly and I had done so well in New York. Our work had been accepted there, we loved the city, and the children seemed to be thriving there. But maybe it was time to move on, just as we had left London several years earlier.

I put the question to Beverly. I told her about the meeting with Don and explained the exciting possibilities that working with one of the best minds in the product business would open up for me. She thought it would be wonderful to be close to her family and old friends, so we made the decision to up sticks and relocate.

Beverly found a Spanish-style house on Bedford Drive in Beverly Hills, and in 1975 we moved into its regal splendour. Almost the moment we arrived in LA, new offers came our way, including a commission to write a general health and beauty book. From my earliest days, I'd been a big fan of trying to live as healthily as possible, eating well and exercising regularly. Beverly was the same. We wanted to share our enthusiasm and, with the help of Camille Duhé, we put together our thoughts on diet, grooming, exercise and, of course, hair. Beverly had a passion for yoga and, because she did it so well, a photo session of her in various incredible postures filled three or four pages in the book. *Vogue* jumped on this and asked her to do a feature in a leotard – which she did with great style. Sadly I was not asked to join her. *A Year of Beauty and Health* was a unique book for its time and we travelled the length and breadth of the

United States promoting it. It was a publishing sensation and went to number three on the national bestseller lists.

With hindsight I think the reason the book did so well was because it demonstrated so many ways to *stay* well. We wanted people to think about, and be aware of, their bodies, the exercise they took, the food they ate, and quite simply how to feel good about themselves.

There was another new development in our lives after we moved to LA. We adopted a three-year-old African-American/Asian boy. Why, when we already had three very spirited children? We wanted the kids to share what they had with a boy from a different background, and we wanted to contribute to society in a meaningful way. When we first met David he was living with a foster family. He was a robust, very bright little boy with twinkling eyes and an irresistible smile, and I'll never forget him looking up at us and saying, 'Are you going to be my new mom and dad?' How could we resist? He was adorable. We welcomed him into our home and our lives. Our children adored him and Catya immediately took on a motherly role, which she thoroughly enjoyed, even if he wasn't always so convinced.

He was also quite mischievous. We had a beautiful front lawn on Bedford Drive, where we did lots of entertaining. At a fashion party we held with Rudi Gernreich – Rudi always got lots of publicity and the press seemed to enjoy the English tea party of scones, crumpets, cream cakes and all sorts of things that were very bad for your health – David stood by a window on the second floor and peed out, just missing Johnny Carson's head. Another time he set the bed alight while he was still in it. Elan was very frightened that he could do something so dangerous and I overheard him giving his little brother some good advice: 'Next time, make sure you get out of it first!' Fortunately it didn't happen again.

Elan and David fought all the time. It was a little unfair at the beginning, as Elan was older and stronger. But as David grew up, the fights evened out. Eventually they developed a great relationship, and as a special treat Elan would sometimes allow him to join his buddies on outings. When they were young, David's hero was his big brother. They still remain very close.

❖

Once we were properly settled in LA, and without really trying, suddenly we were moving in showbiz circles. We spent quite a bit of time with George Hamilton and his wife, Alana Collins. One weekend they kindly gave us the keys to their house in Palm Springs. We left the kids with their nanny and drove two hours to the desert, thrilled that we were getting away to the romantic hideaway our friends had told us so much about and would not have to stay at a hotel. But it was not to be. While the house was as rustic and charming as they had described, it seemed that as soon as you touched something it fell apart. Within an hour, the plumbing had broken down and water spilled onto the carpets. I spent the whole of Saturday afternoon looking for a plumber who never came. We left early Sunday morning, promising ourselves that we would never accept invitations to stay at people's houses again unless they were there to look after their own plumbing.

Not long after, I went with George to a health farm in New Mexico. He was not his usual self and it was obvious there was something on his mind that he did not want to talk about. He made it clear he was taking the week to think through his troubles while having treatments of all kinds. Afterwards, I didn't hear from him for a month, but we learned from mutual friends that he and Alana had decided to go their separate ways. Beverly and I were both very surprised because George and Alana were full of zest and fun, and to see them together you would never dream they were having problems.

George was a wonderful storyteller and had a way with language that had he not been an actor, I believe he would have made an excellent writer. Alana went her own way and eventually married another infamous Scot – Rod Stewart.

I can't remember how we met but Tony Bennett and his wife, Sandy, became good friends, too. They gave a Christmas party each year which was full of music and lovely voices. Many of the people who came were not in the business, but Tony had a way of making everybody feel they could sing, and some even surprised us with their hidden talents. Tony's closest friend, Cary Grant, always came and seemed to take a liking to Beverly and me from the start. Once a year he would invite a select group of friends to join him for the horse races at Hollywood Park, where he had a box. Never in my wildest dreams would I have imagined myself included in such company, but suddenly we found ourselves on his list. Needless to say, my mother was beside herself with excitement when I told her. We had the most amazing day at the races and Cary was not only the perfect host, he appeared to have invented the art. And he wasn't charming only to his guests; he would sign autographs for people with a smile and even had little chats with all of them. I thought I treated people with dignity, but in LA I took lessons from the master himself.

Cary became a client of ours as well as a friend, though he never came to the salon on Rodeo Drive. We sent our people to his home once a month. Male and female alike, they would return to the salon in a trance. Charismatic and kind, Cary was a genuinely inspiring man, distinctive in every way.

Fresh from the success of our book tour, we were approached by the producer of a new daily chat show, which was to be called *Monday Through Friday*. Each night's programme was to be hosted by a different couple. Beverly and I were 'Mr and Mrs Wednesday'. After thirteen weeks, guess who topped the ratings? Beverly and me. And so the following season the other hosts were done away with and it became *The Beverly and Vidal Sassoon Show*. It was a tough gig, but because of Beverly's showbiz experience and my natural chutzpah, we had enormous fun ... and then the show was cancelled. Maybe 'Mr and Mrs Thursday' would have done a better job.

Around this time, Beverly began to drink rather heavily. I didn't notice it at first but at some point, the early evening glass of wine became two, then three, then I started to lose count. I'd had no experience with this kind of dependency and felt totally helpless, as I knew my outbursts of frustration were doing no good whatsoever. I was absolutely thriving in America – the excitement and the energy thrilled me. But Beverly seemed to be losing her identity. Los Angeles proved difficult for her. It was the city where she had been groomed for stardom. She had loved that life – one that was cut short by raising our kids – and was now back there, longing to be the young starlet she had once been. She no longer knew who she was or why, and the need to drink became stronger and stronger. Our whole sense of one another had started to deteriorate. We argued more and more and the atmosphere in the house was terrible, to the extent that the children were beginning to ask why.

In the middle of all of this, Mrs Dorothy 'Buffy' Chandler called. Mrs Chandler was *the* mover and shaker in LA life. Her family owned the *Los Angeles Times* and she was visibly involved in the cultural growth of Los Angeles. By bringing in an editorial team with vision and passion, she had done a great deal to raise the standard of the arts in the city. Whether it was theatre, ballet, opera or the orchestra, Mrs Chandler was behind it. She had never phoned me directly before and I felt distinctly nervous when my assistant told me she was on the line.

'Hello, Mrs Chandler, this is Vidal.'

'Haven't you learned to call me "Buffy" yet?'

'Hmm ... how much trouble am I in?'

'Lots,' she said. 'Margot Fonteyn and the Royal Ballet are coming to town. After opening night, there will be a big party for the whole company, and also many of the Los Angeles ballet fans.'

'Yes ...?'

'And you and Beverly are giving the party at your house.'

'*We are?* Thank you for the honour.'

We hired two companies – one to put up a marquee, which covered the garden, and one to prepare and serve delicious food that we hoped would not be easily forgotten. The ballet was performed at the Dorothy Chandler Pavilion, in downtown Los Angeles. Fonteyn was in her fifties, but her dancing was still superb. Nureyev was not with her that evening but the male lead, Anthony Dowell, danced with extraordinary strength and beauty. Beverly and I were in seats that allowed us to slip out unnoticed before the final curtain. A car was waiting and we arrived home well before our guests. Beverly promised me she would not drink that evening, and to my surprise kept her word, even though the temptation must have been enormous.

We had been asked to greet everyone at the front door. An hour after all the other guests had arrived, Margot Fonteyn, Anthony Dowell and the whole of the Royal Ballet Company made a grand entrance; nobody knew how to do it better than they did. The paparazzi knew our house quite well, but on this occasion were asked by the Royal Ballet to only take pictures outside. This pleased many of Buffy Chandler's A-list guests, not least Shirley MacLaine, a great lover of dance, but who did not want to be bothered by flashing bulbs all evening long.

Suddenly Beverly and I realized we were dealing with a rather unexpected situation. To our surprise, Fonteyn, this extraordinary woman whose posture on stage was superb, could hardly walk by herself. Whether she had pulled a muscle or had put so much into the dance that she was left listless, we will never know. But it was our job to introduce her to the 150 people or more who were gathered in the marquee, and I remember distinctly holding her arm quite firmly as she tried so hard not to appear damaged in any way. Fonteyn stayed for an hour and a half and then left for her bed. For the other guests the evening turned into night and then early morning before the party broke up. It was a great success and it also marked a brief improvement in my marital problems.

✧

In 1977, I was asked to be one of twelve judges for the Miss Universe pageant, which was to be held in the Dominican Republic. The other judges formed an eclectic group. Apart from actress Linda Cristal, former Miss Universe Marisol Malaret, film producer Howard W. Koch and the flamenco guitarist Armando Bermudez, there were Gordon Parks, the African-American writer and photo-journalist turned film maker, who had recently directed *Shaft*; Dionne Warwick, multiple Grammy-Award-winning singer, who was a favourite client of mine and an absolute delight; Yuri Geller, who could bend spoons with his mind; the fashion designers Oscar de la Renta and Roberto Cavalli; Wilhelmina Cooper, whose modelling agency seemed to represent half the top models in the world; and Robert Evans, film producer and general man-about-town. It looked rather a fun list to be on, so with little hesitation I said yes.

Miss Universe was in its heyday in 1977; an over-the-top confection of a beauty pageant that simultaneously took a certain amount of moral high ground. It was more than just gorgeous girls; it was about culture. Televised globally each year, millions of people tuned in worldwide, praying that the representative from their country would win. There was always much interest in the girl who became Miss Universe, and all of us judges took our responsibilities quite seriously. Our year was the usual formula – a bevy of lovely girls, the swimsuit parade followed by evening gowns – but when it came to the final judging, something dynamic happened that thrilled us all: Janelle Commissiong, a ravishing girl from the Caribbean, took the crown. She was Miss Trinidad-Tobago and the first black girl in the history of the pageant ever to become Miss Universe. The final verdict of the jury left me ecstatic, as she had been my number one choice. Dionne Warwick was out of her mind with joy. Gordon Parks, who had been a friend of mine for many years, turned to me and asked, 'Why did it take so long for this to happen?'

The same year, Beverly and I went to the Inauguration of President Jimmy Carter, followed by a function at the White House – a first for both of us. Simcha Dinitz, the Israeli Ambassador to the United States, was there with his wife, Vivian. We had met them at a cocktail party the night before and Simcha and I had an opportunity at the White House to really talk to one another. I respected him immediately. He had a wonderful sense of humour, which must have served him well in the corridors of power.

Two years later, Henry and Nancy Kissinger gave a big party for Simcha in New York and I was invited. I had to look twice to make sure I had not been sent the invitation by mistake. When the day came I duly flew to New York and, after freshening up at the hotel, took a cab to the Kissingers'. Security was very tight, but to my relief they did have my name on their list and after a quick body search, they let me in.

It was quite a party. I don't think I'd ever been in a room containing so many of the political elite. At one point, Simcha invited me into a little huddle with Henry Kissinger, who was, I believe, quite surprised that a hairdresser had come to his apartment.

One day, a Jewish organization in Los Angeles called out of the blue and asked me if I knew Elizabeth Taylor. I said yes, though I didn't know her well. I had met her through Alexandre in Paris, but why did they ask?

It turned out they had the most bizarre plan – to send Elizabeth Taylor to the Middle East to make peace between the Arabs and Israelis, and would I contact her as they didn't know her at all? I called her and she was completely taken with the whole idea. Two months later, I got another call from the same people. Liz Taylor was leaving the following day for Jerusalem and could I please be at the airport to make her feel comfortable?

On arrival, I was escorted to a special lounge where Elizabeth was preparing her notes for a pre-flight press conference.

She gave me a hug and, pulling a brush from her bag, said, 'You know a little bit about hair. Do something!' So there I was, in a lounge at Los Angeles International Airport, teasing Elizabeth Taylor's hair piled high on top of her head. Her trademark style was an affront to everything I had ever stood for, but I found I was enjoying myself, pulling tendrils of hair around her face. It seemed to suit the occasion perfectly. When I'd finished, we both looked into the mirror and smiled. She took the brush from me and squeezed my hand. She looked like Elizabeth Taylor!

Eventually we all moved through to a much larger room, which was full of press and various dignitaries from both politics and the film world who were no doubt wondering, as were we all, how on earth Elizabeth Taylor was going to bring peace to the Middle East, where so many others had failed. She gave a rather nice little speech and explained that it was going to be done with her charm, beauty and intellect. I, who had no seat assigned, stood at the back of the room, listening with bated breath. As Elizabeth finished her speech, she answered questions from a nonplussed press, after which the audience broke out in wild applause – though I'm not sure if it was for her words or the courage of her commitment. She then spotted me at the back of the room, walked up, kissed me on both cheeks and said, 'Thank you, Vidal,' then glided out to board her plane with the rest of her entourage.

I called Simcha and told him about my contribution to the peace process. He laughed for nearly a minute, then said, '*Really?* Well, I'm her Israeli liaison. I'm to pick her up at Ben Gurion Airport and introduce her to all the political whizz kids, both Israeli and Arab.' I asked him to let me know how the show developed.

He called me a couple days later and said that Elizabeth had taken her responsibility very seriously, and charmed everyone she met. Not surprisingly, though, like many world leaders before her, she did not accomplish her mission.

This stranger-than-fiction episode brought Simcha and me even closer and we remained good friends for many years. Whenever we visited Israel, the Dinitzes would be among the first people we called on. One evening at dinner, one of Simcha's closest colleagues told us the story of how, years earlier, he had gone with Golda Meir to a clandestine meeting in the desert where they met with King Abdullah of Jordan to discuss the possibilities of permanent peace. Whenever we were at Simcha and Vivian's we learned something new about the birth and survival of the state of Israel by people who had been part of it.

It was the second week of January 1978, and I was on the road. I wanted to be home by the 16th to spend my fiftieth birthday with the family. When I was on tour I would occasionally call the office but this time, whenever I called, everyone sounded strange. I felt something was going on back home, but didn't know what. And when I arrived home on the 16th, George Shaw, my dear friend whose brilliant PR skills made me look good to the outside world, was there with the family. After the hugs and kisses with Beverly and the kids, he said, 'Sorry to surprise you, but we've organized a small dinner party for tomorrow evening – black tie.' Nobody in Los Angeles gives a small dinner party with black tie, and I hunted around for the truth of what was to come – but to no avail.

At eight o'clock the following evening, the family and I were picked up by a limo and taken to the Beverly Wilshire Hotel. George led the family to the main ballroom, which was packed with people. Suddenly everyone stopped talking and this great sound from the stage took me utterly by surprise. The company had hired the Count Basie Orchestra – led by Count Basie himself – for my fiftieth birthday! It seemed as if half of Hollywood was there. Who were they? Where had they all come from? Of the 750 people who were there, 650 I never saw again. But I wasn't quibbling; it was a small and intimate party LA-style, and what a night we had! We ate, drank, danced and jitterbugged, and swung to the beat into the early morning hours. I knew then that I was the luckiest kid who had ever come out of an orphanage.

Many touching tributes were given. For me, one of the most memorable remarks was by the Count himself, who asked me when they could play this gig again.

✧

Our offices were in Century City, a few minutes' walk from Beverly Hills. One day George Shaw rushed into my office and said that he just taken a call from the police. Our San Francisco school had been blown up the night before. The damage was extensive. Thankfully, no one was in the building at the time. He went on to say that the police had no idea who had done it, but they were investigating.

I couldn't imagine that I had an enemy out there who would blow up an establishment for teaching young hairdressers their craft.

The following day a call came through to our offices. My secretary said, 'There's somebody from the police who would like to talk to you about the San Francisco bombing.'

I picked up the phone.

I will never forget that next moment. A man whose voice I did not recognize said in a conversational tone, 'We got your school. Now we're going to get you.' The line went dead. I went cold. It's a very strange feeling being told that you're going to die by a stranger you can't see. I sat down feeling slightly nauseous and called George into my office. I told him what had just happened. I said I wanted it kept out of the news. He knew by the look on my face that this was no joke.

For the next nine months, five Los Angeles policemen took turns being by my side. Sergeant Jim McGarry was in charge of the case, and – thanks to him – my family and I had a wonderfully close relationship with the LAPD. Gene Fogerty had the sternest look but the kindest heart. Ken Henderson, Tom Andrews and Tom Wyatt were all experienced policemen. They were tough and very able, and I trusted them implicitly.

After the first week of getting acquainted, I gave the law the run of the house. I told them that if they were hungry to help themselves from the fridge. The main thing as far as I was concerned was that they looked out for the safety of my wife and kids.

About three months after the first call, Gene and I were walking through Century City when he said quietly, 'There's a man walking towards us, packing a gun. Walk and talk normally.' Gene already had his hand on the inside of his coat, and said very convincingly, 'He'll get the first bullet.'

I did not want Gene or me to get the second one.

The man walked past us but Gene's eye never left him, as he slowly turned and watched until whoever it was walked out of sight. Gene reported this incident to Sergeant McGarry, who immediately decided that in future, one man would walk with me and another twenty yards behind.

With so much going on in the business, this was a drama I could very well have done without. But Gene looked as though he was enjoying every moment of it – recounting tales of his gunfights and the medals of honour he had earned.

Six months later, the threat just seemed to fade away. There were no more phone calls, but we kept in touch with our LAPD buddies. In the nine months they'd been with us, they had almost become family.

Life appeared to have quietened down. But then one day I was in the garden playing football with Elan when Tisha, our children's nanny, came to me and said, 'Mrs Sassoon would like to see you.'

I went inside. Beverly looked at me and said four words, 'I want a divorce.' Although I didn't show it, a sense of calm came over me. No more frosty telephone calls, tense dinner parties or late-night arguments. We had spent thirteen years together and the last three or four of those had been far from harmonious. All I could think was, *What a relief not to have to live this way*.

I left her at the house and took a flat on Wilshire Boulevard with four bedrooms – enough for all the children to visit me. I was alone but the agony had stopped.

Why did a marriage so good in London and New York fall apart in Los Angeles? How could this have happened to *us*? We had been so much in love. I wondered about the times that I was away doing shows, creating publicity, opening salons and overseeing the business at large. Had it been worth building an empire to lose a family?

When I broke the news to the kids, they were shocked but had been aware that things were not quite right between us. The house had been an unhappy one for some time. When I moved out to the new flat they stayed with me often, but something was missing in their lives, too. The sadness of it all gave me many sleepless nights and I began to make bad decisions with Vidal Sassoon, Inc., which over time I grew to regret.

Not long after we separated, at a time when I was feeling rather adrift, I invited some long-time friends to join me for dinner – Tony Newley and his wife, Dareth, and Jack Klugman, who also brought a girlfriend. I of course went alone. We were at the Bistro restaurant in Beverly Hills when suddenly there was a cacophony of sound as twelve people arrived and were seated at the next table. Tony and Jack knew most of them and said hello. Zsa Zsa Gabor, who seemed to be hosting, came over to our table, gave Tony a kiss, Jack a kiss and me a look of disdain. 'Give her diamonds, give her furs, but get her back.' With that she turned her back on me for the rest of the meal.

Despite all this, the five of us had a nice evening, some great conversation and a wonderful dinner. Tony and Jack were sensitive to my newly single condition and each seemed to give me an especially warm hug as we said goodnight and left. The restaurant valet had brought my car round – a shiny black Roller. When I was young, it had been the dream of every ambitious kid who lived in our neighbourhood to one day own a Rolls-Royce – and I was no exception. Every time I got behind the wheel, I had to pinch myself to believe that it was really mine. I got in the car and drove off. A few minutes later I started looking for some music to play and suddenly realized this was not my car. I immediately turned back towards the Bistro. It must have taken me all of fifteen minutes, but as I pulled up in front of the restaurant, there was an extremely agitated Zsa Zsa, screaming, 'No wonder she left you. You are a thief!'

It turned out I wasn't the only one who had some rather plush black wheels. I apologized profusely and eventually Zsa Zsa calmed down and accepted my apologies. Not long after that I traded the Rolls-Royce in. It was far too ostentatious for me.

After Beverly and I were divorced, Gene Shacove called me up and said, 'You're spending too much time alone. Neil Sloane and I are picking you up in half an hour and we're going to Hef's.' Neil Sloane was without question one of the top hairdressers on the West Coast, and the two of them had decided that the only solution to my monk-like existence was an evening at the Playboy Mansion.

I had been introduced to Hugh Hefner a decade or more ago by a mutual friend – Hugh O'Brian, the star of the TV series *Wyatt Earp*, who had called me up with a rather intriguing invitation. 'Hef would like to see you at the Chicago Playboy Mansion. Are you available?'

I told him that it would be a pleasure.

At the arranged time, Hugh took me to meet the great man himself. We were taken by a bunny into Hef's inner sanctum. He offered us a chair and a drink and though he was more than friendly, his attitude was all business. He had plans for expansion and asked me if I would be interested in opening barbershops in the Playboy clubs nationwide. After I left the meeting and thought it through, the idea of training a hundred or so barbers and neglecting the plans we had already set in motion for ourselves didn't seem to sit well with me. I think Hef must have felt the same way, as the idea never got beyond our first meeting. Nevertheless, when he moved his whole organization to Los Angeles a few years later, my name was on his list as a welcome guest at the mansion.

Hef was very careful about whom he allowed in, and the guests knew that no drugs of any kind were permitted. You came in, had drinks, conversation, dinner, a movie in Hef's rather grand theatre, and you left – either with a girl you had just made your acquaintance with or alone.

As the boys and I were entering the mansion that night in 1980, Hef took me aside and said, 'Use this as your halfway house.' His generosity and kindness were hard to repay as Hef never left the mansion, but for many years we'd send VS hair products round for him and his bunnies to enjoy.

Several years after Beverly and I were divorced she began dating a Spanish bullfighter. George Shaw and I were in Chicago when a call came through. George looked at me, and said, 'I'm not sure you want to take this. It's the manager of that bullfighter Beverly has been hanging out with.'

I took the call. A man whom I'd never spoken to before told me that his bullfighter had married my ex-wife the night before. But they would keep it secret if I would pass over a large chunk of cash. I knew Beverly had nothing to do with this; it was not her style. I started to laugh. I said, 'Give it to the newspapers and television news channels! Send it across the wires. It has absolutely nothing to do with me whatsoever! Too bad you had to pay for this phone call.'

When Beverly heard about the call, it opened her eyes. Her moment of clarity came with such force that she returned to LA alone, determined to start a new life. It took years before she could straighten herself out, but eventually, thank goodness, she did.

12

'If You Don't Look Good, We Don't Look Good'

In 1973 we took America by storm with the launch of our three-step system of hair products. Unlike many salon brands, which took time to build, ours was an instant winner. The shampoo was gentle, but had a lather that cleaned the hair beautifully. The instant conditioner left the hair feeling silky, with a sexy shine. But, for me, the truly inspired product – thanks to Don Sullivan's magic – was the ultimate conditioner. It could be left on for an hour or two, even all day, and it made the hair feel thicker, as if it had absorbed the product. Each product had an almond scent, which we chose after testing many other fragrances. Don assured me that this delicious fragrance would appeal to the clients' senses, making them more open to the stylist's suggestions.

The history of the Brown Line, as it was called – because the packaging *was* brown – goes back to 171 New Bond Street. A very close friend, Eugene Howe – the same man who redecorated my flat after it was decimated by a wild party – had a superb eye for shape and colour, and when we decided to do a revamp of the salon in the early seventies, I consulted with him. Eugene suggested painting the salon a subtle chocolate brown, including the reception area, which would have silver bars running from ceiling to floor, while the picture frames would be – guess what colour? He didn't have to tell me.

I wasn't entirely convinced and gave Eugene's brown decorative scheme much thought, but his enthusiasm won me over and we went ahead. To say that it was a success would be an understatement. Eugene's chic, stylish new look for the salon made a statement about Vidal Sassoon and gave us our long-term branding. It therefore made complete sense to me that our first product line should also be a subtle chocolate brown – and it remained so for many years to come. The bottle design was simple: a brown oval tube with very clean silver lettering. We thought long and hard about the advertising campaign and decided to complement the bottles with rich chocolate-brown packaging, so that our product would stand out in the stores.

During this early gestation period the team and I were in New Orleans doing a show. Laurance Taylor walked into the dressing room with a chap he had told me I would be interested in meeting. That was an understatement. Peter Rogers was the most innovative advertising agent of his time and something of a whizz, having coined the brilliant marketing slogan *What becomes a legend most?* for Blackglama, the renowned fur-coat company. His annual campaign featured some of the biggest names in film and showbiz, including Marlene Dietrich, Claudette Colbert, Barbra Streisand, Diana Ross and Judy Garland, to name just a few.

I carried on cutting a model's hair while Peter crossed the room. He smiled at me and said, 'If you don't look good, we don't look good.'

I stopped in my tracks. It was perfect. Without any further preamble, I simply said, 'You've got the job.' He had got straight to the heart of the matter. Those few words were the slogan that we would run with, and it undoubtedly proved to be one of the main ingredients in our success. When Peter later told me that Andy Warhol would be doing an *If you don't look good, we don't look good* ad for us, I could hardly believe it until I actually saw it in the magazines. I was amazed. Andy Warhol – *how did Peter do it?*

At first we only sold our products to other hairdressers, via wholesale distributors. Word spread via the big hairdressing shows at which our team appeared, using our products. They attracted a thousand, sometimes two thousand hairdressers together at a time. If a ticket to the show cost fifty dollars, the wholesalers would give the stylists fifty dollars' worth of Brown Line VS products in a gift bag upon arrival. The hairdressers would take the products, try them on their families and in their salons, and the orders would come rolling in.

Don Sullivan was the obvious choice to be the spokesperson for the range. He'd developed the products but was no back-room boy. Good-looking and charming, Don had a masterly way of blending science and sales patter and could talk product like no one else. He always had a touch of Hollywood about him, pitching the three-step system in the same magical way that Jackie Joseph had sold his lingerie in Petticoat Lane. As our team cut the models' hair, each snip of the scissors was captured on large screens. That was the draw, of course. Most of the crimpers at the shows had come to study our cutting techniques. But they were curious about the products, too, and once they tried them, they were hooked.

They also enjoyed the profits from the products they were selling. Their clients were happy, too. Much to our surprise, we were sent hundreds of letters of congratulations and thanks. One woman wrote, 'The stuff I have on the top of my head actually looks like hair for the first time in my life.' Not only were we changing the way hair looked, but we were making a distinct and definite statement about the importance of quality product. It was not a miracle cure for a disease, but it made so many people happy. I was thrilled by the reaction, and I had an extra spring in my step as I danced around the chair, cutting hair.

The new product line's growth was astronomical. We had set a rather conservative sales goal for the first year. We doubled it. And by the third year we had a built a very dynamic products company.

❖

In the early seventies, Tommy Yeardye joined the company. I had known Tommy for years. He was a good-looking man and had worked as a stunt double for actors like Victor Mature and had had a pretty racy past, including having a highly publicized affair with Diana Dors. Now, like many of us, he'd put his wild days behind him and was working for the hair-salon operator Glemby Company, learning how to make profits in the hairdressing business. With the high percentages hairdressers were earning and the general expenses involved in running hair salons, it was extremely tough for Glemby to make a 5 per cent bottom line. The company was chaired by Seymour Finkelstein, whose brother, Nathan, was also in the business; they had briefly shown an interest in becoming partners with us but nothing came of it.

Tommy, however, was still keen and after he'd been with Glemby for a few years, we had a meeting in London. He was brilliant with figures and really knew how to produce bottom-line profits. We went into partnership. I gave him the opportunity to oversee and open salons in Europe, and he ran with it. From 1972 onwards, for almost a decade, he opened numerous salons and became hugely successful. Our profits had never been so healthy. I didn't even mind when Tommy bought himself a company car – a Rolls-Royce – and only told me after he'd bought it. He deserved it.

In 1972, Tommy found a property on King Street in Manchester and thought it was the perfect location for a salon. He called me, describing the building – three storeys, large and light. It sounded wonderful. I was in New York at the time and I trusted him so completely that I just gave him the go-ahead, telling him that I would see him at the opening.

The salon had beautifully designed large windows looking out onto the street. The stylists could work on both the ground and the first floor, and colour and perming would be done on the second. We'd never had so much space and despite having opened salons in Chicago and San Francisco the previous year, our school had had so many students that we could provide all the fully trained staff needed for this new salon. I liked Manchester. It wasn't London – but didn't want to be. It was the fashionable heart of the north of England, and the area that our salon was in had great atmosphere, with boutiques and well-known shops all around.

The opening in King Street was pretty wild. Everybody wanted to be there, but British fire regulations were quite strict. Three very tough-looking rugby players stood at the door blocking entrance to anyone without an invitation. I didn't have one and they didn't let *me* in until I was finally recognized. I got a good chuckle out of that.

The hairdressing staff at King Street were a very positive bunch and were soon challenging Bond Street to be number one.

In due course they turned out some fine session work of their own and their loyalty to the organization was second to none. And of course there was also Manchester United Football Club. I would spend three or four days at a time in the city and tried to arrange my trips when United had a home game. Tickets were difficult to get, but fortunately I had a friend who had a friend in the club, and I saw some exciting football.

There's a saying in the North that 'Where there's muck there's brass', and while working at the salon, I fell in with a group of wealthy young Manchester lads who decided they wanted to take me clubbing one Saturday night. I couldn't believe it when not one, not two, not three, but four new Rolls-Royces turned up at my hotel. I thought I must be seeing things. *Each of these lads has a Roller?* I had the good sense not to ask them what they did for a living, but it was clearly lucrative. We visited three clubs that evening and had a ball. My only problem was whose wheels to ride in without offending the others.

The following year, 1973, marked an extraordinary breakthrough for the business. I left the frenzy of product publicity and back-to-back hair shows in the States for London, where I found Tommy Yeardye full of plans for expansion into the untried territory of Germany. He had found beautiful premises in Munich for our first salon on the Odeonsplatz, a very prestigious street. As we looked over the estate agent's details, he showed me that at the back of the building were wonderful gardens that seemed to stretch on endlessly. I noticed Tommy was working quite hard on his sales pitch. It turned out that he was worried that because I was Jewish, going into Germany might be difficult for me. I had no problems with that. Showing Germany why we were the best was a challenge I couldn't resist.

Six months later we opened on the Odeonsplatz. The launch was very different from any other we had had. Various German magazines and newspapers interviewed me prior to the opening and focused on my involvement in the anti-fascist 43 Group, my time in the Israeli Army and my happiness that there were twenty miles of English Channel between Britain and Europe during the Nazi era. I did not hold back, and they printed everything. I suddenly worried that my forthright manner might destroy the salon before it had even opened, but Germany had changed hugely and we had a spectacular opening-night party. Apart from the press, it was packed with stars, high society and all manner of colourful individuals. To my amazement, there was no animosity towards me at all. People were even congratulating me on the press stories. There was only one incident that could have been ugly. I was approached by a man who was not smiling, who said, 'I was a soldier on the Eastern Front and had nothing to do with the atrocities. Your stories hurt.'

I met his eyes and felt very sad for him.

Opening day at the salon was a revelation, too. We had three gorgeous-looking girls on reception who spoke German and English. They were answering telephones and as soon as they put one down, it would ring again. We had chosen Gerald Battle-Welsh, a young English lad who had worked with me in London, to manage the Munich salon and he was looking forward to the challenge of building a clientele there. He didn't have to. Munich, from day one, was as busy as Bond Street. No other salon anywhere had opened with such a ready-made demand for our work. Tommy's choice of location had turned out to be totally inspired. Since that day, we have opened four other salons in Germany, in Berlin, Hamburg, Düsseldorf and Frankfurt.

Gerald was a great all-rounder: a superb chess player, a lover of the arts and an excellent manager. He trained fantastic teams, and if he needed extra staff – which he often did – they would fly in from Britain. Gerald married an English girl, Nicola, who had been one of his stylists. They eventually moved to Hamburg and he ran the German operation from there. He is still out there now, in 2010, doing what he went there to do – make the VS salons a success.

That Germany became the huge player it did for the company was also down to my right-hand PR lady, Ruth Lynam. She had worked with the fashion designer Jean Muir for many years and had also been a journalist on the *Daily Telegraph*. Ruth was a feisty colleague and an outspoken critic of anything that didn't suit her sense of propriety or aesthetics. She would travel with me when necessary and did masterful work with the openings of the German salons. She had an aristocratic bearing and enjoyed the adventure of being with us. We became good friends and I always listened to her constructive criticism. The company had never had anybody quite like Ruth before; she was frightfully posh and well connected. She would host wonderful Sunday evening dinner parties at her house in Islington.

I had got to the stage in my career where I felt totally comfortable whatever class of people I was with. The sixties had put paid to so many of the English class divisions, though there is no doubt that Ruth's dinner table included far more members of the upper echelons than most. As I spent more and more time in America, I sadly saw less and less of Ruth – but when I was in London, I made it my business to take her to the theatre and for dinner afterwards.

❖

After the great success of the Munich opening in 1973, Gerald Battle-Welsh made it clear that we were missing a great opportunity by not being in Hamburg as well – so in 1976, we finally got there. The Hamburg opening on 31 August that year didn't receive the enormous amount of publicity that we'd received in Munich, but after that grand opening, we didn't expect it to. Nonetheless, Hamburg got its share of good press and our opening there had its own delightful flavour. Ruth Lynam and Tommy Yeardye had come with me from London and it was soon clear to all three of us that Gerald had more than proved his point – the receptionists were busy taking appointments even on the opening night. We left the salon that evening in a very happy frame of mind.

An hour later, back at the hotel, Tommy said to me, 'Take a seat, Vidal. I've got some news for you. Ivor died today in London of a massive coronary.'

Apart from the shock of hearing such tragic news, my mind was filled with so many images of my brother: our days and nights at the orphanage, his struggle for an education and the pride the family all felt when he became a chartered accountant. I knew I would miss him in so many ways, as he was involved in every area of my life. He had not only helped me to negotiate every aspect of our business, but he was there to celebrate the joys of success with me, as well. I knew my life could not possibly be the same without my little brother. It was a very sad time for me.

Following his triumphs in Europe, Tommy Yeardye decided he would like to try his hand at the United States. I liked Tommy enormously and wanted to give him a shot at his dream, and he did appear to have something of the Midas touch. But what could he actually do in America? I faced a dilemma. Joe Solomon, who was running the product side of the business, was doing a very good job. Tommy's idea was to franchise the Vidal Sassoon name to a hundred or more different salons across the country. The salon would pay a fee to use the name, as well as a percentage of gross income, providing much-needed cash flow.

The international artistic team was nervous about the idea from the start. They feared that franchising salons would bring down the standard of work, as it would be impossible to train so many people in such a short time. And how would it impact on the thousands of salons who were not directly involved with our franchise? Would they reject Sassoon product and buy elsewhere? Tommy came to the States, bringing his family, and he and his team worked for months exploring the franchise idea in detail. But then a truckload of Vidal Sassoon products went missing and suddenly turned up in stores halfway across the country – and the public couldn't get enough of them. There was uproar in the trade, as people thought that we were being opportunistic and breaking our word that we'd sell exclusively in salons. Salons up and down the United States cancelled their orders.

We had a big decision to make. We loved the hairdressing craft and wanted our products in salons, where they were doing extremely well and making all involved a healthy profit. But once we'd seen the demand for them on the high street, we felt we had to start selling the products direct to the public. We couldn't do that and roll out a franchise operation. I was very unpopular within the hairdressing community for a year or two. There were a few months of unsettling rumblings, and one salon sued, though we settled amicably. But ultimately we were forgiven – other hairdressers realized just what the Vidal Sassoon team had given them. For some, we had changed their lives. Many hairdressers have said to me over the years, 'You helped put my kids through college,' or, 'Learning how to create your haircuts paid for my house.'

I had a long, heartfelt chat with Tommy, who wasn't prepared just to run US salons. The job wasn't big enough for him and he decided to leave the company and go back to England. I understood fully but was disappointed – Tommy had one of the best business minds of anybody I had met.

He later proved this by investing in a brilliant London-based shoe designer, Jimmy Choo, and turning it into a huge success. It was his daughter Tamara's suggestion; she turned out to be just as bright and focused as he was. And although Tommy passed away in 2004, Tamara has made Jimmy Choo even more successful. I've known her since she was a child. She has grown up to be a very beautiful young woman and an enormously successful one. Her celebrity has not diminished the lovely child I used to know.

When Tommy Yeardye moved to the States in 1975 we replaced him with one of our more unusual apprentices – Felicity Green. Felicity was a journalist's journalist. Since her time as my shampoo girl at Ungaro I had watched with pride as she shot up through the ranks to make it onto the board at the *Daily Mirror*. She was an absolute powerhouse. We had remained close friends over the years and when Tommy crossed the Atlantic she took up the offer to join us in London as managing director. She remained as stylish and creative as ever but it was immediately clear that in putting her in the boardroom, we had taken a great lady out of her element. She had no training in running salons but in the years she worked for us did a good job nevertheless. Eventually, however, she realized that her passion was Fleet Street and she was welcomed home to the newspaper business with open arms. Seeing her several months later surrounded by her press associates and peers, I appreciated how much she had given up to join us. But once she left us, she didn't miss a beat – and was soon once again one of the most powerful people in journalism.

✧

At the start of the seventies our business was creating a real buzz and the excitement spread to the City. The investment banker Joseph Sebag wanted to know how we did business. An arrangement was made for me to go to the City and have lunch with, among others, Sandy Gilmour, then chairman of Sebag's. I had always thought of City bigwigs as pillars of the Establishment, hell-bent on keeping people like me out. But upon meeting Sandy, that illusion was quickly stripped away. Sandy was something else. He was young, slim, had sandy-coloured hair, and was full of the joys of his job – which included helping to develop small companies like mine. I was aware that we were close to outgrowing our relationship with the Lanvin-Charles of the Ritz organization and Sandy could be just the man to help us. He had an eye for a deal, and his idea at that moment was to find private backers, who would give us much-needed development cash in return for a piece of the Sassoon pie.

Three months later, in 1971, Sebag's became our partner. Sandy went about selling Vidal Sassoon shares at $3.50 apiece to his clients, one of whom was his brother, Ian Gilmour, who later became a member of Mrs Thatcher's Cabinet. Sandy took a seat on our board and brought in a great friend of his, John Menzies, a fellow Scot who had built one of the largest newsagent chains in Britain. Sandy and his wife would occasionally invite me to weekends in the country, where they lived in a great style.

Sandy and John loved coming out to Los Angeles for board meetings. They never missed one in the winter, when it was gloomy back home, but in the summer would often send their love. It was the friendliest of business relationships and their advice was frequently acted upon. It was a sad day for me when I heard that Sandy and Sebag's had parted company, as the money he had raised from the initial sale of those shares was used to open VS salons across America. The private placement cash from Sebag's also helped us buy our way out of our Lanvin-Charles of the Ritz responsibility. Again, Richard Salomon could not have been more reasonable, as he had suggested we move on. 'Keep in touch,' he said. 'One never knows what lies ahead.'

Stephen Weinrib, of the law firm Franklin & Weinrib, handled the settlement. I had a meeting with him before his first contact with Lanvin-Charles. He was another of those quite extraordinary characters that I met in New York City. I explained that I was absolutely stretched financially across the business and since the separation process from our former partners could go on for a while, it might be some time before I could pay him.

His reply was, 'Don't worry. One day you will.'

I wondered what it was about those New Yorkers I'd met. I was told they were terrible to do business with, but all I found was a depth of generosity and a willingness to take a chance on my future. Stephen Weinrib became so involved with the Vidal Sassoon organization that in due course he left his own firm to join us as legal counsel.

✧

Curling tongs, hairdryers, hair straighteners; for years we had relied on the same companies to supply the salons with the necessary tools of the trade. Just as a few years before I had toyed with the idea of a range of shampoos and conditioners, now I began to daydream about putting my name to a range of well-designed electrical goods.

Helen of Troy, a company that specialized in professional-quality hairstyling tools, had been founded by Louis Rubin in 1969. By 1978, it had cultivated a 25 per cent niche in the market with its hairdryers and curling irons and Louis Rubin handed over the company to his son, Gerald. Although this $6-million business was marginally profitable, it was clear that Helen of Troy needed a boost – it needed an edge in this increasingly crowded market.

When Louis discovered that I was seeking to extend the VS brand into styling tools, he saw a possible solution, and in 1980 Gerald, on his father's recommendation, approached the company about a licence. He ended up in a bidding war with two giants – Gillette and General Electric – but I personally liked the dealings I'd had so far with the Rubin family and found it far more appealing to deal with a small company in El Paso, Texas, than to get lost in the bureaucracy of an enormous corporation. The Rubin family appealed to me because they wanted the business so much. A deal was struck with Helen of Troy.

It seemed to work. Eighteen months later, in 1983, the company had rebounded from the $1.1 million loss it had sustained in 1980 to a profit of $1.8 million. Gerry was motivated by this success to look for a chunk of cash to create real growth, and so on Gerry's behalf I went to see the entrepreneur/financier Michael Milken. I told Michael that with an infusion of cash, Helen of Troy would never look back. Michael was interested and I went with one of his top people to El Paso and an arrangement was made for Helen of Troy to receive $20 million. Raising funds for small businesses was not my usual line of work, but it was rewarding in many ways to help a little company take on the big boys.

In a recent conversation with Gerry in 2009 he told me that his Sassoon business had topped $150 million in the United States and Canada that fiscal year alone. Helen of Troy is now a very substantial company with many streams of income, of which the Sassoon products are slightly less than 25 per cent. But I personally am very grateful that I managed to help at a time when they needed it most, and that my instincts, at least where the Rubin family were concerned, turned out to be absolutely spot on.

I'd made some small mistakes over the years, but my first big one came when the product company was approached by Richardson-Vicks to be bought out. At first I had no interest whatsoever. But their promises and methods of persuasion were very powerful. They owned Oil of Olay and many other fine brands. The only hair-product line they had was Pantene, which was smaller than Vidal Sassoon at that time. And there was no *Mr* Pantene. The Richardson-Vicks people told me they wanted to go international with a name that was well known. I wanted to go international, and I knew it would be extremely difficult without the backing of a large company.

I met with John Scott, the company CEO. He made a good impression on me – it was clear he relished the excitement of working with us and taking us global. For about a year, Richardson-Vicks worked hard promoting Vidal Sassoon products, looking for the most advantageous way of fulfilling both our dreams. In 1985, a year and a bit after they bought us, they themselves were bought by Procter & Gamble for well over a billion dollars. We were never contacted and John was embarrassed about all the promises that this left unfulfilled. I should have known better, as I did not have a release clause for if, by some unlikely chance, Richardson-Vicks was bought out. Back then, it would not have occurred to me to cover my back in this way. Never in my wildest dreams could I have imagined that a company the size of Richardson-Vicks could simply vanish without trace.

13

Wash and Go

The world as I knew it came to an end when Beverly and I split up. The excitement I would normally have felt about the company's growth lost all meaning for me. My marriage was over and I was alone. I had taken a fair-sized apartment so that my children could stay with me but often there was only one person there – me. For the first time in years I thought about the orphanage; I was that little lost kid again, far away from my family. I even grew apart from my friends because I refused so many invitations to parties. People got tired of calling. I began to analyse my romantic past and could not remember once coming out the hero of any situation. The only people I really wanted to be with were my children and we spent a lot of time together.

Once when I was booked to do a show in Poland I took Elan, then aged nine, out of school and took him to Warsaw with me. He loved it. Our next stop was Munich, where he proved such a novelty at the salon that the stylists wouldn't leave him alone for a minute. Elan had a glorious time in both cities and came back to LA speaking a few words of Polish. He had got so much out of the trip and his enthusiasm made me enjoy it too. I'll never forget him turning to me on the way home and saying, 'Dad, can I do what you're doing when I grow up?'

In LA there were puppet shows for children and children's theatre, and the look of pleasure on my kids' faces as they took it all in was a tonic. I once said to the fearsome four, 'There's a film I want you to see, so keep Sunday afternoon free and bring a friend.' Counting my own, seventeen children turned up! As the film was showing in Westwood, over a mile away, I made them all walk with me in a long line. To be safe, I took a head count upon arrival and there were eighteen. Catya had found another friend along the way!

The children stayed part-time with me at the apartment, and when they were with their mother I would go downtown to see a play or listen to the LA Philharmonic, usually with Zubin Mehta conducting. At the Music Center, a lovely girl came into my life; she was even more into music than I was. Jane Branneky was the right-hand woman to Michael Newton, who was the president of the Performing Arts Center. She had studied music in college and could not live without it; she seemed to literally live and breathe it in all its forms. We met a few times casually at the Music Center and I began to look forward to seeing her. She started arranging concert tickets for us both and slowly our friendship seemed to be turning into a romance, which I wasn't sure I was ready for. Far from leading a wild bachelor life, the year after my divorce had been positively monastic. Even the idea of being physically close to a woman made me nervous – I hadn't had sex for a year. I told Jane my fears and she immediately booked a room at L'Ermitage hotel in Beverly Hills. My lost confidence returned that night as Jane told me she loved me and seduced me beautifully.

Not long after this we decided to move in together. Being close to Jane made me realize how lonely I had been. I wasn't cut out for living by myself. And we got on so well, it just seemed the obvious thing to do. Girls usually bring their clothes first, but with Jane it was different – she brought her harpsichord. Her wardrobe came the next day. From the start I loved the private concerts I was given.

I was still making regular trips to Israel and Jane would often come with me. She loved every moment of it. Being blonde and blue-eyed with a superb figure made her very warmly welcomed wherever she went, and Israel was no exception. The Hebrew University in Jerusalem, which I'd become involved with in the mid-seventies, organized a truly magical four-day River Nile trip for us. We absorbed so much – the Valley of the Kings, Aswan, Luxor, the sarcophagi and temples, and the fascinating history of Egyptian culture. We were very compatible travelling companions; Jane had a thirst for knowledge and a refined appreciation of different cultures.

But it was not long before our cosy cohabitation ran into problems. Jane started dropping hints that she wanted more from the relationship. She was in her thirties and she wanted to marry and have children. I had four children of my own and found it enough of a challenge trying to do the right things by them. With great difficulty I told her that if she wished to find a younger man with less baggage attached, then I would not stand in her way. Though I would have liked to.

Eventually, in the summer of 1983, after three and a half years together, Jane moved out. There was no shouting. Her deep desire to have children of her own outweighed her desire to be with me. I kept looking for the harpsichord but it had gone. I missed her quick mind and exquisite body, but I also knew that it was the best thing for Jane. She had been the bright interlude during a very bumpy period of my life.

Although I missed the richness Jane brought to my life, I was very aware that the children increasingly needed me as they were growing up. There is no doubt that the divorce, and shuttling between two houses, had affected them a great deal. There were occasional crises and I often felt powerless to help except to try and be a good dad and be there for them. I couldn't bear the thought of them being unhappy but, like most teenagers, they didn't say that much. I was very consoled by the fact that all of them had such good friends; I knew they had a good support network if things did get tough. But quite selfishly, I just loved their company at the flat. It wasn't highbrow or sophisticated but with them I could let my hair down. Watching movies, eating popcorn, I can't remember how many pillow fights I lost to them. We were happy when we were together and I told myself that perhaps they were finally getting used to living in two places.

I was fortunate – very fortunate – to have Linda Turner running my office during the days when I was travelling to promote the business. Linda and her staff kept me up to date with what was happening back in Century City, where our corporate offices were located. We worked together for a decade and a half, throughout the seventies and early eighties, and she had the looks, the style and the brains that I needed to represent me when I was on the road. Linda was African-American, tall, slim and elegant, with an exotic look. She was also extremely efficient and loyal. Not only did she run my office, but she coordinated many of my children's activities and truly became involved in my life. I would have felt much less secure during my travels if I had not been aware that Linda Turner was in charge at home.

✧

In 1980, I was offered my own national television show. I say 'national' but in some parts of the country it was scheduled to go out at 4.30 in the morning. Fortunately, in the main markets we had some very good time slots and the idea appealed to me. Aside from the short-lived show I had done with Beverly, I'd dabbled a toe here and there in television and always thoroughly enjoyed it. I enjoyed the adrenalin buzz and quick thinking it demanded. Regis Philbin, when he was working out of Los Angeles, often invited me on to his morning show. I would put the finishing touches to a haircut on camera and he'd love to scream, 'Shake it! Shake it!' and the girls would shake their haircuts. My about-to-be-launched show was called *Your New Day*. When I asked Regis for his professional advice he said, 'That's crazy. You spend millions on advertising the Vidal Sassoon brand and they're calling this show *Your New Day*?'

I told him that my production company was taking the sanguine approach. If it were a dreadful flop, they felt it would be better for me if it was called *Your New Day* than *The Vidal Sassoon Show*. Regis, who is known by all as a thoroughly delightful man, gave me some very sage advice about the pleasures and pitfalls of becoming a TV host. He told me to invite some good mates on and just enjoy myself; it would be a doddle.

Your New Day involved me interviewing a variety of guests on everything from current events to health and beauty; nothing too taxing. The great thing about doing a show with a variety of guests was the unpredictability of the mix – you never knew what was going to happen. I remember one show that we created around the subject of 'tea'. It was focused around an English tea party with a very, very proper English lady, a tea specialist flown in from England, who had no idea that Peter Cook and Dudley Moore would be on the same show. The show opened with this delightfully refined lady explaining how you balance the saucer *so*, how you hold the tea cup with three fingers outstretched, and all the other niceties of taking tea in England. After five minutes, Peter and Dudley had had enough. On the table were neatly cut-up sandwiches, cakes, scones, cream, jam and, of course, tea. Peter looked at Dudley and said, 'No, no. That's not how we used to have our tea.' And Dudley said, 'You're right, Peter. Let's show the dear lady.'

It started with Dudley and Peter politely putting sandwiches into one another's mouth. It then turned into the most outrageous food fight. I was almost on the floor with laughter. The real-life Monty Python comedy of the situation caught on with the American audience, who were roaring with laughter. I looked at the proper English lady, whose face was aghast with horror, and excitedly pointed to a camera man to get her expression on film. I don't know if the poor lady ever got over the shock, but she was helped to the car that the studio had sent for her, and took a plane back to England, no doubt cursing the vulgarity of the American networks as she did so.

Strangely, though, all the people who had abused her tea party so badly were English – Dudley, Peter and me. I didn't abuse her, but I didn't stop it either. How could you possibly stop those two in full flight? That was without doubt the most hilarious show I have ever done.

I always felt more comfortable with people I knew personally, whether they were English or American. Several years before this, when I was still based in London, Jack Klugman, star of two hit TV series – *The Odd Couple* and *Quincy, M.E.* – had been making a movie in England and everyone who met him seemed to adore him. Peter Thompson, my movie buddy, introduced me to him and on his last night in England, before returning to the

States, Peter organized two minibuses full of his new mates to turn up in black tie at the house where Jack had been staying during filming. Jack opened the door wearing a pair of jeans and a T-shirt; clearly he knew nothing of this. He quickly dressed and we made a tour of East End pubs, even going as far down river as Greenwich. The magic of the evening was that it was such a delightful surprise. Jack couldn't have been more excited or flattered, as he had loved working with the Brits and developing an English sense of humour. He was sent off the next day with one hell of a hangover to remember us all by.

Now, in LA, Jack did my TV show not once but twice, and both times we told the American audience all about Jack's pub tour. The contrast between the UK and Los Angeles had become much less noticeable now, because I seemed to be seeing the same people on both sides of the Atlantic.

One afternoon I was in the Beverly Hills Hotel when I saw the side view of a man with a beard, grey-white hair and a distinctive profile, and immediately thought it was the playwright Peter Shaffer, whom I knew of old. I called out, 'Peter,' rather too enthusiastically and he turned towards me. Immediately it was obvious I'd made a mistake. I'd got the wrong Peter. I put my hand to my mouth. 'I'm terribly sorry, Mr Ustinov, but I thought you were Peter Shaffer.'

He said, 'Really! I'm sure Peter would be pleased to know that I was pleased that he was pleased that I too thought well of the idea that you thought I was he.' And without missing a beat he said, 'And who are you, dear boy?'

I told him my name. 'Ahhh, yes.' He appeared to be digesting something he wasn't totally sure about. 'I saw you on television this morning.'

I could read nothing into his inscrutable look. I decided to be very brave. 'Is there any hope at all that you might be a guest on my show?'

'Well, since we've had such an extraordinary introduction, I would be very happy to do it.' He gave me the particulars of who to call, and on the morning that it was arranged I had to pinch myself because there, on the set with me, was the great Peter Ustinov. I'm happy to say that I hadn't asked more than two questions before he took over the show. He had a truly individual wit and style and the audience was completely blown away by his genius. At the end of the show, he said, 'Is that it? Can I come back again?' He did. Like Jack Klugman, he actually did my show twice.

I did almost two hundred shows and have to say I enjoyed every one of them, and unlike my previous appearance on the small screen no one seemed in any danger of pulling the plug. If nobody at the network wanted to cancel me, I had a choice to make. Should I carry on with the show, or travel the world showing off our hair products? The decision was an easy one. I enjoyed the notoriety of the show immensely, but the product had to come first. And so I said au revoir to my career as a Hollywood chat-show host, never to return.

✧

Families. My problems just seemed to increase as I got older. My mother was very much on my conscience. She was a widow now, living on a different continent, and every time the phone rang I felt a chill of fear that something bad might have happened.

Nathan G had developed dementia in his late sixties and was eventually placed in a nursing home in South London, as it had become impossible for my mum to care for him at their flat. Over the years they had become like two peas in a pod and it was heartbreaking to see them separated. I still made frequent visits to London and when I went to see him, I would always catch him listening to his Bruckner or Mahler, even as the illness ravaged his brain. I had so much to thank him for; 'Look at Ted "Kid" Lewis, son,' he used to say. 'Anything's possible.' Mother visited him by bus two or three times a week until his death several years later. She lived many years after him, but the heartache she endured never quite left her.

When Nathan died, Mother became even more attached to me. She liked to come to anything that was going on at the salons, especially when it involved foreign travel. As she said, 'I haven't put all these years into you not to get something back now.' If I thought a party might get a little wild, I would try to censor her invitations, but this was soon quashed with a dismissive 'Darling, I've seen it all.' At seventy-five, she was raring to go and you couldn't keep her down. One year the Vidal Sassoon team was asked to do a show for the legendary Italian designer Mila Schön in Milan. She was known for her simple, modern, classically structured clothes and wanted us to design hair that would complement her work. Mother insisted she wanted to see Italy and that I take her there with the team.

On the first afternoon after we arrived, Mother fell up the steps of our hotel and broke her leg on the marble floor. She was rushed to hospital and immediately operated on. She was in her sick bed the whole week of my visit – which made it very difficult, as apart from the show I had individual press interviews and very little time for anything else. But I still managed to visit her every day and could see that she was being well taken care of by the nuns in the hospital.

Being a convent hospital, there were crucifixes over all the beds. 'Does that offend you, Ma?' I asked.

'Not at all. He was a nice Jewish boy.'

She had a cast from her ankle to her hip and my immediate concern was how we were going to get her to the plane. On our last morning in Milan, I went to pick Mother up from the hospital and helped the nuns gently ease her from the bed. We had moved one leg over the side of her bed when she started to groan. 'Oy, oy, oy . . .'

'Are we hurting you, Mother?'

'No, dear. It's just been such a long time since I've had my legs this far apart.' She always tempered her rather regal ways with a very bawdy sense of humour, which put everyone at ease.

We got her back to London and took her to a specialist, who told us that the Italians had done an extremely good job and her leg would mend perfectly thanks to the skill of the Milanese surgeon. Not long after this, I decided to move my mum out to LA permanently so that I could keep a closer eye on her. Little did I expect the city to give her a whole new lease of life in her late seventies.

It was a joy to see how my mum carried on in LA. She completely reinvented herself; she put on her best British accent, white gloves and a hat and loved it when people mistook her for the Queen Mum. She had her own flat in Century City, where the picture of her and Nathan on their wedding day took pride of place. I suggested to Ken Henderson, one of the policemen who had looked after us when we were receiving those sinister threats and who had become a personal friend, that he might become her driver now that he had left the LAPD. I don't think Mother quite believed what was happening to her – her own flat, her own car *and* her own driver. During his police service Ken had lost an eye. I thought it only fair to mention this to my mother, suggesting she might want to re-think the situation. She retorted, 'Ken is an absolute gent and drives better with one eye than most people with two.'

After the horribly hard life she had had as a young woman during the Depression, Mother knew how to turn it around. She would put on her most regal air and grow six inches in height as she left with her driver for the day's activities, whether it was afternoon tea or a trip to the ocean. Ken always treated her, as was his nature, with love and respect.

✧

Harvey Silbert was a man of great passion, much of which was given to the Hebrew University in Jerusalem. I was invited to one or two Hebrew University dinners in Los Angeles, where I learned that this great educational establishment had existed before the state of Israel was founded. Having left school myself at fourteen, I was keenly aware of the importance of education and the opportunities it gave kids to move up in life. Harvey had a wonderful way of drawing you in, making you want to do more, to give more. He planted the seeds for something that became a bit of a mission for me. My first involvement was with scholarships for Israeli kids, whether they be Arab, Muslim, Christian, Druze or Jews. I was very taken with the fact that the university seemed to ignore the political divisions that existed and opened its doors to everyone.

At one of these dinners I caught the eye of a lovely girl sitting at another table. I had a feeling we would talk later and we did. Her name was Jeanette Hartford Davis and she seemed very familiar to me. It all became clear when she reminded me that we had met at Tommy and Ann Yeardye's house. She then told me that her husband had died recently. I felt her deep sense of loss, as they were both quite young and had been very much in love. She hid it well, though, and was boisterous and funny and very charming. I found myself talking to her for ages.

We started to date and soon formed an attachment to one another. She had no desire for children, which made our relationship far more realistic from the outset, and in November 1983 I broke my promise to myself and, in a moment of madness, got married for a third time.

Jeanette's love was horses. She was at her happiest around them and was a natural rider. She chose the most difficult way to go – dressage – but as she led her horse through the movements it was as if she and the horse were one; her eyes lit up and her face showed pure joy. I went with her to the Equestrian Center on many occasions and she taught me how to ride, but I was never in the same class.

Jeanette was high-spirited and energetic, and her thigh muscles from riding horses gave her a power in bed that was very engaging. We often flew to New York on business trips. Kirk Kerkorian had a small airline where you could book a sleeper cabin, and in one of those cabins Jeanette baptized me as a member of the Mile-High Club. Flying with Jeanette could become an addiction – and did.

I was still a regular at the Los Angeles Philharmonic and introduced Jeanette to the Music Center. Simon Rattle was now a guest conductor with the LA Phil. and once, through friends, he invited Jeanette and me to a performance he was giving of Mahler's Sixth Symphony. Simon's way of making an entrance was extremely dramatic. Once the orchestra was seated, with baton raised to shoulder height, curly mane of hair flowing to his shoulders, this majestic figure would walk on stage. The orchestra's respect for Simon was immediately obvious. His presence drew the audience to him, and all of us had great expectations of what was to come. We were not disappointed. It was a stunning performance. Not only did many of us have tears in our eyes, but the orchestra's violinists clapped him for several minutes after the concert. Musicians only do that when something truly special has happened.

As arranged, Jeanette and I went back to Simon's dressing room, where an excited crowd of people were congratulating him on his brilliant performance. I whispered to him that we'd booked a restaurant for a late dinner.

He said, 'No. Let's grab a sandwich instead. Dizzy Gillespie is playing down the road at the Catalina Bar and Grill and I want to hang loose and dig him.'

My face lit up. If it were a question of Dizzy or dinner, I'd take Gillespie anytime. Simon then asked if he could come in our car to the club, as he had actually got a lift to the concert hall that evening. He put his tails in the back of our car and jumped in, and we headed over to the Catalina – the number one jazz club in downtown LA. The three of us sat until the early hours, listening to Dizzy's soaring notes and original sounds. His innovative style was sheer magic and gave me goosebumps. Simon hardly spoke as he was bent on listening to every sound. Afterwards, we drove him to his hotel having heard an evening of extraordinary music.

At seven o'clock the following morning there was a phone call from a somewhat rattled Simon. 'Vidal, can you get my tails to the airport by ten o'clock? They're still in the back of your car, and they'll come in handy for the next concert.'

He got his tails.

This was one of many great moments during my marriage to Jeanette, but quite soon after we'd tied the knot we both realized we'd made a mistake. Our lifestyles were not really compatible and we seemed to be heading in different directions. I could not compete with her horses and she had little interest in my world. We found ourselves arguing incessantly over one another's lifestyles, and after eighteen months as husband and wife the marriage just fell apart. Our addiction to one another waned and she went back to her horses permanently. She bought a horse farm in Florida and has been teaching riding there ever since.

✧

Throughout the 1980s, I was fortunate enough to have Jackie Applebaum working with the company in a public relations position. Jackie's ideas were highly innovative and she had a reputation for getting what she wanted. She asked for a meeting with me and a handful of local politicians, where she announced that she was going to get the account for the Olympic Games, which were to be held in Los Angeles in the summer of 1984. She was full of ideas about how to make it different to anything that had gone before and then she pitched us her master plan. Vidal Sassoon would construct two makeshift salons in tents in the grounds of the University of California, Los Angeles, and the University of Southern California, where so many of the world-class athletes would be staying. Our international team would provide free haircuts, colouring and perming for all Olympic athletes. I didn't need long to think this one through. I had already thought of a handful of our stylists in Britain, Germany and Canada who would jump at the chance to be involved. I told Jackie I thought it was brilliant; we would be honoured.

Jackie was the type of girl who could walk straight into the governor's office without an appointment and with great ingenuity get her way. She approached the Los Angeles Olympic Organizing Committee (LAOOC), who loved her idea, and on 9 February 1984, Vidal Sassoon, Inc. was designated 'the hair consultant for the athletes of the 1984 Games'. It had never been done before – not in any country – and I felt excited by the possibilities it would bring.

Grooming the world's athletic elite proved to be an enormous success – a stroke of genius by Jackie – as more than 1,500 athletes came into our outdoor parlours. The organizers had managed to install hot and cold running water, and so despite their alfresco nature our temporary 'salons' were not without creature comforts. It was fortunate that each country had its own interpreter as the media became very interested in the new looks we were giving their sporting champions and we found ourselves having to discuss at length the new styles we had given them. The 'salons' buzzed with the voices of so many different nations – it really was like the United Nations under canvas. The creative skills of the individual stylists and colourists, whom we had flown in from different countries, fed off each other and were contagious. Being an integral part of this Olympic challenge added to our staff's pride in knowing they were working with a very remarkable company. They were being well paid for their efforts but I think most of them would have happily offered their services for free.

One incident that comes to mind was when a Chinese medalist – a very beautiful girl – asked for the 'Five Point Cut' through her interpreter. I couldn't believe she'd ever heard of the geometric 'Five Point' more than twenty years after I'd first come up with it, but it had obviously found its way to China. One of our top people from the London salons cut her hair, and as the cut was close to being finished, tears streamed down the young athlete's face. I asked the interpreter, 'Does she not like it?'

'No,' she said, 'just the reverse. She never thought she would have the opportunity to get it.'

As she got up, she wiped away the tears and hugged her stylist. A big smile showed off her beauty and her bone structure seemed to fit so well into the haircut. It was one of the most memorable moments of the Olympic Games for me.

Mary Lou Retton, the US world champion gymnast, was a client even before the Olympics, and because of her way with people and her persuasive personality, she dragged many of her more cautious fellow athletes into the tents to indulge in some grooming.

Our relationship with the Olympic gymnasts did not stop there. Just before the final fireworks of the closing ceremony, Jackie came up to me and announced that she had pulled off another major coup. The American men's gymnastics team had just won the Olympic team gold medal and the women's team had won the silver medal. Mary Lou, who had scored a perfect ten in her last event and won five medals, including the all-around gold medal in women's gymnastics, had quickly become America's sweetheart. The whole of the United States seemed eager to see both teams perform live. Jackie's brain was working overtime once again, and the next thing I knew she had talked us into sponsoring a nationwide tour for the men's and women's gymnastic teams. The tour attracted hundreds of thousands of enthusiastic Americans who wanted to express their appreciation, and venues that seated thousands were solidly sold out.

I found myself in city after city, having very little to do except talk to a few press people, being introduced to the crowd as a sponsor of the event, and greatly enjoying every show.

Jane Johns modelling
'The Goddess' cut, before perming.

Jane and 'The Goddess',
after perming.

Cutting Mia Farrow's hair for *Rosemary's Baby* while
Roman Polanski looks on.

With Catya and Beverly.

With the children.
Clockwise from top:
Elan, David, Catya,
Eden.

With Beverly and Cary Grant.

With Joan Collins at the New York
salon opening.

With Jeannette, Altovise and Sammy Davis Jr.

The Rodeo Drive salon
in Beverly Hills.

With Robert Edele
and Jason Peller,
supervising a session
at the Vidal Sassoon
Academy in London.

Vidal with
Yitzhak Rabin.

With Zubin Mehta
and George Shaw in
Southern Lebanon
in 1982.

With Ronnie.

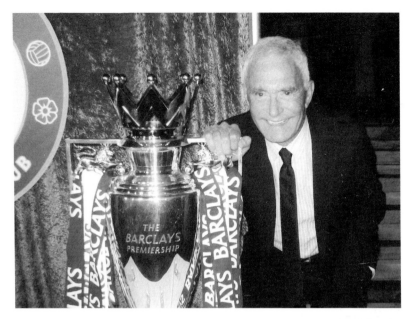

Celebrating Chelsea's title win when the team came to Los Angeles.

With my son-in-law Tomer Devito and my granddaughter Olivia
and members of the Ethiopian immigrant school football team I sponsor
in Kiryat Ekron, Israel.

With my CBE in 2009, just after I had received it from the Queen.

Getting to know the athletes at dinner after each event made me appreciate their dedication to the sport. Finding out what made these world champions tick was a total joy – especially given my own love of sports and fitness. They were proud of what they did, but grateful too for how they had got there and the sacrifices those around them had made. They played jokes, like trying to get me on the parallel bars. They didn't know I had worked out with Nicholas Kounovsky, the famous Russian gymnast, at his Kounovsky's Studio in New York and knew how to straddle the parallel bars. My form was terrible, though, and caused much hilarity. They told me to *definitely* stick with my day job. The twelve members of each team, with their different beliefs and backgrounds, came together in a way that reminded me so much of the strength and character of my own team.

Looking back on those years, I don't think I ever kept still or stayed in one place for longer than a week. Little wonder then that the next product we dreamt up was a combined shampoo and conditioner for people, like myself, who didn't seem to have enough hours in the day to take care of themselves. 'Wash and Go', as it was christened, in its fresh sea-green packaging, seemed to capture the mood of the time perfectly.

It was 1989 and I was in Dublin with George Shaw, a great publicist who worked with me on many shows and events, and the PR girl from London had also flown in. Wash and Go was flying off the shelves in Britain and I was hoping to replicate that success in Ireland. They'd lined up numerous interviews and local and national media for me to do, but the main event was a live TV talk show on the Friday night. Thursday evening was free so the first question I asked the concierge at the hotel was what was playing at either the Abbey or the Gate theatres.

Neither of the plays rang a bell with me, so I decided to take pot luck on a play at the Abbey called *The Real McCoy*.

After a rather enjoyable production with multiple plots, we went to a restaurant nearby that was obviously a popular hangout for thespians. Our dinner for three suddenly became much larger as three or four of the actors came over to join our table. The director of the play, John Lynch, spotted us, walked over and said to me, 'I hear you saw my play tonight.'

I told him I had.

'What did you think?'

'Well, it was eclectic,' I said, choosing my words carefully. 'It had so many aspects to it. I enjoyed it.'

He said, 'Good. Because if you tell Gay Byrne that I'm writing you into the play, you'll be working the Abbey this Saturday evening.'

I thought he was joking. Then I remembered I was in Ireland and total madness was the normal state of existence.

Ireland's biggest television show was *The Late Late Show*. Every Friday evening at 11.30, Gay Byrne would take over the airways. The half of Ireland that wasn't out drinking tuned in. I liked to think Gay and I got on famously (or maybe it was simply because he had space to fill), because whenever my publicist told his people that I was coming to Dublin, I would be booked for the show.

On Friday night, I was sitting in the green room waiting to be called. Gay's show was officially an hour and a half long, but if he was enjoying himself, he stretched it to two hours – the news could wait. Eventually I was announced. I walked on stage and Gay invited me to sit down.

'Hello, Vidal. Where have you flown in from?'

'Beverly Hills.'

He looked aghast. 'Hmm ... I suppose you're going to bore me with stories of all those Hollywood people.'

I retorted, 'No, Gay. I wanted you to be the first to know I'm playing the Abbey tomorrow night.'

He looked even more aghast and said, 'You're doing *what*?'

So I told him the story of how John Lynch was going to write me into the play the following evening. There was a moment of silence. He then looked at the audience and, throwing his arms in the air in exasperation, said, 'Thousands of starving Irish actors and this limey barber is playing the Abbey!'

The audience was laughing hysterically. But Gay looked dead serious. He hung his head and stared down for a few seconds. He then wished me luck with the play and we carried on, talking of other things. Eventually he saw the funny side of a crimper playing the Abbey, and kept bringing it back into the conversation, which brought hoots from the audience. I always had a good time with Gay – and this time was no different.

Saturday at high noon, I had to be at the Abbey Theatre to meet the cast and have my picture taken with them. The press were all there and I was given a script, which I held in front of me while they took their photos. As they left, John said, 'Vidal, drop the script. Ad lib.'

'Ad lib?'

'Yes. You said it was eclectic. Improvise.'

The Abbey is one of the world's great theatres and John wanted me to do my own thing? A few hours later I was in the dressing room beginning to panic slightly. There was a knock on the door. 'Mr Sassoon, five minutes.' Then another knock. 'Mr Sassoon, two minutes. Come to the stage entrance, please.'

Suddenly it came to me and I knew exactly what to do. I composed myself and went on. It was Saturday night. I looked out – a full house – standing room only. Looking at the audience left, right and centre, in a booming voice I pronounced confidently, 'To Wash and Go or not Wash and Go, that is the question!'

Our Wash and Go TV commercial had aired frequently on Irish television so the audience reaction was instantaneous. With their encouragement, and bolstered by the confidence of having done many non-scripted shows of my own, I decided to ham it up. I was supposed to give the leading lady just one line, but the director had told me to ad lib, so for the next five minutes I carried on, talking of the joys of Dublin. The leading man nudged me on several occasions, whispering loudly, 'Give her the line,' but after sweating it out since Thursday night, I was determined to have my fun. The theatre-goers seemed to egg me on. After a much stronger dig from the leading man and another loud whisper of 'Give her the line,' I did. The play went on and when it finished, the whole cast came back and pushed me centre stage to take a bow with them. They were extremely gracious.

Back in the dressing room, John Lynch, the director, confronted me. 'I still don't know if you can act one jot, but hamming it up you're priceless.'

When I tell this story to stage actors, they look at me incredulously and say, '*You* played the Abbey?' It was a memorable evening for me, but I was aware how much I had milked the situation and basked in the limelight. The latent actor in me had clearly been waiting in the wings for far too long.

14

A Girl Called Ronnie

In February 1989, during one of my many business trips to Cincinnati, where Procter & Gamble had their headquarters, one of their vice-presidents, Bill Connell, asked whether I would have dinner that evening with him, his wife and an advertising executive they knew well, named Ronnie Holbrook. As I had nothing else planned that evening, I said yes.

I was taken by Bill and his delightful wife, Gail, to China Gourmet, a rather chic-looking Chinese restaurant in Hyde Park, and for ten minutes we sat waiting for the mystery guest to turn up – with me feeling oddly nervous, not knowing what to expect. Then a gorgeous girl breezed in – brunette, slim, with endless long legs, and I thought to myself *This can't be Cincinnati.* She looked exquisite, as though she had walked straight in from the Faubourg Saint-Honoré or Bond Street at its best. I also knew there wasn't a store or boutique in the city that sold the ultra-chic fashion she was wearing.

I got up to greet her and was immediately struck by her smile. There was instant chemistry on my part and I wondered if she felt the same. The evening was warm; the conversation was warmer – except for one moment that was extremely cold. Ronnie was talking and waving her arms when suddenly a full glass of ice-cold champagne fell into my lap. She was so animated, she hadn't realized what she'd done, or that champagne was dripping down my leg into my shoe. I was so bewitched by her, I pretended it never happened. The evening finished with an exchange of telephone numbers and Ronnie dropped me chastely at my hotel. As she didn't offer her lips, I gently kissed her cheek and said goodnight.

Gail obviously updated her on the champagne incident because when I called the next morning to invite her to dinner again that evening, and opened with, 'I've had my suit cleaned, thank you very much for asking!' she responded with peals of laughter followed by a coy apology. We had dinner at my hotel that night and needless to say, the goodnight kiss was far more satisfactory. I did not see her for a month afterwards, and because of my new determination to avoid permanent relationships, I did not call her either – but I thought of her often.

A month later my telephone rang, and to my delight it was Ronnie. She was making a business trip to California to see a client in Los Angeles, but did not know her schedule. She told me where she was staying, so I sent flowers and a note to her hotel, saying I'd phone her in the morning. After a full week of business appointments and dinners, Ronnie was still unavailable, and I felt totally frustrated as my hopes of seeing her seemed to be vanishing. She was scheduled to fly home that Friday night but curiosity clearly got the better of her and she called to tell me that she would be staying in town for the weekend. I replied, 'Keep the whole weekend open, please,' and booked theatre tickets for the following night. She was happy with the arrangement and when she arrived at my house late that afternoon she asked where we would be having dinner.

'Don't worry about that,' I said. 'I'll make us a health drink.'

She laughed. 'I come from Cincinnati, where we eat food. I was really looking forward to some California cuisine.'

I took the obvious hint and booked a table for an early dinner at Ma Maison, a well-known restaurant downtown. I had never met a girl quite like Ronnie – so self-assured and yet so open to ideas. She had graduated cum laude with a degree in art history and talked knowledgeably about art and architecture. She captivated me that evening. I was totally enthralled and on my way home I thought to myself, *Here we go again* . . .

I was booked to do a show in Holland and decided to throw caution to the wind and ask Ronnie to meet me in Amsterdam. We stayed at a beautiful hotel by the river called the Amstel, which smacked of old-world charm. Our evenings were very romantic and we enjoyed long walks along the Amstel river and the canals, talking, laughing and getting to know each other.

My next show was in Athens and naturally I invited Ronnie to join me there. The head man of the VS product line in Greece was Antonio 'Tony' Belloni. He threw a reception at one of Athens's best hotels on a beautiful balmy evening, and invited an assorted group of Athenians, from society and the fashion and beauty press. I had never met Tony before but after talking to him for five minutes, I sensed he was refreshingly unconventional in his approach to business. He then took no further interest in me and started to chat up Ronnie. He was an Italian working in Greece, and in one evening became besotted with my American girlfriend. Ronnie played along with it, but he seemed to be dead serious.

By the end of the evening, when he saw that his Latin charm hadn't quite worked and that Ronnie was clearly with me, Tony threw himself – rather dramatically given that he was fully clothed – into the hotel's swimming pool. It was a very warm night and some of his junior staff quickly took their jackets off and jumped into the pool to join him. One of his top people later told me that Tony had a marvellous sense of the ridiculous and used it on every possible occasion – making certain he would never be forgotten.

Despite my best intentions, I fell deeply in love with Ronnie. I was fascinated by her and needed her by my side. Although her work was mainly in Cincinnati, she would more often than not fly into Los Angeles on Friday evening, so we would enjoy the weekend together. She would take the red-eye back on Sunday night, and go straight to her office on Monday morning.

From time to time, business took me to Cincinnati, and one day, when we had been seeing each other seriously for a while, Ronnie announced that it was time to meet her parents. I don't remember ever approaching a similar meeting with more trepidation. Ronnie's father, George, was my age – which at the time was sixty-two. He made it quite clear that he had no objection to my relationship with his daughter. However, he did take me for a walk and asked me if my intentions were honourable. I looked up at his face to see if he was smiling, but he was completely serious. It's the type of question you're asked when you are in your twenties, not your sixties, but I did my best to remain respectful. 'After all,' he added, 'she's taking a chance and giving up everything for you.' The love and concern he had for his daughter was quite apparent and his point was well taken. Not surprisingly, George has proved to be one of the most decent people I have ever met.

Ronnie's mother, Jewel – by name and, as I quickly found out, by nature – was warm-hearted and welcoming from the start. A very conservative Christian, she turned out to be totally pro-Zionist, and if Israel gave up an inch of land, she'd give me an hour's talking-to. My somewhat liberal views – and Ronnie's for that matter – did not sit well with her, but otherwise it was clear we were going to have a fine relationship from the start.

Ronnie also introduced me to her great friends Debbie and Curt Tweddell, who had a little boy, Bowen, who had nearly died at birth and has cerebral palsy. He was the most delightful little chap and though he had difficulties with speech and coordination, I found myself completely drawn to his sunny nature. Without really intending to I found myself asking his parents if I could give his head a gentle massage. After that first visit it's become a tradition and whenever I'm in Cincinnati, there is something special I have to do. As I enter their house, I can hear Bowen uttering sounds of glee as he realizes what's coming. For twenty minutes or more, I massage his beautifully shaped head. I've always admired Debbie and Curt's courage and unselfish devotion to their son. They seemed to sense from the moment he was born that he would bring something special into their lives and he is clearly number one in the family. It seems rather silly to say, but I sometimes think those twenty-minute massages help me as much as they do him.

Cincinnati to LA, LA to Cincinnati, after nine months of red-eyeing, Ronnie was getting tired of flying back and forth. She turned to me one day when I was dropping her at the airport and just said that she couldn't fly like this any more. What was I going to do about it? The perfect solution fell into place.

I held her close, and after a long pause whispered, 'Come

and live with me in Los Angeles, where every day will be a weekend.'

She gave it five seconds of long and hard thought and said, 'I'd love to.'

In truth, this had been a tough decision for an independent woman like Ronnie to make. But as she explained to me later, like me she had always put her career first, and, like me, had failed in relationships. She wanted so much to make it work this time and felt that she was ready to give our relationship everything she had.

At the time, I was living in a flat in Century City and I was ecstatic to have Ronnie join me there. She was a fabulous cook and would often spend hours preparing great gourmet dinner parties, which were eagerly looked forward to by me and our friends. I had never been so smitten by a relationship. I knew I wanted to be with her always, but had one worry – which I needed to address with her. I was in my early sixties and she was in her late thirties. Had she really thought the age gap through? I wondered. Would that affect the way she felt about our future?

Without hesitation Ronnie replied, 'You not only look like a big kid, you *act* like a big kid. The age difference doesn't matter to me at all.'

It certainly didn't matter to me. Now that my own children were in their teens and beyond, a child with Ronnie was not out of the question – and we were both open to the possibility.

Once Ronnie moved to Los Angeles, her Cincinnati working days were over. She left her company and immediately started travelling with me. My touring contract with Procter & Gamble was for sixty-five days a year, though more often than not we were visiting countries for between a hundred and a hundred and fifty days each year. I did not mind the extra work if it resulted in extra product sales – which it did.

Procter & Gamble had quite a few hair product lines, and it was in their power to promote or not any of those lines. It was starting to dawn on me that when I had given up control of the product company, I had given up much more than I had ever intended. I started to realize that my voice no longer carried any weight. These days I could only make suggestions – something which, for me, took quite a lot of getting used to. I had worked with a small, tightly knit team for decades. Working with a big company was proving both different and difficult, as there were so many people and personalities involved in the decision-making process. Not long after Procter & Gamble's takeover, I began to wonder if they knew all the promises that had been made to me by Richardson-Vicks.

My best time with Procter & Gamble was in Asia. Denis Beausejour was in charge of VS in Asia. The man working with me on a daily basis was Tom Blinn. He and Denis were based in Osaka, Japan, and were heaven-sent. Tom once flew six hours to Singapore just to meet Ronnie and me for dinner, where we talked for hours planning for the future of this and other tours to the Far East. Ronnie's design background and business acumen, along with her hands-on approach, proved to be a great asset to our meetings.

Since the 'Nancy Kwan' cut, many Asians were keen to have our look. Their thick, black, shiny hair lent itself beautifully to our cutting techniques. Their bone structure was made for our geometric, angular looks too. It would have been a joy for me to work in a city like Tokyo on a daily basis.

Our hair team in Asia was headed by Tim Hartley, who had stepped into Christopher Brooker's shoes as the international artistic director of Vidal Sassoon, a position he held for more than two decades. Tim has an extraordinary talent and a superb knowledge of so many of the arts. This is his life. Nobody could cut hair better than Tim and he made sure it stayed that way. I was aware when he was appointed that following Roger, Christopher and me was not an easy task. He had to make the job his. He still had to create new looks, drawing on the past and developing the future of Sassoon hair, but he did this with such clarity, with such an eye to the future, that young hairdressers just followed in his footsteps.

I remember sitting in the audience once when Tim and the team were on top form. At the end of every show, the audience asked questions. A girl stood up and said to Tim, 'This show was the best I've seen ever, but I also fell in love with your hands.' He presented them to her with a kiss on both cheeks. Yes, he is very special. The shows, particularly in Japan, had a professional producer and director, who naturally were Japanese. Tim worked closely with them to make sure they understood the philosophy behind the work. The Japanese were a very sophisticated audience and we could not let them down; we had trained so many of them. Hairdressers who wanted to learn haircutting the Sassoon way had now been coming to us from many countries for several years.

Back in 1969, a young Japanese hairdresser called Fumio Kawashima had come to London from the Glemby salon in Toronto, looking for a new challenge. He came directly to us because he had heard about the Vidal Sassoon method and wanted to learn our techniques. Joshua Galvin hired him and sent him to the Knightsbridge School, where his teacher was Caroline Hays, one of our best. After a lengthy period of study, he was allowed to take the VS test – to determine whether he would become a stylist with us or not. It was marked by two brilliant stylists, Howard Fugler and Darill Benson, and he passed with flying colours. He was given a position in Bond Street and later was asked to work in Manchester, where he inspired many other young stylists.

Fumio is undoubtedly one of our finest exports. When he eventually returned to his home country he had so many requests from Japanese hairdressers to teach our methods that he criss-crossed Japan many times before opening his own salon in Tokyo. He is a brilliant cutter and teacher, and now owns half a dozen of the very best salons in Japan.

Three years ago, in Barcelona in 2007, Fumio did a magnificent hair show, which I went to see. He spotted me in the audience and invited me up on stage to join him. He then very emotionally told the audience how he had started with us and how, thanks to the training he received while he was with us, he was now able to do major shows worldwide. Fumio is a shining example of how so many of our stylists went back to their own countries as stars.

Not all of our stylists came with such an unblemished record as Fumio. Some have definitely crossed over from the other side of the tracks.

Ron and John Lee are identical twins, born in Oakland, California. Their father is Chinese American and their mother was born in Shanghai. In 1972, Ron and John were chosen by the Oakland police to be decoys for a line-up that the police were forming as part of an investigation into a fatal stabbing at a high-school cafeteria. Of course, they had nothing to do with the incident, but during the investigation they were introduced to Oakland's Suey Sing gang, who were described by the *San Francisco Weekly* as 'a bunch of low-level Chinese-American thugs'. Despite their middle-class upbringing, in time Ron and John were accepted into its ranks. One of the older members of the Suey Sing gang was a young man by the name of Gary Maah, who one day decided to become a hair stylist. Ron, then seventeen, decided that he, too, would like to try his luck as a hairdresser, and – remarkably – eight other gang members followed suit. Ron joined the Vidal Sassoon organization in 1977, becoming a creative director before he eventually moved on. John joined us two years later, and has worked at our San Francisco salon ever since – for thirty-one years – and we are lucky to have him. But how bizarre that ten villains from the same street gang should become hairdressers!

Throughout our tours, I made television appearances and gave interviews to the magazines and newspapers in each country we travelled to. Japan was no exception. The Japanese loved to know that there was a person behind the product and I was always warmly welcomed.

China, being vast, was a different proposition and conquering it would be a major feat. In July 1998, two shows – one in Shanghai and one in Beijing – were organized by a PR company that had international connections, and were very successful. It was obvious that China had been starved of creative fashion and hair shows for some years. It was now opening its doors in a big way, and the turnout for our shows in Beijing and Shanghai was staggering. As the team arrived at the venue, we wondered whether we were dreaming or in Paris during Fashion Week. There were cameras and reporters *everywhere*. Every single facet of the hair show was filmed. After each show, we were invited into the press room, and a two-hour show turned into a four-hour marathon as Tim and I answered questions non-stop from a very eager and excited press. The outstanding publicity we enjoyed as a result of these shows ensured that our products flew off the shelves – we had found the edge we needed to succeed.

Our sales in China and Korea were increasing rapidly. But there were many other smaller countries in the Far East that we visited, some more successfully than others. It really came down to how much time we spent in each country. In one nine-week period alone, the team and I performed in eight different countries.

During the publicity jamboree in Asia, I was interviewed for a Japanese architectural magazine who wanted to know about the ideas behind our work. I spoke of the inspiration I had always taken from architecture and mentioned the superb work of that country's own Tadao Ando, whom I much admired.

About three months later the magazine came out and Tadao contacted us via our people in Japan, to say how much he liked the article, and could we have dinner together the next time we were in Japan? We let him know our return dates and upon our arrival, he took the fast train in from Osaka and met us in Tokyo. He brought with him a gentleman by the name of Kulapat Yantrasast, also an excellent architect, who translated our English into Japanese and Tadao's Japanese into English. Ronnie and I spent a wonderful evening with them, eating at a restaurant with a breathtaking view that served equally breathtaking food. Although Tadao spoke no English, he had a wonderful way of expressing his work – by making lightning sketches on napkins. And the napkins he drew on were probably never washed again, as the maître d' asked him to autograph all of them. There are some evenings you never forget.

Being an avid theatre-goer and inquisitive about Japanese culture, it was only natural to take in some Kabuki theatre while we were in Japan. I found it fascinating, even though I knew only a few words of Japanese. The first time I saw it I left the theatre puzzled but wanting more. I went on a number of occasions and even though I became more and more confused, I was totally enthralled with the voices and costumes of the actors on stage.

✧

Being together for over three years, much of it living out of hotel rooms, cemented the relationship between Ronnie and me. It's very unusual to be able to work together with your partner in this way but with us it just seemed to come naturally. There was hardly a cross word between us. Ronnie was – and is – an extremely savvy woman, very self-assured about who she is and so was never threatened by the girls I worked with every day. We used top models in each country, and there were hundreds of beautiful faces that I got up close and personal with for the duration of the haircut, but both of us knew that any physical closeness ended the moment I put down my scissors.

I knew by the way my heart beat when she was around that Ronnie and I were ready for one another, and that we could face all the challenges of life together. In April 1992, we were in Paris on holiday. It was an exquisite night and the reflection of the moon on the Seine brought out the words that I had sworn all too recently I would never say again. I held her close and whispered in her ear, 'Ronnie, will you marry me – right now?'

'I'd love to, darling, but we can't. We have to go home and get married there. Otherwise, your children would never forgive us.'

On 2 August 1992, we got married in the herb garden of the lovely grounds of the Bel Air Hotel. It was a delightful, intimate ceremony, with just family and a few friends. Mum and my children were there, of course, and Ronnie's warm, solid relationship with them all was a source of great joy to me. Jack Klugman came with his lady, Peggy Crosby. David Soul and Brock Peters were also in attendance, along with Valerie Harper and her husband, Tony Cacciotti.

Ronnie and I stayed at the Bel Air Hotel the night before we were married. There were no doubts in either of our minds that we had found something in one another that nobody else had given us. I adored her with a tenderness that I had not known before.

It wasn't always plain sailing, though – Ronnie's passion for design took a little getting used to. I came home one evening and the dining-room furniture was missing. She told me not to worry, she'd just put it in another room. The following week the furniture was moved back to its original place. Apparently she did this for artistic fulfilment, but I never knew where I would be eating next. Unless of course we were on the road, where she refrained from redesigning our hotel suites.

Ronnie has an extraordinary eye when it comes to art. She can spot an artist who in ten years' time will become highly sought after. She did this with both Anish Kapoor and Lucio Fontana. Not long after we were married, we bought an Anish Kapoor sculpture at a very reasonable price. He had not yet become famous in the United States and he actually flew over from London and personally placed the sculpture in our garden. I'm sure he had other things to do in LA but we like to think he flew over just for us. He and his wife, Susanne, have been great friends ever since.

About three years earlier, a lady on the Upper East Side was selling a Fontana painting. We flew to New York to meet her and instantly fell in love with it. It was white with seven slashes and was painted around 1963. I didn't need any convincing. We brought the painting back to Los Angeles, where it has had pride of place in many different rooms in our home, as Ronnie enjoys rearranging the artwork, too.

Over the years, Ronnie has opened catalogues from various galleries, left a note for me with an artist's name and a page number, predicting a great future for this or that individual who no one has ever heard of – and would I be interested in forking out some cash? Though sometimes I try to protest, I have found over the years that Ronnie's eye rarely lets us down. Our collection is not large, but it's extremely interesting as it focuses mainly on the Italian Zero Movement of the sixties. Ronnie loves anything from the sixties, including yours truly. It's an exciting way to collect art. We're not in the league of spending hundreds of millions on the Picassos of this world, but for us buying art is far more interesting and captivating than looking at the paper each morning to find how your stock has done.

In 1997, Ronnie and I were staying at the Ritz Hotel in Paris and were outside on the front steps of the hotel waiting for our car to take us to Jeremy Scott's first couture show. I was wearing a new white leather coat from Saint Laurent designed by Hedi Slimane during the brief time that he was the menswear designer there, before he went to Dior and became a superstar. Ronnie was wearing a black leather Gucci motorcycle jacket with skin-tight black leather bell-bottomed trousers, with three layers of mink tails on the bottom designed by Tom Ford. I have to say that we both looked rather fetching! As we were waiting for our car, Isabella Blow and André Leon Talley – a man of great stature who couldn't be missed – walked out of the front door of the hotel on their way to the same show. As Izzy walked out she spotted the two of us, clapped her hands and shrieked for everyone within earshot, 'I don't know who I want to fuck first. You both look so fabulous!'

When we stopped laughing, we told them to jump in the car with us and we were whisked away to what turned out to be a stunning show at the Louvre. It was a very rainy night and while we were walking to and from the event, André followed close behind Ronnie, holding an umbrella over her head while chanting, 'Mind the minky tails! Mind the minky tails!' every time we approached a puddle.

With the help of Pierre Rougier, our wonderful fashion PR, the rest of the Paris week was just as fascinating, as Stella McCartney was also showing for Chloe in Paris for the first time and Pierre made sure we had front-row seats. After Stella's fabulous show, Ronnie and I went backstage to congratulate her. After giving us both a kiss she whispered, 'Dad's in the back room. Go say hello.' Ronnie and I went back to see Sir Paul, who I had known for some time. The fact that he kept well out of the way of the press was commendable and the right thing to do. He knew that it was Stella's day, and the vibes coming from him were those of a very proud dad indeed.

That night, dining at Hôtel Costes, we noticed Mick Jagger at the table next to us. When we got up to leave, I said hello to Mick and introduced him to Ronnie – at which point he gave Ronnie a little kiss. Much later, when we were in bed, she turned to me and said, 'Now I can say I was kissed by Paul McCartney, Mick Jagger and Vidal Sassoon all on the same day.'

Being married to me wasn't always so glamorous. In late August 1997, Simcha and Vivian Dinitz were in town and Irwin Molasky – a man of enormous power in the business world – decided to entertain them. A group of us were invited to join the Dinitzes at the Del Mar Race Track, near San Diego. Lovey and Bob Arum were there – Bob is *the* premiere boxing promoter and on occasion invites Ronnie and me to the fights in Vegas – and Irwin, who brought his doctor along, Dr Elias Ghanem. We were dining somewhere rather grand, but Ronnie and I were leaving for an eight-week tour in the Far East a few days later and my prostate was giving me hell. During dinner, I went to the toilet four times without any success. I panicked and eventually gave in and told the table that I truly had to leave and find a hospital. Irwin offered his limo, and he and Dr Ghanem came with Ronnie and me to Scripps Hospital in Del Mar. The relief I experienced once they opened me up was indescribable.

The doctors at the hospital left the catheter in overnight. As it was a Saturday and I couldn't see my doctor until Monday, the catheter became part of me for forty-eight hours. It was quite obvious that I would need an operation – but there wasn't time; I was just about to step on a plane. So, in case there was another emergency, Ronnie was taught how to catheterize me. I was advised by all and sundry to cancel the tour and part of me would have loved to. But since thousands of people in Asia were involved with us on these tours, where we did creative shows and taught our methods and product awareness at seminars, and as I had never backed out of a show before, I wasn't about to start now.

Although a doctor had been put on notice in every city and nurse Ronnie made it clear she felt very comfortable with the catheter, we travelled the Far East not needing it. We got to London and I gave a large sigh of relief – and that's where my plumbing decided to shut down.

We were staying at the Berkeley Hotel – a small, beautiful hotel near Knightsbridge. The hotel had a series of doctors on call and eventually one arrived. As Ronnie explained how we had gone halfway round the world with a catheter and didn't need it until now, he was quite amused to learn that she knew how to put it in and told her to get on with it. He said, 'I will oversee, but you must do what you were taught to do.'

Luckily for me, Ronnie was gentle and quite loving as she inserted the catheter. While she was performing this delicate operation, the doctor had his hand on Ronnie's thigh. I'm sure it was meant to encourage her, but to me, the whole incident was too bizarre for words.

When my usual doctor in LA heard the state I was in, he wasted no time and two days later I was back in LA being operated on.

All the hairdressers loved Ronnie, and when she travelled with me she was an enormous asset with her beauty, wisdom and deliciously wicked sense of humour. Her reputation as a cook was such that while we were in Singapore, she was asked to do a television cookery show, which she did with great aplomb. I was her sous chef and wore one of those very silly hats that smart chefs wear. She cooked linguini with clam sauce. The show was broadcast from the Raffles Hotel, where we were staying. Ronnie's linguini with clam sauce did a great deal for our reputation at Raffles.

Ronnie loved Japan as much as I did, and many of our press interviews were done in our suite at the Okura Hotel. Each day around two o'clock, we would get a break for lunch and order room service. I would go straight to the TV, watching sumo as the Japanese championships were on. I was fascinated by the ritual elegance before and after each bout, which was so different from the slapstick gimmicks of professional wrestling in the West.

Ronnie joined me one day and that's when she fell in love with Takanohana, a sumo champion. When they heard about our new obsession, the people we were working with in Japan said they would get us a box. After a few bouts, the Japanese folk in their boxes surrounding ours would smile, and ask us to share in their saké. Each time we visited the country we saw sumo at least once, and always came away feeling uplifted. It has a beauty and majesty beyond anything I'd seen before in a contact sport.

We worked tirelessly, believing that the work we were doing in Asia was important for the company's overall growth, but we had great fun, too. Much of this had to do with the cooperation and creativity our team received from Denis Beausejour and Tom Blinn. As other territories started to perform less well than we had forecast, I remember thinking, *If only these two gentlemen, with their intrinsic understanding of our philosophy and products, could take over Vidal Sassoon products worldwide.* Asia for me was an enduring love affair. I was inspired and invigorated by its many individual cultures. My work seemed to fit in beautifully with their innate sense of aesthetics.

15

Meetings With Remarkable Men

My relationship with the Hebrew University in Jerusalem began in the mid-seventies. Over the years it was to take up more and more of my time and became increasingly important to me. In 1978, a delegation from Los Angeles, led by my friend Harvey Silbert, who was a leading attorney in LA and a major benefactor of the university, left for Jerusalem and I joined them. As I stepped foot onto the campus for the very first time, I felt the magic of walking Mount Scopus – and I imagined myself as a student there. Over the years, supporters of the Hebrew University have provided funds for numerous extraordinary buildings, within which thousands of students have had the good fortune to study. Since my first involvement with the Hebrew University, I had been introduced to many of the highly distinguished teaching staff but still hadn't put my finger on whether academia was really right for me. On our second night in Jerusalem, the university hosted a very special dinner. There were three remarkable speakers – one being a Druze and the others, two professors at the Hebrew University. But all three spoke with a sense of inclusiveness of Jews and non-Jews alike, and after that evening I didn't have to give it a second thought. I was hooked.

Then Professor Yehuda Bauer came into my life. This extraordinary man was born in Prague. Through one adventure after another he had managed to dodge the Nazis, and arrived in Palestine with his family in 1939. A historian specializing in the Holocaust, he taught at the university and I had read many of his brilliant books on the history of the Holocaust and the Jewish resistance to it. The first time I attended a Yehuda Bauer lecture, the hall at the university was packed with people. He was an extraordinary speaker, passionately relating historical events to his own story, and spoke of anti-Semitism with such power and commitment that I got goosebumps listening to him. Yehuda had belonged to a *kibbutz* for many years and he and the neighbouring Bedouins had enormous respect for one another. He talked of peace and of how Israel's technological skill and advanced society could be so helpful to her Arab neighbours. He totally captivated his audience, and as he finished there was a thunderous roar of approval from about 800 people. There was no question in my mind that he was one of the greatest orators I had ever heard – not just on anti-Semitism, but on many other subjects, as well.

One evening at the King David Hotel in Jerusalem, Yehuda approached me with the idea of creating a centre for the study of anti-Semitism and related bigotries. He felt there should be an independent, non-political place where students of all disciplines – historians, psychologists, literature students – could come to study the relationships between Jews and non-Jews across the ages. As he spoke I kept thinking about my own experience of racial hatred, of all the intolerance I had seen first-hand as a young man in the air force and on the streets of

London, and I could not think of any subject that was more personal or more important to me. He mentioned money. Yehuda had clearly been thinking this up for ages as he'd done his sums and quite straightforwardly told me what this centre would need both to start up and then to run. It was a considerable sum – it would be quite a project – but without any further hesitation I said yes. He had my support – but we would need more.

Yehuda and I went on a tour of America, speaking in private homes and halls hosted by generous people who gave splendid dinners and dug deep for our cause, inviting many of their wealthy friends to do the same. I was the warm-up act for Yehuda, talking about my own experiences with anti-Semitism. One night in Cleveland, Ohio, Yehuda was so powerful that at the end of his appeal there was silence, then rapturous applause. That evening, $250,000 came into the kitty for our centre. Our tour of America, over time, brought $3 million dollars to the Hebrew University and, combined with the money I had pledged, we were able to start the ball rolling. In 1982 space was found for us in a beautiful building on campus and Yehuda opened his office there and hired staff. The Vidal Sassoon International Center for the Study of Anti-Semitism was founded.

Yehuda not only became the expert and adviser on anti-Semitism for Israel and many foreign governments, but he was invited to address the entire Bundestag in Germany on the subject, with Chancellor Helmut Kohl in attendance. He kept the audience riveted for half an hour and received a five-minute standing ovation.

There were well-publicized seminars. I particularly remember one at Oxford University given by Dr Elizabeth Maxwell, a deeply spiritual Christian scholar who was also the wife of the publishing baron Robert Maxwell. Yehuda and I took lunch with the Maxwells, and their financial support for the four-day seminar enabled us to bring the very best speakers to the conference. Elie Wiesel was one of them and I remember more than 1,500 people trying to get seats at one of the university halls to hear him speak. He not only had a brilliant intellect, but his words had the immediacy of having personally experienced the atrocities of Auschwitz as a child. When he spoke about the horrors of the concentration camps you could have heard a pin drop.

Oxford University cooperated beautifully in our venture. A very dear friend and a human being of a rare kind was the Reverend Franklin Littell, who also gave a magnificent address. He was a Methodist minister who was known worldwide as one of the great Holocaust scholars, and founded the first doctoral programme in Holocaust Studies at Temple University in 1976. I once spoke at Stockton College, New Jersey, with Franklin and his wife, Marcie, both of whom were professors there. Franklin's deep love for Israel and what it had achieved gave all of us who heard him much to think about as we left the hall.

These were the kind of people I had the good fortune of getting to know personally through my interest in the Hebrew University. I was hopeful that if I spent more time in such company, a little of their knowledge might rub off on me.

Lou Lenart, who has been a buddy for many years, was a fighter pilot in the American Air Force during the War – and in 1948 led Israel's only squadron, which at the time consisted of just four Messerschmitts, German planes bought from Czechoslovakia. Ezer Weizman, who many years later became the president of the state of Israel, was one of Lou's wingmen. The other two pilots were Modi Alon and Eddie Cohen. Together they were known as the Famous Four. I, who was just a lowly private in the Palmach in 1948, hardly knew a soul higher up the ranks, and it was not until very much later, through my involvement with the Hebrew University, that I began to meet many of the dignitaries who had been involved in shaping the state of Israel.

Some time in the early eighties, Lou heard me speaking at the Hebrew University. Afterwards he told me he was interested in my Palmach background, but not nearly as interested as I was in his flying escapades. We became instant friends, and I would often see Lou in Los Angeles, where he lived half the time, and also in Israel, where he spent the other half of the year. With each year that passed I seemed more and more drawn to Israel and regularly flew over just to be there and take in the history of my 5,000-year-old tribe.

On one of these occasions Lou picked me up at the airport and took me to the Hilton Hotel in Tel Aviv, where the cement had longsince dried. In his suite were two other men. Lou introduced me as Private Sassoon, much to the amusement of the gentleman standing by the window, who turned out to be Ezer Weizman. The other gentleman was Irv Levin, who during the Second World War was a decorated bombardier in the United States Air Force. We polished off a bottle of wine, sang Israeli songs from the '48 period, and a wonderful friendship was forged.

My kids had loved Israel from their first visit when they were still tiny and couldn't wait for their yearly trip with me. George Shaw always came along to look after the younger ones. In 1994, on one of our annual trips, Lou happened to be in Tel Aviv and made arrangements to take my, now grown-up, children and me to the President's residence for brunch. Ezer Weizman had recently been appointed by the Knesset as the seventh president of Israel. He was warm and charming with my family and seemed genuinely delighted to meet them. They were absolutely in awe. Me too. After all, in addition to his own heroic service to Israel, Ezer was the nephew of Chaim Weizmann, who many years before had been the first president of Israel and one of the country's founders.

My time in the Israeli Army all those years ago came into its own when I met another remarkable man who would one day be honoured by the history books. When I first met Yitzhak Rabin, he was a great statesman out of power and in opposition to the then government and, like most politicians who find themselves in this position, not the happiest soul in the world. I had been introduced to him many years before by Simcha Dinitz, the Israeli ambassador, and then had re-met him on a number of occasions during his trips to the United States and also in Israel. There was something about him that mesmerized me, and in 1991, I was amazed to be invited to visit him at his home in Tel Aviv. As I walked into his small apartment with just one guard at the door, I realized how much he had given up for his country. As members of Parliament were not paid a great deal of money, he had clearly given up worldly goods in favour of the pursuit of wisdom. I don't know how or why I had the good fortune of spending two hours with Yitzhak Rabin in conversation in his apartment, but it was an afternoon I will never forget. He was clearly a man of frustrated ambition who needed to use that energy by being in office, and he talked of winning the next election and becoming prime minister again – which he eventually did. There was so much that separated us, but we had one thing in common: we were both *Palmachniks*, and we seemed to talk Palmach for an hour. I learned much about his beginnings in the military and about his passion for the land. Here was a lieutenant-general and chief of the general staff, giving me – a private – the benefit of his knowledge and experiences. I had to pinch myself to believe it was happening. I came away exhilarated and didn't tell this story until years later, as I was sure no one would have believed me. Even now, long after his death, I think of that day often.

In late 1982 Yaacov Agam, the famous Israeli artist and one of the pioneers of optical art, was in Los Angeles and I found myself sitting opposite him at a dinner party thrown in his honour at the home of a mutual friend. We hit it off and he asked me to call him the next time I was in Israel, which I did when I flew into Ben Gurion about a month later. He was very happy to introduce me to his artist friends and give me an insider's view of Tel Aviv – a city so colourful that its music, dance and arts were an intricate part of the country's existence.

A week later he called me and said he'd like to introduce me to a special friend of his – Menachem Begin.

I had to get him to repeat this. Surely he was joking?

He wasn't. Agam made all the arrangements and we arrived at the Parliament building about three o'clock the following afternoon and were shown into the Prime Minister's quarters. My first impression as we shook hands was that Menachem Begin's reputation for being an impeccable dresser was clearly well deserved. Every detail, from the polished shoes to the pressed suit and the matching shirt and tie, was beautifully coordinated and immaculate. But debonair attire aside, as soon as he spoke his statesmanlike qualities came to the fore. During the troubles in 1948 before Israel became a state, Menachem Begin was the leader of the Irgun Zvai Leumi, which was considered by many to be a terrorist group. He was profoundly knowledgeable and though he spoke kindly and softly, he obviously carried a big stick. He seemed a little perturbed; I wondered if it was about the situation in Lebanon, which was very much in the news then. Slightly neurotically I began to worry whether he was annoyed with Agam for bringing a lowly hairdresser to meet him at a difficult time.

Prime Minister Begin and Agam went off into Hebrew for a few minutes. Agam must have told him that I had been in the Palmach because suddenly his attitude turned very friendly and he put his arm around me. He asked me which battalion I fought with and who were my officers, and we talked of the Negev Desert and what a deep, almost spiritual effect it had had on us. As Agam and I left, the Prime Minister said, 'Come again,' but I never had the opportunity. I only met him that one time, but he made a lasting impression on me.

In the early nineties, Ronnie and I made a trip to Israel with my lawyer and good friend Ron Litz and his wife, Gloria. I was due to make an appearance at the Hebrew University to meet some young Arabs who had just won scholarships there. A call came from Brigham Young University, which has a large and beautiful campus on Mount Scopus near Jerusalem, asking me if I would give a presentation there about my experiences in Israel.

The hall at Brigham Young was full of blond, blue-eyed, eighteen-year-old Mormons doing their year of community service overseas to broaden their minds and expand their knowledge of the world. Their questions were far-reaching and I wasn't sure my answers were developed enough to satisfy their curiosity, but I quickly decided to put aside the lecture I had prepared, dug deep and just shared my personal experiences with them. It was a very satisfying evening and it certainly seemed that they didn't want it to end. I learned that night how much the Mormons believed in something that we all could gain from – a dedication to service, giving of oneself without monetary compensation. They were a delightful bunch and as they left, I wanted to hug them all one by one for the insight they had given me.

As the Litzes, Ronnie and I were preparing to leave, a distinguished-looking and rather beautiful Arab couple came over to us, saying how much they had enjoyed the evening. They were husband and wife, and both taught Islamic history at Brigham Young. After an opening *Salam*, they said they enjoyed my passion and even-handedness, and wanted to know if we would like to visit Ramallah, the West Bank town where they lived.

The four of us joined them after their morning commitments at Brigham Young and drove to Ramallah. They showed us the town, entertained us in their home and took us to a kindergarten school where the children were dressed in smart uniforms. When we arrived, they were having a sing-song. After they finished, I said how beautiful their voices were and how charming the song sounded. Our host and his wife gave a knowing glance at one another and then he said, 'It may have sounded beautiful, but the words in Arabic mean "It is our duty to kill all the Jews."'

When I asked why this was allowed, our hosts explained sadly that the recent history of the Arab people had led to this attitude being taught in schools; they could not teach another point of view. In the 1967 war, Israel took over territory that they believed was rightly theirs. The Arabs felt exactly the same way; they believed it was *theirs*. The professor told us that the children's parents and grandparents were terribly frustrated because since 1948, each time there had been peace proposals, they had come to nothing.

We made arrangements to meet this intriguing couple again, and we shared a delicious meal together at a superb Arab restaurant in Jerusalem. The restaurant's clientele was mostly Arab, but many Israelis were also patrons. Our friends seemed to know everyone there and, much to my admiration, could converse fluently in Arabic, English and Hebrew. It is quite obvious why I cannot mention their names, but we all left with a sincere wish that enlightenment and peace were just around the corner.

❖

My first meeting – a very wet one – with Zubin Mehta was in the early eighties. He was in the swimming pool of the Hilton Hotel in Tel Aviv, throwing children up in the air and catching them. I was trying to swim laps. There was no chance of me finishing with kids flying all over the pool, so I gave up. I glanced over at the guilty party to give him a dirty look. To my amazement it was the great conductor. I introduced myself and told him that I was a great fan of his work. Zubin has always been involved with the Israel Philharmonic Orchestra and in 1981 had been appointed their music director for life. He invited me to join a group of his friends for dinner at an Indian restaurant that evening. Listening to Zubin ordering delectable-sounding spicy dishes for everyone with the passion he usually reserved for music was a wonderful experience, and I remember wanting to eat everything in sight. There was a quirky end to the meal, as our waiter rushed across the street to Ben & Jerry's to bring back ice cream. Zubin, being a national hero, was the only patron who was allowed to request American ice cream for his dessert. Nobody seemed to mind.

When I got back to Los Angeles, a lady called Ruth Gold called. Zubin had asked her to get in touch with me. Ruth and I met and discussed ways to raise funds for the Israel Philharmonic, and she asked if I would be prepared to help. There was no doubt in my mind that it was a good cause so I said an unequivocal yes. We decided on an outrageously expensive evening to be held on 15 December 1991 – at $25,000 a couple. We would keep the format simple. Zubin would arrive with another celebrated musician who would play and a lovely dinner would follow.

First I had to find a house that was big enough to hold between 100 and 125 people. Given the occasion, it seemed fitting to approach the world-famous composer Henry Mancini and his wife, Ginny, who had a very beautiful house in Beverly Hills. When we told them in strictest confidence that Zubin would be bringing the prodigiously talented young violinist Midori to play for the guests, they jumped at the idea of giving their home for the evening, as it could easily hold the required number of guests comfortably for dinner. The delightful Mrs Gold helped me with the guest list, which was no mean feat. Although at that moment America was enjoying an economic up-turn, $25,000 a couple was a lot of money for dinner and a bit of violin playing. But once Kirk Douglas and his wife, Anne, said yes, the evening became far easier to sell.

Henry and Ginny Mancini were wonderful hosts. My old friends Jack Klugman, Steve Lawrence and Eydie Gormé, and the Hollywood producer Sherry Lansing came, as did many other well-known music lovers. Zubin gave an impassioned speech about his orchestra and then Midori, just twenty years old, backed by three members of the Los Angeles Philharmonic, played her heart out. She played the violin so sweetly that when I closed my eyes I thought I was listening to Itzhak Perlman. There was something extraordinary about listening to music of that quality and intensity in the intimate surroundings of a private home. At the end of the evening, when it was announced that we had raised $1.1 million for the Israel Philharmonic I think that everyone felt as I did that we had given wisely. The Israeli Orchestra members were certainly not overpaid and needed all the donations they could get, and that night had topped their coffers up considerably. From that moment on, I seemed to see a lot of Zubin.

Ronnie and I, with half a dozen others, flew to Berlin with him, where he conducted the Berlin Philharmonic, and then to Tel Aviv, where, two days later, he conducted the Israel Philharmonic. His extraordinary power with both orchestras was a sight to behold.

Many years later, while doing a hair-product promotion in Seoul, Ronnie looked at the one English-language paper and announced that Zubin was conducting the Vienna Philharmonic that night in the city. I had a free evening and Ronnie called the concierge, who, when asked for tickets, laughingly said, 'They've been sold out for six months.' Ronnie, being so much smarter than me, realized that there could only be two or three hotels in that city of the right calibre for the Mehtas, and after two phone calls she tracked down Zubin's wife, Nancy, who immediately insisted we take their house tickets and join her for that night's performance.

As they had been on the road for quite some time, Nancy was as delighted to see us as we were to see her. Ronnie and I had never heard the Vienna Philharmonic live. Like all great orchestras, it had its own enviable sound and for us, with Zubin conducting, it was all the more special. Afterwards we had a lovely dinner with Nancy and Zubin. During dinner, Nancy looked across the table and said, 'I've got two tickets for the Michael Jackson show. He's playing Seoul tomorrow night.

Zubin can't come, he's conducting.' I couldn't go as I was working, so the following evening Nancy and Ronnie saw Michael
Jackson live in Korea.

Twenty-five years ago, I heard one of the fearless leaders of the
Druze, Zeidan Atashi, speak at a Hebrew University dinner in
Los Angeles and made a point of getting to know him. He was
not shy in asking for scholarship funds for his people and I was
pleased to contribute to such an important cause. In 1948 the
Druze fought on the side of the Israelis. Zeidan was a Druze first
but a loyal Israeli second. We became steadfast friends and have
visited one another's homes ever since. His fellow Druze, being
aware of my involvement, always treated me like family. Zeidan
had been an honours student at the university, a member of
the Israeli Parliament, and is now an ambassador-at-large for
his birthplace, Israel. Once, while visiting him, I met his great
friend Muhanna Kenaan, a fellow Druze who had worked his
way up through the ranks to become a general. Muhanna was
one of the high-ranking officers in the Israeli Defense Forces
who had held various commanding and combat posts, among
them commander of one of the brigades in northern Israel. This
encounter reinforced for me something I have always believed –
that wherever you come from, if you have what it takes, the
possibilities are limitless.

I adored Zeidan's wife, Zahvia, who sadly passed away
recently. She was an exceptional cook and took great joy in treat-
ing people to her culinary delights. It was advisable not to eat for
two days before visiting the Atashis because a dinner with them
was a feast. There was dish after dish of delicious Middle Eastern
food and not to eat two helpings of everything would have been an
insult. Zahvia would invite neighbours who spoke English to join

us, as throughout the British sojourn in Palestine, most people had English as their second language. The Druze had their members of Parliament and seemed to be so well informed regarding Israeli politics and how it affected the outside-Arab world. At one of their dinners, there was one delightful man who wanted to know when Israel was going to have its first Druze prime minister. I told him that in Britain there had only been one Jewish prime minister – Disraeli – and his father had had to change the family religion before they would allow him to serve.

❖

Having a foundation named after you is a privilege, but you have to have the money to fund it. In the eighties and nineties, black Ethiopian Jews were pouring into Israel in large numbers and the Israeli government paid for their health, education and housing. Students going to college were given grants by the government, but needed an allowance to pay for necessities like books, lab fees, transportation, clothing and food so that they could afford to stay in college and receive an education. In 1991, I was asked to help in a programme that had been founded by Middie and Jonathan Giesberg two years prior and was struggling to provide these necessities. The name was changed to Vidal Sassoon Adopt a Student programme and our foundation took over the administrative costs, so that all donations could go directly towards the students' needs. People's generosity continues to surprise me and large numbers of people 'adopted' these students, who are now young professionals – among them doctors, lawyers, engineers, scientists and politicians. The programme is funded yearly and in 2010 it costs $1,200 a year to provide for the basics that allow the students to complete their courses without getting themselves into unnecessary debt.

In 2005, I visited a school at Kiryat Ekron, a small town south of Tel Aviv, and saw lots of Ethiopian kids kicking a football around goal posts marked by pieces of clothing. They were completely absorbed in their game and I found myself transfixed. It reminded me so much of my own early days in Petticoat Lane that I decided to create a football programme for the school. In due course the foundation I set up provided sports kits and proper coaching and the football squad developed an unshakeable team spirit. As well as the physical practicalities – nets, training, transport – the sponsorship also provided an after-school study programme to help nourish both the mind and body. With all this on their doorstep my little team soon became a force to be reckoned with. In 2006, the Maccabee Junior League realized how serious we were and made me proud by accepting my kids' team into the league. In the opinion of the head coach, Chaim Levy, four of the youngsters presently in the programme have the potential to be professional soccer players.

There's a photograph of me with the team that I treasure. I can almost imagine myself as Roman Abramovich surrounded by my squad. I can't get there as often as I'd like, but sometimes I think I've had as much joy and satisfaction out of my little Ethiopian Israeli football team as all the so-called celebrity that helped build my name.

Both the Adopt a Student and youth football programmes are run by the North American Conference on Ethiopian Jewry (NACOEJ), an organization that runs important programmes, without whose total caring and efficiency nothing would get done.

In 1994, I was asked to develop a seminar for the Hebrew University in Los Angeles. There was a well-established format whereby each year professors from the university lectured to a thousand or more Los Angeles residents on subjects ranging from new advancements in science to philosophy, psychology and some subjects the names of which I can't even spell. The event was held at the Century Plaza Hotel, as it had a large ballroom. I wanted my day to be different, so I invited the Reverend Jesse Jackson, James Zogby, founder of the Arab American Institute, Dr Alan Keyes, an American Conservative political activist, Professor Yehuda Bauer and the Reverend Franklin Littell. To my great surprise, they all accepted and the diverse views we heard on that Sunday were mind-boggling. The conference was billed as 'Fighting Bigotry through Education: The Challenge of Xenophobia, Racism, and Antisemitism' and I was the conference chair. There was not one subject that all five agreed upon, but as was expected, their opinions were passionately held and tenaciously argued.

Later that year, I stood on Mount Scopus in Jerusalem being presented with an honorary doctorate in philosophy. For a kid who left school at the age of fourteen, this was the highest honour I could possibly dream of – from a university I not only love, but which has an extraordinary reputation as one of the world's finest institutions for the dissemination of ideas. Dr Sassoon! I toyed with the idea of having new business cards made up. But only briefly.

Many major cities around the world have a museum or a piece of architecture to remind us of the Holocaust. Not that we would ever want to forget, but neither will we be allowed to. I've been to quite a few of them on my travels and they have all affected me in their different ways. Twenty years or so ago, I was in Miami Beach, Florida, with Ronnie and some friends who insisted on showing us Miami's memorial. It's set around a water garden and the architect has played on the multiple reflections created by luminous Jerusalem stone, sombre black granite and the stillness of the water. All well and good on paper no doubt, but as you walked over the black stone at night, it was very hard to tell where the walkway finished and the water began. At least it was for me. As I walked closer, to get a feel of the memorial, I inadvertently stepped into three feet of water. Ronnie heard a splash and was in absolute hysterics, as she knew my tendency to be accident-prone and this did not surprise her. Her friends, on the other hand, were quite concerned about my unexpected dip and said that they would run us back to the hotel. Eventually as we reached the hotel, we had to decide how to get in, as every time I moved, I squelched. As we said goodnight to our friends, Ronnie came up with the perfect solution. 'Take your jacket off and your shoes and march through the lobby as if you own the place.'

I took Ronnie's advice, but as I dripped my way across the hotel lobby she kept laughing hysterically that someone who had created a centre for the study of anti-Semitism in Jerusalem had been so easily done in by a memorial to the Holocaust in Miami Beach.

16

Letting Go

By the early eighties the product division had become so all-encompassing, so time-consuming that I felt it was in danger of eclipsing the core business. Yet no one was more aware than me that without the hairdressing salons we would never have had the ever-expanding range of shampoos and conditioners. How could I show the people who worked in our salons and training schools that had it not been for them and their work, the products would never have happened? I wanted them to realize that they were still leading the craft. After much deliberation I decided that the only way to show them how important they were was to give them autonomy. I called a meeting with our top management sometime in 1983 and told them my feelings. We all agreed that we wanted to keep the salons and schools in the family – the hairdressing family – and it was decided to give three of our very top people a leveraged buyout and allow them to run the salons and schools themselves.

Christopher Brooker, who had been with me more or less from the beginning, was the brilliant artistic man the board chose as creative director as we knew he had the ideas and the charisma to inspire the young up-and-coming hairdressers. If evidence were needed of his overwhelming suitability for the job, I only had to think back to the time Chris had beaten the great Art Buchwald at chess while we were travelling from Fort Lauderdale to Rio on the *Queen Elizabeth*, doing hair shows. Art, who was the on-board entertainment, said, 'I can't believe I was beaten by a hairdresser!' I remember saying, 'There's more to us crimpers than meets the eye.'

My first choice for the role of management would have been Joshua Galvin, but he had left us after he fell out with Tommy Yeardye. Phillip Rogers was a young hairdresser who had joined us in the very early days, noisily working his way up to become a manager. You always knew when Phillip was in the salon as he had an extremely forceful personality. Phillip, then, seemed to be an obvious choice, as he had done a splendid job of management in the past. The board ruminated a long time over who should manage our extraordinary business, which was constantly growing. We were very divided on this one but in the end Phillip got the vote.

For the third choice, we didn't have to look any further than Annie Humphries. Annie, who had become the teacher to all colourists worldwide and renowned for her extraordinary expertise in creative colour work, was another obvious choice. Annie may have been tiny but she was a mighty dictator in her department and commanded everyone's respect. She would create the wildest colours and her ingenuity inspired the whole company; colour is such an important aspect of how a haircut looks.

The three of them reacted to the news with considerable excitement, of course – they were being given the opportunity of a lifetime. And for some time, they worked together beautifully. But after three years I got a call from Christopher, who said he could no longer work with Phillip as their philosophical approach was so different. Apparently there had been numerous arguments and he had come to the conclusion their differences were irreconcilable. Had the situation been allowed to go on any longer, it would have jeopardized everything we had worked for in the past. Annie, to my surprise, sided with Phillip. They arranged to buy out Christopher – which saddened me, as I felt he was the most likely person to stay true to our original vision.

Christopher's departure left something of a gaping hole in the role of creative director. Fortunately for Annie and Phillip, there was a new boy on the scene who was just beginning to make a name for himself. Tim Hartley was given a great opportunity to fill Christopher's spot as international artistic director. He did this for more than two decades, going from country to country, salon to salon, developing shows that were so individual that his work with the company created a standard of work that equalled Christopher's. It had always been my dream that among the young artists and managers there would be hairdressers with the ability to create, manage and eventually buy the business. It was clear to me – and many others – that Tim had the talent and charisma to carry the name forward and truly step into Christopher's shoes. If he had been made a full partner, and allowed to take over his share in the business, his voice might have carried the day. Unfortunately, this was not to be. Twenty years after they had first taken over the reins, Phillip and Annie announced that they were selling the company to the hairdressing giant Regis, who had literally thousands of salons everywhere. On 18 December 2002 Regis bought twenty-five salons and four academies. Sadly, our management team had failed miserably to realize my dreams.

When my son Elan heard what was happening to the salons and schools he leapt into action. He was in his thirties by this time and making a name for himself in the beauty business just as he had always said he would. He got together a consortium of people with the money to buy the salons. He made an offer, but the deal with Regis had already been sealed. The only asset that has come out of all this – and it is a very important one – is that Regis allowed Sassoon to remain Sassoon and keep its standards of excellence intact.

To say that I was distraught would be an understatement. I had given a group of people I trusted the chance of a lifetime. Not only did I feel let down, but I wondered why I had been stupid enough to create the situation in the first place.

During that ghastly period, wherever I was travelling and there was a Sassoon salon, I felt compelled to visit – not only to see our people, but to see the work. I was encouraged enormously by the standard they kept up and by the great warmth they always showed me. It was as if people were saying, 'Don't worry, Vidal. We won't let you down.' And they didn't. In London last year, at a fashion party, I kept staring at a girl whose haircut and colour were quite superb. Finally I couldn't resist going over to her and asking her where she had it done. She looked at me and smiled, saying, 'At your place. Where else?'

Although I have no particular relationship with Regis, I have met Paul Finkelstein, their CEO, on a few occasions. He has had the foresight to let Sassoon be Sassoon – for a very good reason. If he decided at any point that Sassoon truly didn't belong to his group of salons, the standards would still be so high that he could get a good price for it.

❖

VIDAL

Annie Humphries, uber-colourist, still with her finger in every
pie, was colouring Ronnie's hair in Japan in January 1994 and
she mentioned that London Fashion Week was working out of
a small hotel. 'It's a total disaster, and will go under unless
somebody comes along to save it.' Apparently it had dwindled to
the point where a few brave designers were showing their
collections in a London hotel to a handful of the fashion press.
Annie was quite concerned about a dying London Fashion Week
and asked Ronnie to enlist my help. At the time, Ronnie and
I were touring with our team in Japan. Ronnie must have
badgered me at least half a dozen times to do something and
quickly. London Fashion Week had played an important role in
inspiring Britain's young designers since it began in 1984 and
Ronnie was determined that I should be the one to try and save
it. She was so persuasive that eventually I called Procter &
Gamble and they were more than willing to help with a
rescue operation. I was delighted that they acted so speedily,
as time was of the essence, though I was disappointed that
the fashion stores in Britain were not as helpful as they could
have been. It appeared they did not have the vision
to see how critical London Fashion Week was to the British
economy.

It was arranged that Annie would contact Clinton Silver,
the chairman of the British Fashion Council, and set up a
meeting for the day after our return from Japan. The results of
that meeting were so positive that the very next season tents
were erected once again in the grounds of the Natural History
Museum in the hope that the majority of British designers would
participate. Fortunately many of them did. Procter & Gamble
insisted that the event be highly publicized and the Vidal
Sassoon name be prominently displayed over every tent.

Suddenly young fashion designers who had given up hope of ever being recognized had a venue to show their talents. Great designers like Alexander McQueen and John Rocha – who was the Designer of the Year in 1994 – gave the lead. It is extraordinary how with a little initiative things can change drastically in a hurry. Just six months later, the international press decided that, after New York, they would cover the London shows before Paris and Milan. The effect of this was wide-ranging and, more importantly, long-lasting. London was firmly back on the fashion map. Ronnie said to me, 'With all the money there is in fashion, they had to get a crimper to save it.'

The rush created from all the excitement not only brought top designers from so many other countries, it gave London the edgy, creative feeling it had in the sixties once again. On 22 January 1994, Alison Veness wrote a piece in the *Independent* headlined SASSOON STEPS IN TO SAVE LONDON FASHION WEEK. I still have that cutting on the wall of my office.

Six months later, we had to rent considerably more space for Fashion Week, as word had spread and booths were taken by many companies who were not walking the catwalk but did want to show their wares for the following season. By making it more of a public spectacle again, interest had been stirred and many ordinary people expressed a desire to get tickets to see the shows. We organized separate shows for the public, which pleased the designers enormously, as many of the people who came would see their clothes at their launch and would want to buy them even more when they hit the stores. Many of the new designers became famous because of their ground-breaking shows at London Fashion Week and afterwards were invited to design for many of the big houses in Paris and Milan. This only served to heighten the appeal of the week as so many other young designers happily took their place.

Of all the great fashion designers who came through London, Alexander McQueen was in a league of his own. With Alexander you could forget the runway. Girls would sometimes be surrounded by fire. Sitting in the audience, one always had a sense of great expectancy and he never let us down. There was one show where they actually walked through water. There is no question in my mind that he could have produced and directed a West End stage production for the theatre. Actually many of his shows *were* first-class stage productions and we were his first-night audience, whom he never failed to surprise and delight. With all this showmanship, he was still one of the finest cutters and designers in the industry. His death was such a tremendous loss to fashion.

I greatly enjoyed my involvement with London Fashion Week. I believe it was one of the most important events that Vidal Sassoon, as a company, ever became involved with, but after eight years it was time to hand over the reins to others and move on.

17

A Bypass Round My Heart

Catya, my eldest child, started acting as a teenager. The studios had taken an interest in her and we dined with many of their executives. They wanted to make her a big star in the Hollywood way. She never made it. Drugs got to her first. When she was just fourteen, I remember her coming to the house; she wasn't herself at all, and it was far too obvious what was making her different.

By the time she was fifteen, she had become a model in New York. We got her a flat there and arranged for someone to look after her, as a sort of minder figure. It didn't help. It came to a head when she was invited to do *The Morning Show* and asked me to be on it with her. I flew in from Los Angeles, looking forward to having fun with her on TV.

We met at seven in the morning in the green room. She was totally stoned. For Catya and me, and probably the audience, too, it was the most embarrassing ten minutes of television. I insisted she return to LA with me, but she was soon in trouble again.

We booked Catya into the Betty Ford Center, and after a

month there she seemed to have regained her spirit. Just before her sixteenth birthday, she married a lovely guy called Luca. When they came to me to say they wanted to get married, I had a long chat with him. I was desperate and thought it was possibly her last chance and asked him, 'Can you handle it?' He thought he could, but he couldn't. Their marriage lasted just a couple of years.

Cat was shooting a film in South Africa when she met a guitar player from Zimbabwe. They came back to the US together, got married, and had a son, whom they named London. Soon after, they moved to Zimbabwe, but in a short while, that relationship ended, too. Before too long, Catya was in a very bad way. Our friends from New York, John and Nitza Heyman, recommended a recovery house in Israel, just outside Tel Aviv, with which Nitza was very actively involved. She told me they were tough but kind, and would not take any nonsense. But after several weeks in Israel, Catya phoned her mother, who flew her and London back to LA. Very sadly, Catya's problem came with her.

She started misbehaving badly in the Beverly Hills salon. Etienne Taenaka, the very experienced manager of our West Coast salons, went up to her and said, 'You are embarrassing yourself, embarrassing the salon and, even more, embarrassing your father. I do not want you to come here any more.'

It had to take a lot of guts for Etienne to bar my daughter from a salon that bore her last name on the door, and for a while I felt a mixture of anger that he should have done so and remorse for my daughter's terrible behaviour. It was a great shock to me, but I did not reproach Etienne when I heard about it and we have never discussed it. I don't think he knows to this day that I knew then what had happened. And – as I watched him work, handling his staff with discipline but also great kindness – I realized he had been in the right.

Sometime later Catya was very fortunate to meet a young man named Joe Meyers. He was tender and cared for her with all his heart; we liked him immediately. Joe's a great guy and a wonderful dad to their twin girls, Skye and Mycca, who are now ten years old. For a while it seemed as if things were at last going well for Catya, but the effects of Joe's well-intentioned influence could not last.

There was only one moment in our relationship when Ronnie turned to me and said that she couldn't take it any more. Catya always seemed to hit her lowest lows with her drug addiction when Ronnie and I were either touring for the company or on holiday. After one particularly bad episode it became clear to us that the situation was putting an intolerable strain on our marriage and we needed professional help. For over twenty-five years, I had been the patient of Dr Soram Singh Khalsa – a brilliant man who had all his medical degrees, then decided that his true calling was in holistic medicine. Ronnie and I spoke to him about our situation and he recommended a marriage and family counsellor, Dr Sat Kaur Khalsa, who had her offices nearby. She saw Ronnie and me, sometimes as a couple and sometimes separately. For five years Dr Sat Kaur counselled us and brought us closer together. We owe her a lot.

A couple of years into our counselling, we were in London, preparing for a visit to Prague. Ronnie was so shaken up by the latest Catya events, she announced she was not carrying on with the trip and was going to go back to Los Angeles. I spent a couple of days alone in London, fearful that she might really be about to leave me. You never give up on a child and even though

I knew Catya's case was fairly hopeless, I now had the added concern about Ronnie. I cancelled Prague.

When I got back to Los Angeles, Ronnie was waiting for me at the airport and, with all the warmth she could muster, kissed and hugged me and welcomed me back. It really hit home that my wife had been living through a nightmare situation, which without her natural strength could easily have overcome her. But at that moment I knew we were a team and could get through almost anything together.

New Year's Day 2002 is a date I will never forget. We were in Cincinnati visiting Ronnie's family for the holidays when we got the call. The phone rang and it was not well-wishers ushering in the new year; it was the worst news a parent can ever receive. My beautiful daughter had been found dead.

Catya had done so much damage to herself, maybe she just knew her fate. She must have had some kind of premonition of what was to come. During 2001 she kept saying, 'Let's do this together,' and, 'Let's get the family together for that.' She had tried to get herself clean so many times but it was as if she knew her time was up. She was thirty-three when she died. Catya had overdosed at a New Year's Eve party and closed her eyes for the last time. You never completely recover from the loss of a child, whether they fulfilled their potential or not. And there still are Catya days. How could there not be?

✧

Elan, our second child, has grown up to be a very handsome lad. He's six foot two and has a great gift for friendship. He is still close to lots of the same kids he grew up with. As a young man, he had a great passion for Brazilian legs and the women who grew them, and the summer before his last year of high school he chased a girl to Rio. He called me and asked, 'Can I do my last year in Rio?' Apparently there was an American school there that would accept him.

I said yes, on the condition he became fluent in Portuguese. He took private lessons three times a week. After one year in Brazil the girl he had chased had moved on, so he enrolled in the American University in Washington, DC. Bill Cohen, who would later become Secretary of Defense in Bill Clinton's Cabinet, was a senator for Maine at that time and he happened to know Beverly quite well. It was the first week of school and I went to Washington with Elan to see him settled in. He said to me, 'Dad, Mother has made arrangements for Bill Cohen to take me around the Senate. Would you like to come with me?'

I don't think he realized that not every boy studying at the American University was taken around the Senate during his first week by a member of that august body.

You could make a bet that when eventually Elan met the love of his life she would be Brazilian. After graduation from college, he met a girl from San Paolo in Los Angeles named Adriana Kfouri. She has long legs, brown eyes and a very pleasing bone structure – essential if you're going to produce little Sassoons! They got married in LA and Adriana's parents came from Brazil for the wedding. Her father spoke no English and her mother had to translate the ceremony for him. They are now living in Boston, where Elan has opened salons and developed his own line of hair products – his gracious way with people has won him many lucrative business arrangements. He and Adriana have two gorgeous children – Ariel, who is ten, and Isabella, who is five.

Isabella is bright and saucy, and I'm delighted by her personality when I see her – which unfortunately isn't all that often.

It wasn't until they went to school that the kids became proficient in English. The last time I saw Isabella, in fluent English she said, 'Grandpa, no more bottom biting.' Her elder brother, Ariel, has the spirit and chutzpah to be a creative force in his own right. He speaks beyond his years and his middle name is 'Trouble'. Elan delights in his children and takes Ariel with him everywhere. For his age, the kid is a spectacular soccer player and has been chosen for one of the top boys' teams in Boston. I adore them both and their father fills me with great pride.

My youngest daughter, Eden, is like me in many respects. By the time she was fourteen, when not studying at school, she would be either working as a waitress or selling clothes in a boutique just to earn a little cash of her own to give herself some independence. I told her that if she behaved, I'd find her a newspaper round.

She changed schools quite often. She had so many interests, she never quite settled on any one thing, though eventually she spent a year at Pepperdine University. She married an Israeli boy, Tomer DeVito. Not a typically Israeli name, but then his father is Italian. Tomer and Eden have two children, Olivia and Tyler, five and three years old respectively. These are the two grandchildren whom we see the most, as they live nearby, in LA. Olivia is very shy around me, just as her mother was when she was that age. She's adorable, and guess what? *Very* beautiful. Tyler, blond, blue-eyed – haven't a clue where that came from – always charges into the house head first with fists flailing. This delightful young tearaway keeps me in hysterics with his antics. He's caught me a couple of times in a very unfortunate place, but we know he will grow and my life will become less painful.

Eden and a business partner have opened a Pilates studio

in Beverly Hills that seems to be full from morning till night. She loves the excitement of seeing the physical improvement of the people who regularly train there. Eden has a wonderful get-up-and-go mentality and it's great to see her enthusing the inhabitants of LA into donning their workout gear and doing the same. She is very precious and will always be my little girl.

Some years ago, Jim McElman, a friend of ours, a police sergeant whom I knew through Beverly, called and asked if I would come down to the station. *What could he possibly want?* By this time David was thirteen and, as it turned out, getting into all kinds of trouble that I hadn't heard about. He and some friends were jump-starting cars, driving them a few blocks and then abandoning them.

Sergeant McElman said, 'Get him out of town. Otherwise, I'll have to send him downtown.'

David spent a couple of years at a reform school near Sundance, in Utah. There was a chap there called Smith, a very skilled psychiatrist. He took David on and did wonders with him. He came back to Los Angeles but still didn't seem to fit in. I had done a bit of homework and found out about a great school called Morehouse in Atlanta. It was an African-American facility and I thought this would be the answer for him. Naïvely I thought he might learn something about the other half of his birth culture which could give him a sense of pride.

I got an appointment for us at Morehouse and looked around the campus, feeling more and more sure that this was the right place for David. David came to his own conclusion. I asked, 'David, is Morehouse for you?'

He said, 'Not really, Dad. There's no white chicks here.'

David never found his roots, but he enrolled at college –

Franklin Pierce College in New Hampshire – and seemed to enjoy his time there, becoming a quite brilliant speaker. He also became an avid reader and would sometimes read three books at once. After college, he came back to LA but still hadn't found his true calling. One day he left and went to Montreal to work as a sous chef, then to San Francisco. He talks to his brother and sister all the time and recently moved back to Los Angeles. Regrettably, in the past few years I've not been on his A-list of people to phone. We have not spoken at all for a year and a half, but recently David told Eden that he has many regrets and now feels so much closer to the family and wants to see me. He is clearly going through a soul-searching period, trying to understand who he is. I can't wait to see him and spend time with him once again. He has the ability to do something great with his life. I regret enormously that I might have been the cause of his leaving town, as I expected so much from him and was always on his case. We will see one another soon, but one thing is certain – I will not be as forceful, and I'll allow him to develop at his own pace.

❖

In April 2000, shortly after my seventy-second birthday, Procter & Gamble demanded that I had a total physical examination, and asked if they could use my cardiologist's office at Cedars Sinai Medical Center for the exam. I'd had routine physical exams before from them but this was in connection with a large insurance policy and the company involved were demanding more exhaustive tests. I was still touring for the company an extraordinary number of days each year and they wanted to be sure I was up to it. They sent two rather portly insurance doctors to conduct a whole host of examinations. After the tests, which included some physical activity, the two medical people declared themselves quite happy with my health.

My cardiologist, Dr Rick Gold – who was present at the exam – suggested differently. He said that what would normally be considered a healthily low heart rate was in my case significantly lower than last recorded. He told me that given the workout they had made me do, my heart rate should have been more rapid, and immediately made arrangements for an angiogram, which I had the following morning. He wanted to rule out any possibility of a blockage. Ronnie came with me with some apprehension, worried about possible complications with the procedure. She was asked to stay in the waiting room while I had the angiogram. A Dr Neil Buchbinder did the exam, and after half an hour he and Rick Gold approached me. I could tell by the look on their faces that the news wasn't good. They told me as kindly as they could that my condition was serious. They would operate in the morning. Ever the optimist, Ronnie came bounding in when she saw the consultation was over, telling me to get dressed and that we were going for breakfast. When I told her that they were keeping me in for surgery she said I was just groggy and confused. I told her they were scheduling a heart bypass for the following morning and poor Ronnie literally collapsed in shock.

That evening, just like in the movies, the family gathered around my bedside. I cracked jokes and the kids and I sang the old songs that I used to sing to them so many years before. It was so good to see them all. If I was to go, it would be with a smile on my face.

The following morning I was given a quadruple heart bypass by Dr Alfredo Trento. The operation was apparently a success and I owe my life to Rick Gold, who first spotted the danger, and the rest of that wonderful team at Cedars Sinai. During the operation I felt as though I was out of my body watching the whole procedure take place. I awoke in recovery just as Dr Trento was making his rounds. He approached me and said, 'I've given you another twenty years.'

'But I wanted twenty-five,' I replied, surprised to find that the words came out oddly slurred.

The very next day I got up and walked the halls of the hospital. I met Ronnie coming towards me. *Was she real, or was I dreaming?* I felt nothing like myself.

It never occurred to me that for the next six months I would be just half a person. I was back in the hospital twice while they extracted liquid from around my lungs, and once more with atrial fibrillation. I was thankful the day they finally allowed me to get into the pool, but it took six months before I conquered the mile again. I had always been thin but I'd lost a lot of weight after the surgery and now looked like a gaunt Sinatra. I was often cold even when bundled up – and needed a lot of cuddling. Ronnie said it took a year before she got her husband back both physically and mentally.

Naturally my touring for Procter & Gamble came to an end. I do not know what happened to the two overweight gents who gave my health the thumbs-up. I just know how lucky I am to be writing this book.

18

Hairdressers in a Hurricane

On 28 August 2005, Hurricane Katrina pounded the southern coast of the United States with devastating effect. According to the US Department of Health and Human Services, more than 1,800 people lost their lives and more than $81 billion of damage was accrued. I watched the scenes on television in horror, as story after story of people's personal disasters left me feeling totally helpless. It seemed unbelievable that New Orleans had been razed to the ground, leaving so many of its inhabitants homeless. Seeing the sheer desperation on the faces of people who had lost everything, I felt very uneasy endlessly watching the news on CNN from the comfort of our home. I caught Ronnie's eye. She was clearly thinking what I was thinking. *We need to do something about this.*

Poor housing, shoddy foundations, the more the story unfolded, the more it showed up the huge gulf between rich and poor in our society. After a rant about this with my son-in-law Tomer, he called Habitat for Humanity to see how we might help. Habitat, as it is commonly called, is an international Christian non-profit organization devoted to building simple, decent and affordable housing for those in need. Ronnie and I decided that – as a start – we would personally provide the funds for two houses to be built.

We needed to enlist some more support, and what better place to start than the industry where I had made my name. Mary Rector-Gable, who owns the beauty industry's biggest networking site – behindthechair.com – in Chicago, was keen to come to New Orleans with Tomer and me to get a feel of how she could help, along with Winn Claybaugh (founder and co-owner of Paul Mitchell the School), James Morrison (co-founder of Toni & Guy/TIGI USA) and Marilyn Esquivel, my business manager, who is involved in every aspect of my activities. Mary's website receives over half a million visitors per month – and through her promotion of our endeavours on her website, she encouraged many thousands of hairdressers to give what they could to this very worthwhile cause.

Habitat for Humanity took us by car on a complete tour of the city, including the areas that had been hit the hardest. New Orleans now looked like a bombed-out city after the Second World War. In the worst areas, where everything had been destroyed, the smell was rank. The bodies of those who had drowned had been fished out and taken to makeshift morgues to be identified. As I began to learn the truth about the city's infrastructure, I was horrified. The levees, supposed to hold back the water, were built on sand and mud, and as Robert Bea, Professor of Civil and Environmental Engineering at the University of California, Berkeley, wrote, 'If it had been built as it should have been built, we would be repairing some shingles and mopping up some wet carpets.'

At a higher level what I met with was inertia. It was then that my frustration turned to anger. How could people just get on with their lives and allow New Orleans and its people to drown? I just kept asking myself why would any government allow a whole city to sink? New Orleans desperately needed 50,000 new houses. The only positive thing I could cling on to was the knowledge that the hairdressing community had galvanized themselves when the people of New Orleans needed it most.

Mary Rector-Gable, to her great credit, organized a tour of major hair shows in many cities across America for me, and she would often join me on the road. Together with my right-hand gal Marilyn Esquivel, Mary and I launched the Hairdressers Unlocking Hope campaign. I spoke at many events that year and slowly but surely the money started to pour in from the hairdressing community. When Toni Mascolo, the brilliant crimper behind Toni & Guy, heard me talking about my plans to build a village in New Orleans funded by hairdressers from across the United States, he said without a second thought, 'Vidal, you've got a house.' I was floored. I had not even asked him for anything, but a large cheque from the Toni & Guy Foundation was quickly given soon after.

To date we have raised close to $2 million and have built twenty-three houses. The generosity of our hairdressing family, so many of whom rose to the occasion and donated unselfishly gives me an enormous sense of pride.

As the keys to the newly built houses were handed over to their new owners, many of us who had contributed to the project had the pleasure of seeing their sheer joy as they entered their homes – young kids squabbling over which bedrooms would be theirs and who would take the first bath in the new tub, parents crying and laughing with happiness because, at last, they had a roof over their heads once again. It was impossible not to be touched.

Marilyn came with me three times to help organize everything we were doing, whether it was building houses or catering for all the hairdressers who had so generously volunteered their time and resources. A certified public accountant who had come to work with us in 1992 shortly after Ronnie and I were married, she really came into her own in the aftermath of Hurricane Katrina. Apart from being quite brilliant with figures, she loves being involved in all our activities. As my contract with Procter & Gamble gradually unravelled, Marilyn worked many extra hours each day to help the lawyers. She has helped organize many projects for the Foundation and through her astuteness, she has always been able to spot anyone who is not particularly honourable, or who might try to exploit us. It gives me great satisfaction that Marilyn is still with me today.

❖

It sounds sentimental to describe one's work colleagues as family but that really is the best way to describe how I feel about the people with whom I've worked closely, especially my fellow crimpers. It amazes people who don't work in our business quite how close-knit it is. If you were to draw up a family tree of who started where and worked with whom, it's amazing how we all overlap.

It would be beyond my capabilities to write about every talented hairdresser I have known, but I would be remiss if I did not mention a few of them by name. They are all people who have more than proved their worth at what they do and I admire them enormously. Many of them, I might add – though not all – began their careers with us.

Paul Mitchell joined one of our London salons and then came over to join the American team – in a rather unique way.

When he led that group of Vidal Sassoon luxury liner, the *Queen Elizabeth*, travelling from Southampton to New York City, doing a show each day, it seemed to mark him out as a and for all. Without doubt, one of our most brilli London, by the time he got to New York, he had alr uilt a clientele for his Manhattan debut. The switchboard was literally deluged with refined ladies from the Upper East Side requesting the services of the delightful young man they had met on their cruise. He was one of the brightest young businessmen that ever worked with the company. In 1980, after his time with us in New York, he teamed up with John Paul DeJoria and together they built one of the most creative empires in the history of hairdressing, based on an overwhelming belief in developing quality products that could only be sold through salons. Paul sadly died, far too young, of pancreatic cancer, but his son Angus trained with us at our academies and became a very fine craftsman in his own right. He has the gentlest nature and a wonderful sense of humour – just like his father – and he calls me each year on my birthday and other special occasions. Angus is very involved in the Paul Mitchell franchise, and they continue to break all records in our business.

Trevor Sorbie has taught many hairdressers worldwide his methods and he has a wonderfully individual talent. It gives me a great deal of pleasure to know that he started in a Vidal Sassoon salon in 1972 and within a year rose to the rank of artistic director – something that nobody else has done in such a short time. He just seemed to take our methods and run with them, reinventing them totally – everything he did had a definite 'Sorbie' touch. Some of his world-renowned looks were photographed while he was still at Vidal Sassoon. He opened his salon in Covent Garden in 1979 and was named British Hairdresser of the Year for so many years that we felt the award belonged to him on a permanent basis.

In 2009 Trevor interviewed me for a column he was writing for a newspaper. We met at his salon and when I walked in, I made it my business to greet the receptionist, the stylists, the shampooists and the cleaning lady. I'd always do this in any salon – especially my own. It is so important to make people feel they are needed and appreciated. Trevor picked up on this and made it the focal point of his article. When he was awarded an MBE in 2004 I couldn't have been more delighted. I hold him in the highest esteem as a hairdresser of the most outstanding creative abilities, and I enjoy the mutual respect we have for one another.

John Frieda always knew where he was going. Sadly I can't claim him as one of our own, but though he is a few decades younger than me he has built a business that is an example to us all. But it's his product division that I envy the most. If there is one product I would love to have invented it is Frizz-Ease, which is undoubtedly one of the must-have items of the last twenty years. John spotted a niche in the market and really went for it. He has a rare talent for that, but he also has a wonderfully gentle and generous nature. As a young man he had worked with Leonard Lewis in his salon in Upper Grosvenor Street and when Leonard became seriously ill in 1997 and lost his business and his livelihood, it was John who came to his aid. John felt that Leonard had taught him so much that he simply had to do something positive to help. He invited me – and many of our crimper colleagues – to a fund-raising evening. It was a great success and £75,000 was raised for Leonard's future. We were delighted to help out of respect for all that Leonard had done for the craft.

Fernando Romero joined our Beverly Hills salon in 1969. He was born in Acapulco and as a teenager he was one of those crazy boys who dive off cliffs to entertain the tourists. He brought that spirit with him to Los Angeles and within two years of starting work with us, he had become West Coast artistic director.

Not long after that, an amazingly beautiful Japanese girl walked into the salon. I greeted her and the receptionist seated her. I then walked over to Fernando with a big grin on my face, to tell him about the beautiful girl whose hair I thought he should do. Perhaps I could have had an alternative career as a matchmaker. It was love at first haircut and Fernando and Kay got married very shortly afterwards.

I encouraged Fernando to move to our London salons and while there, he often went to Paris to work with magazines such as *Harper's Bazaar*, *Vogue* and *Mademoiselle*, and in shows for some of the great international designers. Eventually he became one of our artistic directors, remaining with me for twenty years before opening salons and launching products of his own.

Fernando and Kay are still dear friends of mine. When my family went to Mexico to celebrate my eightieth birthday, a whole mariachi band came to the house and played for an hour and a half – a lovely gift from Fernando, who is not just one of my favourite hairdressers, but one of my favourite human beings.

Mark Hayes has been with the Vidal Sassoon organization for more than three decades. After having been with the company for twenty-eight years, he finally took hold of the reins as international artistic director in December 2005. A perfectionist whose whole life has been dedicated to the quality of the work coming out of the salons, he has also shown admirable patience in waiting for his moment to come. There have been four artistic directors since my time in the job: Roger Thompson, Christopher Brooker, Tim Hartley and now Mark. I watch him, abounding with energy, creating looks that inspire not only the many hairdressers who work in our salons but also the thousands who don't.

In the sixties, almost fifty years ago, I received a wonderful letter from a hairdresser called Denise Moody, who ran a small three-chair salon in Darfield in Yorkshire. She had realized that something was happening at the Vidal Sassoon salon that was changing hairdressing and she asked if she could spend some time in London learning our methods. I invited her down. Much to her husband's chagrin, Denise closed her salon, abandoned her four-year-old son, Stephen, to the neighbours and left for London. She spent three months studying with us, then went back to Yorkshire, picked up her son and re-opened her salon. Eventually, when Stephen was old enough to become an apprentice, he was sent to London to learn our methods and never left. He was soon expert in all our methods and studied to be a teacher, which seemed to be his forte. Now based in Santa Monica, California, he has been with the company for thirty-one years and is the executive director of international education and the overseer of all sixteen VS academies.

After the leveraged buyout of the salons, I had dropped out of the picture in terms of making any decisions as I no longer retained a title in the company. Emotionally, though, I was still very involved and paid close attention to what they were all doing, which remains the case to this day.

My friend Michael Gordon is an extraordinary man, the creative and business genius behind the New York-based empire Bumble and bumble. Although a relative youngster, he has done so much for our industry with his salons, products and hairdressing schools, as well as his very individual way of teaching young stylists.

Our backgrounds are similar. We're both kids from London who had the ambition and drive to become internationally successful. His father had been a hairdresser in England and Michael began working in the craft at the age of fifteen. Although I didn't know him in those early days, he was very much in the same neighbourhood, firstly at the House of Leonard and then with René of Mayfair.

In 2002, Michael wrote a book called *Hair Heroes* about the hairdressers who had inspired him. He showed his impeccable judgement by asking me to be in it. When he interviewed me he impressed me from the outset by only asking the questions that mattered; he had gone through the process so many times himself and knew what was relevant. Some months later when he sent me a finished copy, the words brought to life with his excellent photographs, I knew he was on to a winner.

Over the years we have become close friends and in January 2007 Michael mentioned that he would like to give me an eightieth birthday present. I told him there was nothing that I truly needed or desired, but his reply left me quite flabbergasted. He wanted to make a documentary of my life.

I hardly knew what to say. Just as I was about to protest weakly he continued, 'I already have a professional team lined up.'

It has taken two and a half years of constant travel, filming in the streets of London, New York, New Orleans and Los Angeles, and in hair salons and studios in those cities to make the documentary, but we have never had a bad day. And

Michael, with Craig Teper, his brilliant director and screen-writer, whose first feature-length film this is, and Jackie Gilbert Bauer, his super-efficient producer, along with executive producer Jim Czarnecki, never lost faith in the project. And they were rewarded when *Vidal Sassoon the Movie* premiered at Robert DeNiro's Tribeca Film Festival in New York in 2010. There were four showings in different cinemas and each one was completely sold out.

Strangely enough I didn't mind having the camera constantly intruding in my life. In fact I'd go so far as to say I perform better under its constant scrutiny, and, as the adrenalin flows, my memory travels back to fifty years ago as if it were yesterday. And I'm not the only one. When Mary Quant and I met in the studio, it was supposed to be a ten-minute conversation. But Mary, who'd had a hip operation just ten days before filming, ended up reminiscing with me for an hour and a half. If she was in pain, it never showed. She is quite a lady that Mary Quant; age has not withered her one bit and Craig captured her at her most enchanting.

Craig and his team never missed a beat. When I was presented with the CBE in October 2009 he even managed to somehow get into the grounds of Buckingham Palace and film the occasion. Right after the ceremony, there was Craig, in the courtyard, waiting to film me in full regalia. Prior to this, in the privacy of the state-rooms, where even Craig wasn't allowed to venture, the Queen had pinned the medal to my lapel. In a moment I will always treasure, she quietly said, 'You've been at it a long time, haven't you?'

19

A One-Man Salon on Capri

When the comedian Ali G was 'interviewing' various establishment figures with his unique brand of political incorrectness, Gore Vidal was one of his victims. Having mentioned the splendid novels and other learned books that Gore had written, Ali G turned to him and said in all seriousness, 'You also cut hair, don't you?'

'No,' said Gore.

Ali G held up his notes. 'I've got it here. Gore Vidal created many new haircuts for women.'

By this time Gore was starting to get mildly tetchy. 'No, no. That's Vidal Sassoon. I've known him many years. We're friends of a sort.'

On another occasion, I was due to speak on beauty and health at a fashion college in California when a lady I had not met gave an introduction that had nothing to do with me whatsoever, though I quite liked hearing the words 'formidable' and 'intellect' attached to my name. With a grand flourish, looking at the audience, she said, 'Please allow me to introduce ... Gore Vidal.'

The students of the college had known in advance that they were getting the hairdressing Vidal, and as I walked out they started to giggle. The woman who had introduced me went a dozen shades of red when I appeared on stage, thanking her for the many compliments she had paid me and promising to send her a first edition of every book that Gore had written. I tried to console her by telling her she wasn't the first person to confuse us, but she obviously hadn't done her homework, and got more and more flustered, which only increased the students' amusement. I told them about the mix-up at Grayshott Hall back in the sixties and had them in stitches.

The last time I was confused with Gore was when he was a Democratic candidate for the United States Senate. Half a dozen letters enclosing generous cheques arrived at my house – campaign contributions for Gore. When I called him to ask what to do with them, he said, 'Send them over immediately, dear boy. I need every penny.'

'Minus fifteen per cent as an agent's handling fee?' I suggested cheekily.

Poor Gore Vidal. He never could get me out of his hair.

After my heart bypass I was advised to take life at a slower pace, which was easier said than done. The one concession I did make to a more leisurely pace was taking a house on Capri for a month in the summer, which we did four years running. David Codikow, *the* host of LA, who has become one of my closest friends, would usually bring at least two girls, and the house was always full of people who would stay a week or so and then, the moment they left, their beds would be occupied by others. There was usually a very eclectic mix. My friend David Philp came one year with his wife, Hunter, an art critic and author. Back in Los Angeles,

David sold property by day, but by night he would put on his leather and go out with his band, the Automatics, playing pubs and clubs all over town. After their first visit, David and Hunter came out to Capri every year.

On one visit, I found myself staring at David soon after he arrived and saying, 'If I've got to look at you for a week, I'm going to cut your hair.' This I did – to everybody's surprise, including mine. It had been years since I had actually given a human being a haircut – although I would quite often shape the hair of our three darling shih-tzus at home. The only other hair-cut I've done recently was also on vacation in Capri; it seemed to be a place that brought the scissors out in me. Our good friends Fred Specktor and Nancy Heller were staying. Fred was always on at me to cut his hair, but until we were back on our little island I had no interest. Then, suddenly, I found myself again saying, 'If I have to look at you all week, I'm going to cut your hair.'

Once we'd found an appropriate chair and I'd put a makeshift gown round him, Fred asked me when I had stopped cutting hair. I told him it was more than twenty-five years ago, which made him squirm a bit in his seat, until I told him it was like riding a bike. There are some things you never forget.

His next question was, 'Why?'

It was always my intention to go out at the top of my game. My love for cutting hair was driven by a creative instinct, the knowledge that anything was possible. When I was in my thirties and forties ideas came to me all the time, often when I least expected. But as the business matured, I had to give so much time to other areas – such as products and shows – that new ideas came less easily to me and I realized I was beginning to copy myself.

Although I could cut with the best of them, my inner voice was telling me to stop while I was ahead. By the time I was in my early fifties, I had a strong, talented team behind me who could cut hair every bit as well as I could. But only I could do the other bit. I suppose there was a certain pragmatism in me that said, *Standing behind the chair cutting hair all your life will not build an empire*, and my team were expecting international growth so that they, in turn, could share my adventure. The world was wide open to us and we intended to conquer it. I accepted invitations for myself and my artistic team to visit so many countries where I cut hair, but more and more often I found myself acting as MC for the shows. Very gradually I stopped cutting hair altogether. It took a while and it certainly didn't happen overnight; there was no grand announcement, no fanfare – no 'last haircut'.

But now, for Fred, I picked up the scissors. It was instinctive, and I looked at his face in the mirror, and cut to his bone structure. It was fun and rather emotional – it had been such a long time since the desire to cut hair had struck me. For about half a minute, I thought of opening a one-man salon on Capri.

Not long ago, when I was in my seventies and he was in his eighties, I had the pleasure of seeing Kirk Douglas once again. It was my daughter Eden's birthday and Ronnie and I took her to a restaurant called Drai's in Beverly Hills to celebrate. Eden had invited her closest girlfriends and they were every bit as glamorous as she was. Even I could see that we must have made quite a striking table. Out of the corner of my eye I noticed Anne and Kirk Douglas sitting at a table close by. As they were leaving the restaurant, Kirk stopped and said to me, 'You are a lucky fellow. Do you always take out seven or eight beautiful girls at a time?'

I said, 'Mr Douglas, it's my daughter's birthday and these are her friends.'

'I'd like to talk to you,' he said, and suddenly in my hand was a piece of paper with a telephone number. Ronnie and I were both surprised, but we've become good friends. We occasionally dine together, and Kirk adores Ronnie's cooking so much that when we invite them to dinner, he insists that Ronnie cook at home. Recently, aged ninety-three, Kirk gave four performances of a one-man show in which he told stories of his life while behind him a large screen showed clips of the many films he has made. Ronnie and I went to a performance on a Sunday afternoon at the Kirk Douglas Theatre in Los Angeles and we were riveted. If you hadn't known Kirk's age, you would never have known he was in his nineties; there was so much youthful vigour in his performance. He mesmerized a packed house. There was one moment when he talked of his son, Eric, who had tragically overdosed and died. Catya came to my mind and tears streamed down my face. Without saying a word, Ronnie put her arms around me, and wiped away my tears. Seeing another father express his pain – so similar to my own – had opened the floodgates.

❖

For nineteen years, Ronnie and I lived on a street called Calle Vista Drive in Beverly Hills in a U-shaped house designed by architect Hal Levitt. It is a work of art in itself and has a bridge inside the house that crosses over the swimming pool. When Ronnie added an extension, it was pure Levitt, and nobody could tell it wasn't part of his original design. As it was her first venture in renovating a home, she worked with Larry Totah, a well-known designer. Together they did a splendid job.

Then, in December 2004, Ronnie took on an extraordinary project. A Richard Neutra house in the hills of Bel Air with breathtaking views on both sides came up for sale. It was the perfect canvas for Ronnie's talent. She had studied the work of fine architects for years, including many of the greats, among them our friend Zaha Hadid, whom we met in 2003, and – of course – Neutra himself. For the three years that it took to restore the house, Ronnie focused on his work, keeping the design as true to Neutra's thinking as possible, while adding her own unique flair. After the restoration project was completed, we fell so in love with the house, we decided to live in it ourselves. The house has a certain spirituality and serenity, and we are loving the change.

In October 2007, Ronnie and Eden approached me about my plans for my eightieth birthday, which was three months away. Did I want to celebrate the day with a big party?

I shuddered at the thought. I just wanted something small and intimate with my family around me. Eden found a house in Baja, California, that would accommodate all of us, and she and Ronnie began making plans with the help of the super-efficient Marilyn.

We brought my grandson London in from Johannesburg, where he lives with his father, Kevin Bird, and Catya's other two children, Skye and Mycca, also flew in along with their father, Joe Meyers. Elan brought his son, Ariel. His daughter, Isabella, was in Brazil with her mother at the time. Eden and Tomer brought Olivia and Tyler and my son David was there too. Two of my brother Ivor's grown children also joined us. My nephew Simon came in from New York. Ivor had a second son – Damian – with another lady and he joined us too. Unfortunately, my niece, Esther, who lives in London, was unable to attend, but her son, Alex, was able to join in the celebration and we were glad to have him. As everyone started arriving I remember thinking, *This is going to be fun . . .*

There was no shortage of activities for the eight days we spent in that glorious mountain-top house, overlooking the sea. It had something for each and every one of us, almost like an enormous playground, with a games room, a putting green, a cinema and a lovely swimming pool. It was a joy to watch the family get to know one another – many of the grandchildren had not met before, and even the adults behaved themselves beautifully.

At dinner on the night I turned eighty, as I looked at my family all gathered around me, it brought back memories – some good, some sad – of those who weren't there. My brother, Ivor, would have loved this first-ever family reunion. He had his children years before me and was always enthusing about the joys of family life. And, boy, did he love a party. When Ivor died in 1976, I didn't realize what a huge gap he would leave and how much I would miss him. Over the years, when we were in business together, *he* had become the big brother, looking after every aspect of our lives. I was terribly proud of him with his keen brains and ability to always think things through. Had he lived, I know that some of the mistakes that I had made would not have happened. More importantly, I missed my kind, generous little brother for his compassion and his care for the family. I had a sudden image of his contented face asleep in the banana box the day we lost him, and it seemed like only yesterday.

Gone, too, was Catya. But I still cannot let myself dwell on her for long – I always find myself asking why? How she would have adored seeing her children growing up. They seemed to share their mother's lively spirit, careering around wildly, enjoying the excitement of just being with each other.

My mother – she would have loved it too. There's a picture planted firmly in my mind of her walking hand-in-hand with Nathan G down Kilburn High Street, as they did wherever they were. Their closeness and the many ways in which they had cared for one another was a powerful testament to their love – and as I thought of them, I was grateful that I had found that kind of lasting happiness with Ronnie. Nathan G was my first teacher, and I thought of how much he had given me and how lucky I was that he had become my dad. I felt myself start to well up when I thought of him offering me his life savings to start up a salon. He and my mother had been such a strong motivating force behind many of the successes of my eighty years. As we celebrated in Baja, Mother was so sorely missed. Two nights before she died I had sat with her, holding her hand, as she said to me, 'I'm so tired. I must go to sleep.'

'Ma,' I said, 'another three years and you'll be a hundred.'

'I'm tired now, son. I'm quite content with ninety-seven,' she replied.

Two days later I was in my office when I got a call from one of Mum's nurses, Rory. 'Your mother passed away in the night. She seemed to have a peaceful look on her face.'

She had lived a very full life and she would have definitely put her stamp on my birthday week in Baja. Had she been there, she would have rearranged the whole affair, and would have insisted on making chicken soup and matzo balls to keep us all out of hospital and get us into the synagogue.

Although four of the people who have meant so much to me were gone, there was an enormous life-force present in the house that week. The next generation had inherited so much of the spirit of those who weren't there and as I watched them enjoy themselves, I came to see this very vividly. And it chased away the ghosts somewhat as I welcomed in the next decade.

After we arrived home, we received letters and phone calls from all the family, talking about a magical eight days. It *was* magical and it left no doubt in my mind that I had made the right choice for my eightieth birthday.

When Ivor died, I became guardian to his son Simon, who was then in his early teens and living in London. He had been studying classical piano for many years and I wanted to send him to Juilliard – but he had other ideas. Shortly after moving to the United States, this wonderfully extrovert and adventurous young man decided to change direction. He loved rock and roll and decided to give it a try, forming a band with Corey Williams, the son of Billy Dee Williams, and four other musicians. Simon was the pianist and lead singer. The competition out there was really tough and the band eventually broke up. Simon still plays the piano beautifully, both rock and roll and classical. He's now turned his considerable talent and energy to business, always thinking of new discoveries and inventions.

He's also a kind and generous young man. Just recently I found myself in hospital with pneumonia. It wasn't looking too pretty and the family were all called in to see this eighty-two-year-old relic deteriorate. Fortunately I didn't; I turned the corner and am at home at this moment writing these few words. Ronnie, who was nervous of my condition, asked Simon if he would stay a few days beyond his scheduled departure time. He answered, 'I'll stay as long as you need me,' and he did –

for close to a month. He even bathed me. I asked him why he was doing all this and he said, 'You've been my dad since I was thirteen. How could I not look after you now?'

Simon's sister, Esther, who inherited Ivor's sensibilities, majored in French and German in college. She speaks both languages beautifully and became an interpreter for major corporations. I've always had a special relationship with her. She now has joined Simon in his new venture – which at the moment is not public knowledge, but she will no doubt bring some sanity to the proceedings; she is very level-headed by nature. I am fortunate to have such a kind and caring young woman as my niece.

Ivor, who had always been an outstanding pupil himself at school, would have been extremely proud of his grandson, Alex, who some years ago won a scholarship to Harrow, spending four years there. From the East End to one of England's top public schools in two generations – there's no doubt that one's a chip off the old block.

✧

Recently, on a trip to London, Ronnie and I were having lunch at the Ivy when Michael and Shakira Caine stopped by our table. Michael glanced down and said sardonically, 'They haven't found anyone to replace us yet, have they, Vid?'

Our old London is gone for ever. Whitechapel, Petticoat Lane and Aldgate have all changed beyond recognition. Gone are the public baths, Tubby Isaacs and his seafood, the sounds of Yiddish on every corner. A different culture has moved in with great success and breathed new life into it.

My heart is still in London and Ronnie and I spend as much time there as we can. I took a drive round my old haunts not so long ago, looking for places that reminded me of my journey from reluctant shampoo boy to respected crimper.

The old tenement building in Petticoat Lane is no longer there, but the market traders are still on Wentworth Street doing a roaring trade in sari fabrics and mangoes. Adolph Cohen's salon on the Whitechapel Road was no more, though. It had vanished along with so much of the old East End. Aspiring artists and shoestring entrepreneurs now sit in pavement cafes where the tailors for hire used to stand. Maida Vale hadn't changed very much. The orphanage is not an orphanage any more, but the building is still there next to the Lauderdale Road Synagogue. I remember the dark, dreary room I cried in when Mum left me there – I've spent a lifetime surrounding myself with beauty, trying to forget that. But life goes on and the picture of me with Ivor outside the home in our rather dapper suits is one I shall always treasure.

I drove by the Chelsea Club, which had made me an honorary member three years ago, and which is run by my beloved Chelsea Football Club. The Chelsea offer gave me an extraordinary feeling of satisfaction, and I had to laugh as I remembered all those other clubs that wouldn't let me through the door when I was younger. Every other day that I'm in London I try to swim a mile in their pool and I'm convinced it has given me the energy to keep going, and I owe them my gratitude.

Not long ago I took Liza Bruce, one of Europe's top swimwear designers and an absolute knockout-looking girl to the Chelsea Club. She'd confided to Ronnie and me that she wanted to flip-turn at the end of a length at the swimming pool but couldn't. After ten minutes of my expert instruction, she actually performed the movement more gracefully than I did. I hear she's been flip-turning at the Chelsea Club ever since! I still find it amusing that the queen of swimwear had to rely on an old crimper to teach her to flip-turn – but stranger things have happened in pools. And it's done wonders for my standing at the club.

I walked into the sauna the other day and there sat Frank Lampard being bothered by a couple of other Chelsea supporters. He recognized me and we had a good chat. I have more in common with these down-to-earth English guys than I do with most of the celebrities I meet in Hollywood.

When I was fourteen, my buddies and I would go to Stamford Bridge and watch Chelsea play. Players like Tommy Lawton, Chelsea's centre forward, could head a ball into the net harder than most men could kick it. Over the years Chelsea has been my respite and my therapy. Most of the time I counted myself extremely fortunate that I worked with ladies five and a half days a week, but Saturday afternoon was time spent with the boys and it was necessary for my equilibrium. Any weekend that Chelsea was at home, between fifteen and twenty-five of us would meet at Alvaro's Restaurant, near the ground. There would be pasta however you liked it and a great salad, all for the princely price of one pound – which Alvaro eventually put up to two as he knew a captive audience when he saw one.

The stadium was in the most dilapidated state but it really did not matter. The shed, as it was called, was full of tough-looking guys hoping for a fight – but thousands of well-meaning people just wanted to enjoy the football and would pass young-sters down over their heads so that they could get closer to the front and have a better view of the game. As soon as I could afford it, I got myself a season ticket in the one stand that had seats. It was right on the end, nowhere near the best seat in the house – but as I recall it cost the princely sum of fifteen pounds a year. As my income got better, so did my seat and eventually I moved closer towards the centre, where I saw much more of the game. I knew I'd made it when the chap sitting next to me looked awfully like someone I recognized from the movies. And then he spoke to me and I realized it was Richard Attenborough, so my income *must* have improved. Like me, he was an extraordinary enthusiast for Chelsea and could not have been more friendly. Eventually he was invited to become a director and moved into the director's box. About the time he moved into the boardroom, I moved to New York and my attendance became much more sporadic. But my heart never really left Stamford Bridge.

Over the years, Chelsea has had some fantastic teams – and some others that you rather want to forget. One superb team had Jimmy Greaves as inside forward, and I often thought that if that great Italian Zola was playing alongside him, Jimmy's goal total would have been even more outrageous. I remember once going to Liverpool to watch Chelsea in a cup round. Bobby Tambling scored the winning goal as Chelsea won 2–1. We travelled back to London with some of the team and many of us stood in the train and talked about the exciting game. The players earned so much less in those days. Today they could buy the train.

There was something brilliant about the team when Peter Osgood was captain. They were a joy to watch – and Charlie Cook on his day was another Georgie Best. When Peter Osgood died, I was invited by Kerry Dixon to the memorial service, which was held in the stadium. As his ashes were laid on the penalty spot, I felt deeply moved. What a class player. He played quality football with such distinction. His passing was superb and he always seemed to turn up at the right time to score a goal. After the service, drinks were served in the club, but I just could not bring myself to join the party.

In recent years, Roman Abramovich has created at Chelsea a world-class squad and it is thrilling to see that there are four or five English internationals who regularly play for the team. He brought them to Beverly Hills two years running to play the local football elite, and I had a great evening chewing the fat with John Terry, Joe Cole, Didier Drogba and so many others.

There seems to be an informal Chelsea supporter's breakfast club developing here in LA with the comedy writers Ian La Frenais and Dick Clement along with myself and three others. In order to watch the game live this happens at 7 a.m. over a bowl of fresh fruit and boiled eggs, or oatmeal and mugs of coffee, rather than a pint of beer as is more customary. My friendship with Ian has become stronger over the years and on occasion he'll call me to go over to Dick's house with him to watch the Chelsea matches. Just last week, both of them were at my place watching one of the big games with me. When it comes to football, the Brits really do hang together. At eighty-two, I have been a firm supporter of Chelsea for close to seventy years. I have sweated blood and tears for those boys. Do I regret it? Given the silverware they've brought home recently, winning both the Premier League and the FA Cup, not for a minute.

When the legendary tailor Dougie Hayward died in 2008, Ian La Frenais called every Brit in Los Angeles, booked a room at Mr Chow, and about twenty die-hard Dougie Hayward fans turned up to celebrate his life. It was an extraordinary evening. Each of us had to tell our own story about the great man; many of us had more than one. The evening, which started at 7.30, seemed to fly by, with everyone wanting to tell their second or

third story, too. We were all going strong when the maître d'
informed us it was time to go home.

The streets of the West End are still so familiar to me. Curzon
Place where my first flat was, Mount Street where Dougie
Hayward's emporium was, now lined with grand boutiques and
changed almost beyond recognition, but Bond Street will always
be Bond Street. The odd building has been bulldozed and a new
one replaces it. But it does not alter one bit the buzz of this great
street where I did business for so many years and which I always
visit when I'm in London. I park the car and take a stroll down
those very familiar pavements, walking the distance between my
two salons, and memories come flooding back. It seems hard to
believe that fifty-six years have passed since I opened my first
salon. Professor Cohen occasionally used to pop in and see me
once he retired. I always made sure we got the red carpet out.
When I saw those immaculately polished shoes and neatly
parted hair making their way through reception, it was like
being reunited with family. It's hard to think that without my
apprenticeship with him there might never have been a Vidal
Sassoon on Bond Street at all.

Seeing Michael Caine again at the Ivy reminded me of the
times we used to wander around looking up at the skyline admir-
ing the architecture, dreaming of what was around the next
corner. We see each other so rarely now but he's still a great
friend. However, I have to straighten him out on one or two
points. Obviously he's an incredibly talented actor whose views
are taken seriously and, on occasion, I'm mentioned in his interviews. In one magazine I was described as '*his* barber *who had
done rather well for himself*'. In another he said he stayed with
me and Terence Stamp in my flat. He is at all times a wonderful

storyteller, but the truth is I was never his barber. He was a scruffy young pup when I hung out with him, getting thirty quid a week in a West End play and he couldn't have afforded me. And he and Terry stayed in my flat *while I was in New York*. The important point there is that I was absent. But it doesn't really matter, it's water under the bridge as they say. As for the barber quip, had he asked I would have happily cut his hair *gratis*.

From Bond Street I head back to Notting Hill, which is home now when I'm in town. It's a wonderful place to see the world – it's really like a village. At the weekend when the market stalls line Portobello Road, I find myself drawn to the patter of the stall-holders. There's something so comfortingly familiar about the hustle and bustle of a market. It doesn't seem so long ago that my brother and I were two little scallywags pinching the fruit while the barrow boys turned a blind eye.

The other week I saw some delicious-looking blueberries on one of the stalls and asked the vendor for a couple of boxes.

He said, 'What's wrong with a third?'

'I won't be able to eat them,' I said. 'They'll just go rotten.'

He put the two containers in a bag and charged me for them. Next thing I knew he was wrapping up the third one as well. 'It's a present. On me.'

As I walked away, smiling to myself about his generosity, he shouted out, ''Ere – when you've got time, come back and give us a haircut!'

Index

Index

Index

Index

Index

Index

Index

Index

Index

extracts reading groups
competitions books new
discounts extracts
competitions extracts
books new discounts
events books extracts
reading groups new extracts
reading groups books
new titles reading groups
interviews extracts
events extracts events
discounts events
new books events interviews
events new books
discounts extracts discounts
www.panmacmillan.com
extracts events reading groups
competitions books extracts new books